Ivor Heller fell in love with Wimbledon FC when, at the age of nine, he went to Plough Lane to see his first football match. He saw the Dons meteoric rise from the non-League to the Premier League, he witnessed the infamous Crazy Gang years, and he rejoiced when his heroes beat Liverpool to win the FA Cup. Ivor was an ordinary fan until 2002, when he did something extraordinary to save his beloved club. Not only did he help launch AFC Wimbledon from his printing-press office, he served as the club's commercial director for 21 years and remains a life vice president.

Mike Dunn is a former Head of Sport for some of the UK's biggest national papers, including *The Sun, News of the World, The Independent, The I Paper* and *London Evening Standard.* He has previously written five books, including the official AFC Wimbledon history, We Are Home, which catalogued the club's return to Plough Lane. The book was shortlisted in the *Daily Telegraph*'s Sports Book of the Year awards.

WE SHALL NOT BE MOVED

How Wimbledon Fans Beat the Football Association

THE IVOR HELLER STORY

WITH

MIKE DUNN

ARENA SPORT

First published in 2026 by Arena Sport
An imprint of
Birlinn Limited
West Newington House
10 Newington Road
Edinburgh
EH9 1QS

www.birlinn.co.uk

ISBN: 978 1 913759 26 1

British Library Cataloguing-in-Publication Data
A catalogue record for this book is available from the British Library

Typeset by Hewer Text UK Ltd, Edinburgh

Papers used by Birlinn Ltd are from well-managed
forests and other responsible sources

MIX
Paper | Supporting
responsible forestry
FSC® C117931

Printed and bound in Great Britain by MBM Print, Glasgow

CONTENTS

AUTHOR'S NOTE

The following book contains outspoken and controversial remarks about the Football Association and a club in Buckinghamshire. They do not represent the official views of AFC Wimbledon.

FOREWORD

I first met Ivor Heller in 2014 because I had an idea: What if I used money I made from streaming videogames online to sponsor an actual, real-life football team? Ivor may not have understood the economics of YouTube livestreaming, but he needed a back-of-shorts sponsor for AFC Wimbledon, whose rebirth and rise he has fuelled for 25 years now.

Ivor is, above all else, an enthusiast. His enthusiasm for AFC Wimbledon is so infectious that I've been that back of shorts sponsor for twelve seasons. He loves Wimbledon so much that he makes you love Wimbledon, makes the world love Wimbledon. Some of us might've responded with despair or hopelessness to having our football club wrested away by the English football authorities. But Ivor is allergic to despair. He and others instead responded with hope: maybe the FA would say it wasn't 'in the wider interests' of English football to have a football club in Wimbledon, but Ivor and his band of merry football fans would go on to prove the FA wrong again and again and again.

Every other Saturday, around 8,000 people gather in a stadium built by the fans of AFC Wimbledon – a stadium that the authorities and rich football investors thought was impossible. They watch professional football played by a team that, again, the authorities and wealthy football investors thought was impossible. And this dream, this wonder, would've been impossible without Ivor and the other cofounders of the club that means so much to me and to many. He literally made his dreams come true.

Ivor has spent his life proving people wrong. He has prevailed where others said it was impossible over and over again, and both his Wimbledon story and his life story are reminders to me that hope is always the right response to the miracle of consciousness. His book will make you believe in the impossible again, the way you did when you were a kid, the way we all still should.

John Green

ACKNOWLEDGEMENTS

I have had many amazing people help and support me throughout my life so far.

This book would not have happened without Mike Dunn. He has sat through all of this, and there's a lot of info that has not made the cut!

Peter Miller has advised and told me off many a time throughout my Wimbledon life and throughout the process of making the book. Thanks also to David Barnard for his love of Wimbledon and his constant guidance.

From the club, Erik Samuelson stands out along with David Charles, Nigel Higgs and one unsung hero, Tim Hillyer. These people have always been there for me. They have never closed their door or not communicated with me.

Thanks to my Commercial Team, Keith McGuinness and Sam Grayson. Pietro Palladino made the transition to Plough Lane a pleasure and is the most personable person I know. Jim Piddington, my travel partner and good friend, and Carlo Vendettelli, an eternal enthusiast, all deserve special mentions.

The Batsford Boys have been a constant in my life for well over 50 years. You know who you are, and I will always be a BB.

My best friend, Alan Tucker, has always been the witness to the ups and downs of my life. Although we support different teams, he is my football rock. My other best mate, Keith Grossmith, went missing soon after we started the club. I hope he reads this book and it makes him smile.

My family took a back seat but always understood. My brother, David, is solid as a rock and always there. I'm extremely proud of his achievements and always will be. His wife, Esther, is an inspiration to all of us.

Then there's a long list of other valued family members: Daniel, Karin, Rebecca, Simon, Sammi ('The Gooner'), Adrianna, Adam, Dianna, Pedro, Diego, Lucas, Miguel, Paul, Sam, the inspirational Aunty Myra, Cristina and Dan plus the grandchildren – Meghan, Mia and Jennifer. Thank you all for moving the family celebrations so I could go to more or less every game!

Then there's Dickie Guy and his amazing family, Craig Wellstead – a giant of a man – and Craig Cope, who is a top bloke.

The women in my life – you know who you are – thank you and some. Aideen is the third woman, friend and supporter extraordinaire.

Finally, thank you to every fan, volunteer and player who takes the time to say hello, smile or shake my hand.

What a wonderful group of people to thank in bucket loads. If I've missed anyone, I am really, really sorry.

MY RULES

1) I will never call them by the name they've adopted;
2) I will only call them The Franchise;
3) Frannies is acceptable;
4) I will never offer them hospitality;
5) I will never accept hospitality from them in return;
6) I will never spend money in their food and beverage outlets;
7) I never want us to buy or loan a player from them;
8) I will never treat them like an ordinary club;
9) I will never mix with them at any level;
10) I will never forgive them.

INTRODUCTION

THE Football Association did not want this to happen. On 27 May 2025, Wembley Stadium was awash with yellow and blue. I was one of 32,000 fans going wild, ecstatically celebrating my club's promotion. Television cameras beamed our joy into homes across the globe – and yet the images were never meant to be. Why? Because my club was the club the FA wiped off the map – and then ordered to lie down and die.

On 28 May 2002, the most shameful decision ever taken in the history of the English game was rubber-stamped. A three-man commission, appointed by the FA, allowed a famous football club – us, Wimbledon – to be airlifted from its community and moved 70 miles away to Milton Keynes.

It was football's crime of the century. The FA could – should – have stopped it but chose not to. Instead, they facilitated the crime. The sense of loss, the injustice and the outrage, were immeasurable. A community that had supported its local club for over 100 years was about to see it vanish while the FA stood back and allowed it to happen.

How could you?

Nothing like this had ever happened before and it left our national game dangling. Did we want to be like the United States, where it's called franchising and is commonplace in baseball and American football?

The nightmare that was happening to my club could also happen to any other club up and down the country. The FA had made it clear: they wouldn't stand in the way. Who might be next? Perhaps: 'The FA are today announcing that Sheffield United will replace Barnsley in the Championship after the decision was taken to move them to Birmingham.' You get the picture.

My name is Ivor Heller and I had a choice to make. Either accept that my club was about to be erased from the map, or fight like fury to keep it alive. But this wasn't just a fight to save my club – it was a fight to save the entire structure of the English game. To stop Barnsley becoming Birmingham.

I chose to fight. I chose to defy the FA, with their riches and rule books and lawyers and committees and anonymous people in suits. They were all a million miles away from the heartbeat of the national game. Clueless, aloof, up themselves. Never again would I simply be Ivor the Football Fan. Me, Ivor bloody Heller: working class, an ordinary football fan, bit of a cheeky chappy – once courted by some of London's nastiest gangland villains – a snooker and poker player, not averse to selling a few coats on the black market.

I'd no experience of running a football club. I was first and foremost a fan, so how could I possibly trouble the gentrified FA elite with their old-school chumminess? It's fair to say I would be small fry in their eyes – quite literally. Barely five feet tall, my only claim to fame was comical to say the least: I played an elf in the Hollywood blockbuster *Santa Claus: The Movie*. Seriously. I'm the short-arsed one next to Dudley Moore. And he was pretty short as well.

The FA completely changed my life with their decision. They might squeal they didn't actually make it, that, technically, it was a ruling made by the three-man commission. But the FA appointed them – so it was all the same to me. Their decision was a blasphemy against football, whomever you blamed.

But my club was worth fighting for. It had been one of the original 20 teams to start the Premier League in 1992 and it stayed in the top flight for eight consecutive seasons, regularly beating the likes of Manchester United, Arsenal and Liverpool. It also spawned the infamous Crazy Gang – notoriously tough players who included Wally Downes, Dave Bassett, Vinnie Jones and John Fashanu.

Wimbledon Football Cub was a quintessential part of why the Premier League was the envy of the world. Shamelessly uncompromising, brutally hard and combative, we embodied the romance of the game: the possibility that David could beat Goliath and when he did, the beautiful game was enriched. Renowned underdogs, Wimbledon had risen from the bottom of the pile to become living, breathing proof that a club with barely any resources could not only live alongside the game's elite, it could regularly beat them, too.

My club blazed a trail for the likes of Wigan, Brentford and Bournemouth today. If you didn't support Wimbledon, it was highly likely they were your favourite second team. Nothing epitomised that more than our infamous FA Cup triumph in 1988 when we beat Liverpool at Wembley to lift the coveted trophy. That 1-0 triumph inspired legendary BBC commentator John Motson to declare: 'The Crazy Gang have beaten the Culture Club.'

But the FA had no concern for any of that in 2002. Instead, their commission ruled that Wimbledon could be torn out, like some wilting rose bush, and replanted in Milton Keynes. All the history, all the triumphs, all the romance were considered irrelevant. Just to make their absurd decision even more farcical, the FA commissioners ruled the new club in Milton Keynes could still be called Wimbledon.

And they weren't finished there, either. They still had a handful of spite to add to the mix. Worried that some tearaway Wimbledon fans – like me – might rebel and start a new club to replace the one taken from us, the FA pompously proclaimed that such a move would not be in 'the wider interests of the game'. In other words, they told us to lie down and die.

But this was the same Wimbledon that had been defying the odds since the club was first formed in 1889. Refusing to take no for an answer, pulling off victories against mightier and richer opposition, fighting back and standing up to the man – all this was deeply ingrained in my club's DNA. The players took that on to the pitch with them. Now it was our turn. If we were going to beat this and keep Wimbledon alive, then it was going to need the very people the FA wanted to silence – the fans – to do what our club had been doing for years.

Fight back. Do something miraculous and do it with no resources and against all the odds. The Crazy Gang had outrageously won the FA Cup; now it was up to us, the fans, to do something even more remarkable: save our club.

The following is my account of how I stuck two fingers up to the FA and their poxy commission. Along the way, my marriage collapsed and the struggle cost me very many sleepless nights. I was bullied during my schooldays and there were times when this felt exactly the same. It was a David vs Goliath battle all right. Just like it had always been throughout Wimbledon's history. The question was, could the little man really pull off the biggest victory in my club's history – or would Wimbledon be literally wiped off the map and our national game turned into a franchising free-for-all?

THE WARM-UP

Chapter 1
THE CALL

MY MOBILE rang unexpectedly around 7 p.m. as I was packing up to leave the office. I glanced at the number. *Why's he calling now, it's too soon?* I anxiously pressed the green button to answer and immediately heard a familiar voice. He got straight to the point: 'Ivor, I've got bad news.' Wow. My mind clouded. This wasn't what I'd anticipated. I think I'd clung to the belief that if he did call, it would be to say something like, 'They can't make their minds up, there's going to be a delay.'

I'd have settled for that.

'What? Tell me, what?' I shut my eyes tight, possibly to shield myself against what might be coming.

'You've lost. They're going to let it happen. It's all over.'

My heart sank. I suddenly saw all the people I knew, and the thousands more I barely knew, who would be devastated by what I'd just been told. Loyal, passionate football fans who organised their lives – their holidays, their weddings, their anniversaries – around the fixtures and the matches they couldn't bear to miss. All that was about to stop. Our club was about to be erased and the game's spineless governing body, the Football Association, was going to let it happen. A club that had played its first game in 1889 was about to be wiped off the map. Literally.

'Fuck.' Then silence. I didn't know what else to say. I wanted to scream wildly, I wanted to tell the world: 'This is wrong, this is evil, they're all bastards. Why is this happening?'

The voice on the end of the phone maybe sensed this. 'You can't tell anyone,' he said, almost pleadingly. I noted his sense of panic.

'Don't worry, you've got my word, I swear. And thanks for telling me – really, thanks,' I replied, probably unconvincingly. My scrambled mind was still swirling viciously between fury and disbelief. 'Nobody will ever know it was you who called, I absolutely promise,' I added. 'But listen: I will have to break the news to two or three people I trust totally because we need to start again, and we need to do it right now.'

I knew that more than anything else. Even at my lowest point, I already knew what the next move had to be. I just never thought it would actually come to this. And before I could end that sentence, he interjected: 'That's the spirit. Go on, my son.' And then he hung up. To this day, nobody knows who called me at 7 p.m. on 27 May 2002. The voice belonged to one of the FA's most senior and respected executives and I will never forget the favour he did us in that moment. He risked his own position to phone me with highly confidential information so we could have a head start. More importantly, he was on our side. He knew this was a calamitous error, a stain on the governing body he worked for, a betrayal of what it was meant to stand for. A gross perversion of our beautiful game.

He was willing us to fight back.

So that's what we'd do. Nobody else in the world knew in that moment. There wasn't a hint of it in any local or national newspapers the next day, or on any television coverage anywhere. Believe me, it was the story they all wanted.

Chapter 2
MY PLEDGE

I SLUMPED back in my office chair and stared at a line of photos on the shelves directly opposite. My eyes immediately focused on one picture in particular: a cherished snap of a golf day with Wimbledon's legendary goalkeeper, Dickie Guy. He'd been my boyhood hero, but I'd got to know him as I got older and had invited him to play in my golf team. I was absolutely thrilled when he came along to play at Farleigh Court. Dickie embodied everything I loved about football and my beloved Wimbledon FC and now the bloody Football Association were about to obliterate my club – and his legacy. They were going to shut down Wimbledon FC once and for all and let it be moved to a town 70 miles away called Milton Keynes.

Milton Fucking Keynes.

Suddenly the memories came flooding back: standing on the West Bank behind the goal, giving Dickie some banter, making him smile. He seemed like a giant to me; he could save anything: 'Dickeee, Dickeee.' And then I saw me, aged 11, banned from travelling to Elland Road on a Saturday afternoon in 1975 because I was too young to go there to see my heroes – still part-time players in the Southern League – play mighty Leeds United in the FA Cup.

Instead, I sat alone in our lounge, listening furiously to faint reports that were barely audible against all the crackling from inside my small Roberts transistor radio. I'd spent most of the game twisting and contorting the aerial so it vaguely pointed towards Yorkshire – wherever that was.

'And now we go to Elland Road where Peter Lorimer is – *inaudible crackle* – penalty against the part-timers from Wimbledon, who – *more crackle* – for 82 minutes against the First Division champions . . .'

And I rammed the radio tight against my ear and squeezed a cushion even tighter as the tension mounted. I'd already turned the lounge into a Wimbledon shrine, the walls splattered with newspaper headlines and cuttings and photos stuck on with blobs of Blu-Tack and rolled-up Sellotape.

'And Lorimer places the ball – *crackle* – walking back. This is going to break the hearts of these Wimbledon players – *inaudible* – miracles here at Elland Road . . . Lorimer is moving forward . . . and: 'Guy saves! Guy saves! Dickie Guy has saved Lorimer's penalty – *crackle* – ball has been cleared. The score remains Leeds United

0, Wimbledon 0 . . .' In my mind, Dickie must have athletically flung his giant frame through the air to finger-tip Lorimer's monstrous strike off target and somehow divert the ball inches past the right-hand post.

I remember then storming out of my bedroom, screaming and yelling so hysterically that Dad – downstairs serving a customer in the shop – roared back: 'Ivor, for God's sake be quiet; what's all that noise about?'

'Dad, Dad – Dickie has saved a penalty.'

'Oh, is that all? Now please shut up, I'm serving someone down here.'

And then the memory vanished as quickly as it had emerged. I spun my chair round, stood up and thought: 'Right. Fuck the lot of you. Let's go again. Let's keep our club alive.' And I hit the phone immediately. The first call was to Marc Jones. 'Marc – we've lost. They're going to take our club away. We've lost, end of story.'

'Fuck. But how can you be sure . . . who told you? Maybe it's just a rumour?'

'No, I'm 100 per cent sure, my bloke cannot be wrong, so get in here tomorrow, early, and we'll start again. We only have a few days to get stuff done and if we don't get it done then we won't start next season and if we don't do that, I don't think this will work.'

I was acting on impulse. I knew we needed someone with Marc's skills – a creative wizard who could design everything from a club badge to a kit, to all the messaging we'd need if we were going to get people to follow us.

We'd also need Trevor Williams and Kris Stewart on board. We'd all talked about this moment but only in airy-fairy ways, pub conversations that inevitably got drowned by beer. In reality, it couldn't have been any other way: how could we react until we knew what the decision was. We couldn't have got the ball rolling before that moment.

Next, I phoned Kris. 'It's bad news, mate. I'm telling you we've lost.'

He was more aghast and even more sceptical about my informant. 'But you can't know for sure, Ivor,' he said, clinging to hope.

'Listen, Kris, you go to the FA's headquarters tomorrow and hear it announced officially. Someone has to represent us there and that's you. But I won't be coming because we are going to start again. As far as I'm concerned, though, you must be our first chairman. People react to you, Kris, they like you, you're not divisive and they will look at you and realise you have nothing to gain personally from this. That's why we need you. So do what you must at Soho Square tomorrow – but please, please, be back in my office the next morning.'

Kris was vital if we were going to pull this off. He had the ability to rally people and win their confidence, a perfect statesmanlike front man. We were going to need his skills in bucketfuls.

Finally, I phoned Trevor. 'I don't believe it, I don't fuckin' believe it, the bastards. Right – let's get cracking.' Out of the four of us, he was the true football geek. He'd know the players that might be out there, their statistics and form and where we'd need to go for everything we'd need to physically put a team together.

And me? I'd bring in commercial and business contacts. I felt the four of us had a perfect blend of different skills. There was just one problem. None of us had a fucking clue how to start, or run, a football club.

Chapter 3

NOT IN THE WIDER INTERESTS OF FOOTBALL

SEVEN words. Seven nails the FA couldn't resist hammering into our coffin. It was bad enough they were going to permit our club to be airlifted from its natural home. Just as spiteful were the seven carefully selected words they used to spice up their appalling decision. Seven extra words that exposed the maliciousness. Words that laid bare the FA for what it truly was – cowardly, unprincipled and utterly out of touch. Ironically, those very words – as repulsive and unnecessary as they were – simply motivated us more than ever. In the end, they did the polar opposite to what the FA had intended.

None of us knew anything about those words, though, until the FA formally confirmed its decision to take our club away. As agreed, Kris went to Soho Square to hear the official announcement. The three-man commission of Aston Villa director Steve Stride, Ryman League chairman Alan Turvey and FA legal advisor Raj Parker had inexplicably voted two to one in favour of us being relocated (we know Turvey resisted). Unbelievably, they tried to sweeten their decision by saying the club in Milton Keynes could still be called Wimbledon. As if that would make everything okay.

To erase any hope that common sense might prevail, the FA also confirmed there would be no right of appeal – although none of us had any intention of going down that route. Then came the seven words. In a calculated bid to nip in the bud any plans we had, the commission ruling added: 'Resurrecting the club from its ashes as, say, "Wimbledon Town" is, with respect to those supporters who would rather that happened . . . not in the wider interests of football.'

Despicable.

There it was: everything you needed to know about the FA in seven words. Seven deadly sins. We were 'not in the wider interests of football'. What did that even mean? How could it be that *we* (a bunch of penniless, powerless fans) weren't in the wider interests of the game, yet moving our historic club from its natural home to Milton Keynes was? What possessed them? Hadn't they done enough damage? Why did they need to twist the knife in deeper? Was it to flex their muscles and show us how powerful they were? I think that's the truth of it. The FA wouldn't dare take on the likes of Manchester United so why bully the likes of Wimbledon instead? They bullied us because they could get away with it and it made them feel good about themselves. Big and important and powerful.

We've shown those Wimbledon upstarts who's really in charge.

That's why they issued those seven words. To put us in our coffins and keep us there. But they'd fucked with the wrong people.

FIRST HALF

Chapter 4
KICKING OFF

IF I HADN'T been so bloody short I might have made it as a professional footballer. And if it hadn't been for football, I might have won a gold medal at the Moscow Olympics. I fell in love with kicking a ball when I was three years old. I vividly remember watching older kids playing outside in the street and desperately wanting to join in. Mum and Dad would tell me I was too young but I wasn't having it. I guess my refusal to do what I was told, my defiance and determination to prove everyone wrong, started back then with those street games.

Round the back of where we lived were some council-run pitches where local schools would play matches. Luckily for us, the fencing had collapsed so my brother David and I would clamber through and spend as much time there as we possibly could. There'd be loads of other kids there, too – we'd have 13, 15, 20-a-side games – and some of those youngsters eventually turned professional.

Chris Dibble played for England schoolboys, then Millwall and Wimbledon; Mike Fillery played for Chelsea and QPR. They were two or three years older than me but you could tell, even then, they had what it takes. Jimmy Bolton was on the books at Spurs and became a record non-league goalscorer for Carshalton. Gary Waterman, whom I'm still in touch with to this day, also played for England schoolboys and was an early Wimbledon apprentice.

They were all out on that pitch every day. Although my height was always against me, I had a good centre of gravity and could twist and turn with some pace. I played in what you'd call a number 10 role today, but my speciality was chipping the ball from distance on to the crossbar – long before anyone invented the crossbar challenge.

Then came my reality check. When I was 13, in my last year at Chaucer Middle School, our football team made it to a local schools' cup final. The game attracted scouts from top London clubs – not to see me, but kids like Jimmy Bolton, Harry Waterman, Keith Hider and Robert May. I played well that day and, when I came off the pitch, three or four scouts talked to me. They all said the same thing: 'You've definitely got something, son, but you're too small right now. We'll come back for a serious look once you've grown a bit.'

I went home that afternoon and ploughed through all my football sticker albums, pouring over the statistics. I knew there were two short players who'd made it – Scottish legend Billy Bremner and Wales's hero Brian Flynn. They were both five foot four inches and the shortest players in the top flight.

I went to my mum and dad and said: 'How tall are you?'

'Five foot, two inches,' Dad replied. Mum added: 'Four foot, 11.'

'So, correct me if I'm wrong,' I said, 'you're usually taller than your mother and maybe a bit taller than your dad. That's about right, isn't it?'

They both nodded. 'Dad, has anyone in our family ever been above five foot, two inches?'

'No.'

'In that case,' I replied, 'I ain't ever going to be a professional footballer.'

And that was it. I knew. There were no tears. I was smart. I knew there was no point hankering to be something I could never be.

Instead, I became the Sussex junior archery champion. My parents ran a shop and one day I overheard a customer talking to Mum and Dad about archery. My ears pricked up and I said: 'I fancy having a go at that.' His club was nearby at Willows High School and they had some spare bows and arrows I could use, so off I went. I had an eye for it straight away and was soon good enough to enter the regional and national tournaments, which were huge events. All the Olympic competitors were there but I started winning trophies, prizes and plenty of medals. Then I got asked if I'd like to train with the England team and prepare for the 1980 Moscow Olympics, which were still six years away. Training would be every Tuesday, Thursday and . . . Saturday.

And, just like an arrow piercing the bull's eye, a single thought shot through my brain: football. I'd have to miss football on Saturdays – and some Tuesdays as well. I talked it over with my parents and said: 'Name me the most famous archer you know.' In a flash they both quipped: 'Robin Hood!' And that was my point. I'd never heard of a single archer ever. I wasn't saying I didn't want to shoot arrows for England. But I absolutely was saying, 'I'm not giving up football to go to the Olympics, thanks very much.' Archery and I went our separate ways.

I was born in King's College Hospital, Dulwich, in 1963. Both my parents, Barry and Estelle, were skilled tailors, altering and making clothes as well as selling ladies' shoes and handbags. They eventually ran a dance shop – ballet shoes, dance and theatrical costumes, stuff like that – with a dry-cleaning service at the back.

We lived in a two-bed maisonette with my older brother David above a parade of shops in Green Lane, Morden, on the sprawling St Helier estate – the second biggest council estate in the country. Our parade had everything you could ever need. It was real old school: a baker, butcher, greengrocer, post office, pharmacy, fish and chippy and even a bicycle repair shop and car workshop. It was a great little community – everyone knew everyone else and we'd often go on holidays with the neighbouring shop owners.

Mum and Dad's business – Barry's Valet Service – was on the ground floor, with a shop at the front and a workshop at the back. It became well known, not just with locals but with the London theatre world as well. The comedy actress Bella Emberg was a regular customer – as well as TV celebrities like Windsor Davies and Harry Secombe. I got used to people like that coming in and out regularly and I learned a lot of social skills in the process. I'd come back from school, there'd be people in the shop and all of a sudden I'd be serving and talking to them. It made interacting with people natural to me at an early age.

We all lived upstairs, where there was a living room, sitting room, separate kitchen, bathroom and two bedrooms. There was no central heating, though, and in the winter the frost would be on the inside of the windows. We were an extremely close family and I stayed there until I was 17 years old. I never saw Mum and Dad argue; they were far too busy for that. Dad worked for several of the big high street retailers, like Hepworths and Burtons, picking up clothes from them every day that needed altering. He'd frequently work until 11 p.m. in the shop and I'd often creep downstairs to watch him cutting and sewing cloth.

The business never appealed to me, though. I saw how hard my parents had to work for starters. Other dads came home from work and relaxed in the evenings, but mine never stopped, 24/7. Besides, I much preferred football – playing and watching. I didn't really support a specific team when I was very young, although I had a favourite player: George Best. Sometimes I'd bc allowed to stay up late to watch *Match of the Day* and I'd pray that Manchester United would be one of the first matches so I could see my hero. And that's when I became aware of our next-door neighbour.

Tommy Appleby should have died in 1958, along with the Flowers of Manchester, their lives tragically cut short in the Munich air disaster. Mr Appleby was a Manchester United director, as well as manager of the prestigious Manchester Opera House. He'd been to all United's European Cup games that season and was due to fly with the team to see their quarter-final tie at Red Star Belgrade. Instead, Mr Appleby gave his ticket away to a successful businessman he hoped would join United's board of directors – Willie Satinoff, who owned a nationwide clothing company.

Satinoff was one of the 23 who died after the plane, which had stopped to refuel in Munich, crashed on its third attempt to take off in driving snow. The Flowers of Manchester – eight of the greatest players of their generation – also died, while legendary United manager Matt Busby and England hero Bobby Charlton were left fighting for their lives. A few years ago, I was talking about the Munich disaster with my best mate, Alan Tucker. I couldn't believe it when he said, 'My great-uncle was on the plane – Willie Satinoff.'

Mr Appleby spent a lot of time up north, but used to come back every four weeks or so. I'd never seen anyone like him. In fact there were times when Mum and Dad would sit outside on the balcony above our shop with David and me and wait to get a glimpse of him walking down the road.

Tall and graceful, he usually wore a Crombie coat with a gentleman's trilby completing the refined look. He looked like a Second World War spy. To us, he was the most connected man on the planet. For example, he got us tickets for the *Bar Mitzvah Boy* play in London. Mum, Dad and I were sitting in the best stall seats when suddenly a guy in front turned round, looked at my mum and said: 'Are you Estelle?' It was Barry Manilow! My mum adored the American singer and was reduced to a quivering wreck as he leaned over and gave her a kiss on the cheek. And they talked for ages after that. Mr Appleby had arranged the whole thing.

My best memories of Mr Appleby, though, were when we sat on our balcony outside and he'd tell us what was really going on at Old Trafford. He knew that George Best was my favourite player – 'he's mine as well,' he confided – and I'd listen in awe as he told us about the players and what they'd been up to. We knew, for instance, that Bobby Charlton had thumped Best long before the story of their fight got in the papers.

On one occasion, Mr Appleby took my brother to Manchester to see United play QPR. But that wasn't all – he also arranged for David to have lunch with Sir Matt Busby. He got me a signed copy of Charlton's testimonial programme and, for my bar mitzvah, he gave us four tickets for United's FA Cup final against Southampton. But they weren't ordinary seats: we were in the

Royal Box, just behind the Queen and alongside Sir Matt. There was only one thing we never talked about with Mr Appleby: The Flowers of Manchester.

Chapter 5
BULLIES

I'M A VICTIM of bullying. Bullying takes many forms. When I was a child, it was in my face, naked, out in the open for all to see. During my adult life, though, it's been more insidious. The cowardly impact of that has been just as painful as the bullying I endured in my schooldays. I detest bullies. I've learned they come in all shapes, sizes and guises – every one of them grotesque. How the Football Association snuffed out my football club was a form of bullying: it had the same cowardly, telltale characteristics. Believe me, I should know.

My personal nightmare started at school. I only survived because my father taught me an invaluable lesson when I was very young: 'Ivor, if you don't stand up to them, they will never go away.' His words never left my side, especially when we defied the FA.

I definitely enjoyed a treasured, loving home life, but, sadly, it couldn't shield me from bullies who were gifted two easy reasons to target me: the religion I was born in to (Jewish) – and my height, or lack of it.

Short and Jewish. What a combination.

The bullying started at Morden's Canterbury Junior School: I'd walk down the corridors between lessons and kids as young as seven years old would snarl 'Jew boy' as I walked past them. It was the way it was said. In isolation, the words 'Jew' and 'boy' don't sound too horrific, but these were spat at me like poisonous bile. It stung and kept on stinging as I progressed through Chaucer middle school and finally Garth High.

In those upper schools, groups of lads from my class – and the year above – would have a go on a regular basis. By then it became physical: I was regularly getting punched and pushed to the ground. I needed hospital treatment on one occasion for a suspected broken right arm after I was deliberately tripped and shoved.

The teachers were told but they did nothing and I became an all-too-easy target. I dreaded going to school and dreaded getting up in the mornings. I'd often come home broken and wretchedly unhappy. 'Please, Dad. Can't you move me to another school? I can't stand any more of this,' I'd sob.

But my father wasn't having it. Instead, he said: 'You know what, son. There comes a point in everyone's life when you have to sink or swim. You'll have to do something about this, take some action yourself, or it will carry on with you for the rest of your schooldays – and maybe the rest of your life. And we can't have that; that's no good. Moving you to another school won't solve it because it'll just happen all over again there. Word will spread, it's all local, kids will find out you were moved because you were being bullied and that will give them the idea to do it themselves. That's the nature of the beast.'

A couple of days later, I was back at school and it kicked off again. But this time, Dad's words were going round and round in my head and I was getting increasingly wound up. I was heading towards a meltdown and that moment came when I was in Mr Myatt's metalwork class.

As often happened, he left the classroom halfway through the lesson, leaving us kids to whatever we were doing. A sixth sense told me trouble was brewing, so before anyone could make a move, I turned to the class and said: 'I'm warning you. I'm telling you right now: I will batter the next person who says a word to me.' I'd snapped before like this, promising them I would do something, but it was always just words. Silence. Nobody said anything for a few minutes until, suddenly, there was a towering body in front of me – the tallest boy in my year, almost six foot even by the age of 11. He'd never really bothered me before. Today was different, though.

What he said wasn't particularly grotesque – he just chose the wrong moment to say it. 'You little weed, you little weed' – over and over until it utterly overwhelmed me. Then I heard Dad's words, also over and over – 'you have to take some action, you have to take some action'.

I had a mallet in my hand as he was goading me, and the more he chanted, the harder I started smashing it into an aluminium sheet on the table top in front of me. The class was captivated and that's when the tallest boy in my year made another mistake. Instead of backing off, he came over again, digging at me, in my face until I snapped: 'You say one more thing and I'll smash your head with this mallet.' He was back a minute later, this time with a sickly grin. 'I've warned you,' I yelled. 'Yeah, yeah, Jew boy, what are you going to do then?'

In a flash, I raised the mallet and swung it straight on to his forehead. The blow sent him crashing to the ground, but instead of backing off, I jumped on top and smashed him again – like I was pummelling that aluminium sheet. I had completely gone, years of provocation erupting out of me, and I would have landed more blows if Mr Myatt hadn't walked in at that exact moment and dragged me up.

I got marched to the headmaster's office but I didn't feel the tiniest bit of remorse or concern. In fact, I was elated. I had taken action and it had shut them all up. The headmaster didn't see it my way. He loomed over me as I sat on the other side of his desk and thundered: 'You do know what you've done is abominable, don't you, Heller. There is no excuse for extreme violence and I will not tolerate it at my school.' At that moment, my parents walked in. 'We will have to suspend your son immediately,' the headmaster announced, his chest all puffed out. But my dad wasn't having that.

'Our child has been subjected to horrific bullying for far too long at this school and you've done nothing to stop it,' he roared. 'If you suspend him, then we will go to the papers and tell our side of the story. Believe me, that won't look very good for you – or your school.'

Surprise, surprise, I didn't get suspended; they knew they'd fucked up. Dad tried to pretend he was annoyed as we left but, once we got into the car to go home, he said: 'Well done, son. I know that was hard. But you will have to go back to school tomorrow because there is no hiding now. When you get there, you will hold your head high and you'll walk through those gates and I guarantee there won't be anyone waiting there to bully you. That's all over now.'

I wasn't entirely sure that would be true but, hey presto, the moment I walked through the school gates every single nutter in the school suddenly wanted to be my best mate. My life changed completely. I never heard the words 'Jew boy' ever again in that tone. Everything turned round: every tough bastard in the school wanted to be my mate. I was elevated to hero status and it changed everybody's perception of me.

The bully eventually returned to school and stayed right out of my way. I held no more grudge against him, but in later life, long after we'd left school, I saw him in the street. To my surprise he came up and said: 'I want to talk to you.'

'Oh yeah,' I replied, not sure where this was going.

'I owe you an apology. I should have never done that. It was diabolical; I can't believe I said it. I didn't mean it, I was just trying to impress everyone else, and I don't hold anything against you for doing what you did to me.'

I hadn't expected that. 'Good,' I replied and we shook hands.

As far as I was concerned, Dad had been right: there comes a moment when you have to stand up for yourself. But my ordeal didn't disappear, even when I left school. It just kept resurfacing in different ways and for different reasons. Sometimes it was employers – like Tesco in Wimbledon, where one of their managers pushed me into working illegally long hours. The store was raided for mistreating staff after I reported them. Sometimes it was bosses, who refused to pay me the commission I was legitimately owed. Sometimes it was London's gangland and, specifically, one of the Krays' most notorious henchmen, who tried to make me hand over a winning betting slip at the bookies. And sometimes it was the people I least expected, like the Football Association. Thanks to my father, I was better equipped to deal with them all.

Chapter 6
PLOUGH LANE

WHAT made Wimbledon Football Club such a big deal? Why couldn't I just lie down and die? That's what the FA wanted, after all. Here's why. I doubt they'll understand . . .

We jumped off the train at Haydons Road station, just the three of us, and walked past the second-hand car showroom until we reached Mr Bissell's fish and chip shop, his name emblazoned in bright red lettering on a white panel above the main window. It was a dark, frosty night, and even though there were shops lit up on both sides of the road, his stood out the most – mainly because of the deeply seductive smell. The sweetest cocktail of chips and vinegar wafted through Mr Bissell's open door and hung tantalisingly over the pavements outside. I stared enviously at clusters of men standing outside, each clutching scrunched-up white paper bags. I wanted to join them – but there was no time to stop.

We carried on, past the newsagents, until we reached the church on the corner. Suddenly there were a lot of people at the crossroads, all heading in the same direction, all loud and boisterous, some singing and chanting songs I'd never heard before. Everyone except me seemed to have a blue and yellow scarf wrapped tightly round their necks – or slung over their shoulders so they dangled alongside each arm as they walked along.

And that's when I saw them for the first time. That's when the magic really started. I'd never seen anything like them before and for a few seconds I stopped and just looked up, mesmerised by huge square blocks of brilliant white light, suspended high in the black night and blazing down ferociously into the darkness below. Someone tugged my arm and I moved forward, slowly making out the faint outline of giant spindly legs that seemed to rise up and up until they reached the lights high above.

I was close enough now to see wispy clouds of cold night air illuminated by the incessant glow. Night was being turned into day and I was spellbound. That image and the sheer thrill of excitement that surged through me in that bedazzling moment has never left me to this day. Whenever I go to a night game, no matter which ground, the moment I see the floodlights is a moment when I once again become that nine-year-old boy going to his first-ever competitive football match in 1972. And that was just the start of it.

I was with my brother David and our local football coach who had agreed to take us to see Wimbledon play Guildford City at Plough Lane in the Surrey Senior Cup. David had already been to a match but I was forbidden because Mum and Dad thought I was still too young. I howled and screamed and protested so much that, in the end, Dad begged the coach to take me.

I'd no idea what we were walking into but, as we approached the ground, I could see three or four thin door frames punched into the exterior brick wall, with poster signs advertising the next fixtures and entrance prices daubed in white paint above each one.

Then came something else that was new to me: the clunk, click of rusty old turnstiles. They were only waist high but I was so short the top bar was still above my head. I watched David go through first, then lifted my arms up to push the rickety mechanism forward.

Once through, I saw the pitch for the first time: a vast, green, glowing carpet under the bright white floodlights that were shining down from all four corners of the ground. It was way bigger than I'd ever anticipated and way bigger than anything I'd ever kicked a ball on before.

I'd barely absorbed that shock when the Plough Lane smell struck. I'd never smelt anything like the aroma coming from the Wimbledon food kiosk. 'What's that smell?' I called. 'Hotdogs and fried onions,' came the reply. 'Oh Lord, it's delicious,' I rejoiced. I didn't even know what a hotdog was, and, being Jewish, I'd never eaten a pork sausage.

We carried on walking, shoulders bumping into shoulders, incoherent music coming from somewhere on high and unidentifiable voices all around – either guffawing or swearing or both – as we headed for the South Stand and the halfway line, where we stopped close to a low, metal fence that separated the pitch from the terracing. It looked like the sort of fence I'd seen in the local park, circling the rhododendron bushes. It was so short even I could see over it, so I stared out at the vast, empty pitch and took in my first football ground.

Plough Lane. It looked magnificent to me. I didn't spot its pimples and imperfections: the decaying corrugated panels, the crumbling concrete, the complete absence of things like hospitality lounges, executive boxes and, heaven forbid, clean toilets. To me it was majestic and it took my breath away. The Ivor Heller Theatre of Dreams and I quickly got lost in my own dreamland as I gazed out, thinking about the goals I'd be scoring on that pitch one day.

Suddenly the crackling music stopped, replaced by an indistinct voice that sounded like it was being strangled inside a tinny speaker. It was impossible to tell what this voice was saying but it triggered a roar around the ground and two lines of players slowly appeared from a gap in the middle of the stand opposite us and ran out on to the pitch. Almost instantly another powerful smell

I'd never experienced invaded the night air. Something vaguely medical I thought. 'What's that?'

'Liniment. It's what the players rub into their skin before a match,' came the reply from our football coach. Liniment and hotdogs. Oh, this is bliss.

Everything felt so real, so raw, so alive – so adult, like it was dangerous to even be there. This was proper men's territory and I half expected someone to shout: 'Ivor Heller, you're far too young for this. Go home immediately.' I looked around, relieved not to hear anyone picking me out. It wasn't a huge crowd, there were spaces here and there, but it was definitely loud and raucous and vulgar and incredibly, incredibly funny.

Grown men with tough-looking faces and black jackets were spontaneously breaking out into chants and, somehow, they all magically knew the words. Then, when they weren't singing, they were shouting out, using words and language I'd never heard before. 'Pick your fucking legs up, you dozy tosser.' That would be followed by delighted howls of laughter and I'd laugh, too, desperate to be part of this thing.

It was hilarious and intoxicating and beyond anything I'd ever imagined. I'd never heard grown-ups swearing so much in public. It was mind-blowing. I loved it. I spent most of the game watching the crowd, but when I did glance at the football, there was one player who stood out more than anyone else. Ian Cooke.

Like me, Cooke was so much shorter than the others yet, time and again, he would plough into colossal opponents, who uniformly towered over him in height – and width. He should have been poleaxed by them but, instead, they were the ones left sprawling on the floor, or simply stranded by his lightning speed. Cooke was everything I wanted to be: fearless, skilful and extremely capable of looking after himself when tempers boiled over.

Ian Cooke could never be bullied.

Wimbledon won 3-1 but when I returned home, and Mum and Dad asked me how it had gone, I could barely remember a thing about the match. Instead, I remembered the laughter, the swearing, the smells, the ground, the sense of belonging and excitement, the night air trapped inside the gaze of the floodlights, the grown-up-ness of it all. And Ian Cooke. So, I decided there and then that Wimbledon were my team. For ever.

I went to school the next day and told everyone about my night at Plough Lane. 'I'm telling you, Wimbledon are better than Chelsea and Arsenal and Fulham,' I proclaimed. But none of them were convinced. So I went to Plough Lane without them, and started to befriend a slightly older group of lads who all congregated on the West Bank, behind the goal. That's where I got to know lifelong pals like Steve Elson, Russell Smith, Dickie Mason, Martin Newton and Dave Snowdon (RIP).

That's where I got close up to our keeper, Dickie Guy, for the first time. That's where we'd shamelessly chant his name – Dickeee, Dickeee – and he'd wave and give us some chat when the action was down the other end.

Our little group grew until there'd be 30 or 40 of us, and the more we went, the better it got: Plough Lane was rapidly becoming the best fun I'd ever had in my life. Every game felt like a knees-up. I was still too short to actually see much of the football but that didn't bother me, either. Crowd surges were all the rage and getting swallowed up in human tides lurching backwards and forwards was heaven enough for me.

There was only one obstacle to all this joy: Mum and Dad were determined that I attended the local Sutton synagogue on Saturdays. They were never overtly religious parents – the most I remember is Mum lighting candles in our flat on Friday nights – but they were adamant that I completed my bar mitvah by the age of 13. 'I don't care what you do after that,' said Dad. I had no choice. But Saturday was already holy to me for an entirely different reason: Saturday was matchday and somehow I'd have to juggle the two.

So, I'd get to the synagogue by 10 a.m. and while everyone dutifully prayed and listened to sermons and readings, I'd fidget furiously. I spent every second watching a clock on the wall tick painfully slowly towards 12.30 p.m. when the ordeal would end. That would still give me enough time to get home, ditch my good clothes and get into my match gear.

By now I'd made my own top hat and that gave me great notoriety among my new mates. It was basically a giant cardboard tube I'd made at school with 'Dons are the Greatest' written across the front around a blue rosette. I even got it signed by the players and religiously stuck it on my head at every game. A lot of the lads wore Doctor Martens but we couldn't afford them so I made do with some cheap lookalikes, with army green trousers rolled up to show off the boots. My Elvis shirt and tank top would complete the look, along with as near to a Harrington jacket as we could afford. Replica shirts weren't a thing back then, so I'd show my allegiance with a home-made yellow and blue scarf that Mum had knitted slung around my neck. I looked a right state but I also looked like one of the lads.

Once dressed, I'd run down to the station. I adored waiting on the platform for the train to come in and could always tell what size crowd we'd be getting by how many people were on it. I'd clamber in, my top hat perched proudly on top of my head. Everyone loved that hat – people would pull it off and chuck it merrily around the carriage, but it always came back to me undamaged, like it was the Pope's holy mitre or something. At each stop, lads would stick their heads out of the windows so fans getting on would know which carriage to go to. There'd often be 30 or 40 of us wedged in, jumping up and down and chanting. Morden South, Merton South, Wimbledon Chase and Wimbledon passed by in a blur until we reached Haydons Road, where we'd all get out.

I still couldn't persuade anyone at school to join me at Plough Lane, but I did get an unexpected bonus one day when the PE teacher walked up to me and said: 'You're a Wimbledon fan, aren't you, Heller?'

'Yes sir, 100 per cent,' I replied, wondering why he'd asked.

'In that case, we've been given a season ticket by the club to give to a fan at the school and you're the only one. So you can have it.'

And that teed me up for the 1974–75 season. The greatest in the club's history.

Chapter 7
SLAYING THE GIANTS

THE biggest single thing that kept me going as we fought to save our club was the memory of what happened in the 1974–75 season when we were still non-league minnows. I was 11 years old and about to witness and feel something so wonderful that it never left me. It started in the 92nd minute of our first-round FA Cup tie against Bath City, when Mick Mahon blasted home a late winner from 30 yards out. Mahon's thunderbolt didn't just win a match, it put Wimbledon on the map. If we hadn't beaten Bath it's highly likely the entire Wimbledon story would never have happened. Instead, we cruised past Kettering and reached the third-round draw for the first time in our history. The excitement was off the scale.

This was an era when the FA Cup really mattered – so much so that one of our schoolteachers, Mr Haydock, actually stopped his lesson so we could all crowd round the transistor radio I'd brought in and listen to the draw, praying we'd get Manchester United or Arsenal at Plough Lane. Then we heard: 'And Burnley will play . . . Wimbledon Football Club.'

Shit.

I remember the radio commentator adding: 'That's a tough one for the Southern League part-timers, who must travel to Turf Moor and face a Burnley side currently third in the First Division.'

It was such an anti-climax and all the kids started laughing. 'You should support Chelsea like us, Heller.' Even Mr Haydock was shaking his head knowingly. Burnley weren't the glamour side I'd wanted, although they had a string of internationals like Leighton James, Brian Flynn and Peter Noble, all household names.

We've no chance.

We had a new manager back then, though. Allen Batsford had only taken over in the summer and had immediately raided his old club, Walton and Hersham, to bring in players like Dave Bassett, Dave Donaldson and Billy Edwards. He'd also added two strikers who'd played for him before – Keiron Somers and Roger Connell. Plus, we had Selwyn Rice. He was an absolute thug on the pitch, but off it one of the nicest, meekest human beings I ever got to meet. It didn't add up at all. 'Selwyn bites yer knackers' was a popular chant back then.

The bookies gave us no chance and made Burnley 1-25 favourites to win. Mum and Dad insisted I was too young to travel up to Lancashire, so I tuned into my radio while simultaneously watching *Grandstand* on the TV. My brother was working in a pharmacy in Morden and my parents were running the shop downstairs, so I sat there alone – with my blue and yellow scarf round my neck – surrounded by the newspaper cuttings I'd plastered all over my bedroom walls.

It quickly became apparent that my idol, Dickie Guy, was performing heroics. 'It's all Burnley but Wimbledon are defending well and whenever they have broken through, Guy is saving everything,' said the commentator. Then came an unexpectedly excited voice on the radio. 'And we're taking you live to Turf Moor where there's been a goal.' My heart practically exploded out of my chest.

It's all over.

'It's remarkable, it's remarkable. Wimbledon have taken the lead – Mick Mahon has scored.' And for some reason, the commentator added words that I've never forgotten to this day: 'It's not totally ridiculous!'

I jumped around like an idiot and got shouted at for making a noise. I completely forgot the game wasn't over and ran out into the streets, screaming and yelling and swirling my scarf maniacally over my head. When I got back, we'd won 1-0 and become the first non-league team to win at a top flight club for 54 years.

Then it was all about the draw and this time we really did hit the jackpot. It wasn't a home tie, but we were drawn against the reigning First Division champions, Leeds United. They were favourites to win the European Cup at the time. They were probably the best team in the world, never mind the UK. Allen Batsford and Dickie Guy and Selwyn Rice and Dave Bassett and Ian Cooke and Mick Mahon – up against Jimmy Armfield and David Harvey and Billy Bremner and Peter Lorimer and Johnny Giles and Eddie Gray.

Once again, nobody fancied our chances. The attitude was: 'You've had your fun at Burnley; there's no way you're getting past Leeds.' Once again, I was deemed too young to go, so I made more home-made banners and slung them across my bedroom walls. This time I had two radios as well as the TV on and I'd gasp every time someone said: 'And now we go to Elland Road for an update.'

Each time it was the same: 'Dickie Guy is having the game of his life. Dickie Guy is Wimbledon's miracle man as the part-timers continue to defy Leeds.'

Then came the 67th minute when Leeds were awarded a penalty, then came the agony of waiting for Lorimer to hit the spot-kick. Then came the elation of hearing: 'Lorimer shoots and . . . Guy saves, Guy saves! Dickie Guy is the super hero; he will surely have the freedom of Wimbledon after this,' proclaimed the commentator. He was right, too, although it took a hell of a long time for that to happen – 15 September 2021 to be precise. We held on for a goalless draw, which meant only one thing: Leeds United would be coming to Plough Lane for the replay.

Fucking hell.

My brother David phoned the club that same night and discovered tickets would be on sale the next morning because the replay would be the following Tuesday. I was the first up at 6 a.m., dragging my dad and brother out of bed so we could head straight to Plough Lane. There was already a colossal queue snaking round the ground when we arrived, but I had my school's season ticket so I could join the much shorter priority line.

The actual replay ticket was blue with the match details printed in black. Even I thought it would be easy to forge – which is exactly what happened, although I didn't know that then. I woke up early on Tuesday morning – matchday – and pulled back my curtains, only to see torrential rain outside. It didn't stop all day long and I got a sinking feeling at school that the game would be called off. It was. Instead, it moved to the following week. That was okay, but then came another bombshell: the fixture was being transferred to the much bigger Selhurst Park, home of Crystal Palace, because so many forged tickets had done the rounds. Some 15,000 tickets had been sold but there were at least 3,000 forgeries apparently. Waiting and waiting for a week to crawl by felt like purgatory. The draw for the next round went ahead in the meantime and, once we'd beaten Leeds, we'd be away at Derby.

No worries, we can beat them as well.

There were no advance tickets for the rearranged replay, just pay on the day. The whole of London wanted to see this game; sadly, hooliganism was rife and fans from other clubs fancied the prospect of a punch-up with Leeds's own notorious supporters. I bunked off school that afternoon and David and I were literally the first people in Selhurst Park at 4.30 p.m. so we could stand right behind the goal. The crowd slowly built up and there were definitely groups of hard-looking men everywhere. Fights broke out sporadically inside and outside the stadium long before the game actually started. In the end, there were 46,000 of us in the ground – with many more locked out. It was almost a dream start when Roger Connell scored an early goal, frustratingly disallowed for pushing.

Once again we held Leeds and Dickie was saving everything that came his way. We even had some decent attacks of our own and there were plenty of gasps, oohs and aahs ricocheting around the stadium. Then came the sucker punch. Just when it was all going so well, Johnny Giles unleashed a speculative shot from miles out. Dickie clearly had the ball covered until it took a wicked deflection off Dave Bassett. I remember thinking, 'Dickie's going the wrong way, the ball's changed direction. There's nothing he can do: this is the end.' And it was. But what a ride.

Our league crowds went up and up after that. Plough Lane was buzzing and, no matter who we were playing, everyone kept singing: 'We all hate Leeds and Leeds and Leeds.' That went on for years.

Batsford's team had everything. It was a golden period when I fell truly, madly, deeply in love with Wimbledon FC. I was convinced we were going all the way to the top with these players and I remember telling my best friend, Alan Tucker: 'In 10 years' time we will be in the First Division and we'll have won the FA Cup.'

Despite losing to Leeds, the season was still very much alive, although we had a massive backlog of games caused by the cup run. At times we were playing Saturday, Tuesday, Thursday then Saturday again – with a squad of just 14 part-time players. We reached the London Senior Cup final against Leatherhead in April. They were considered one of the best non-league sides in the country, but we won 2-0 at Dulwich's Champion Hill ground and invaded the pitch afterwards. Next, we won the Southern League itself after a 1-1 draw at home to Telford. That was the first time I ever invaded the Plough Lane pitch – although someone had to help me climb over the fence first. I loved being on the pitch, especially when the players came back out to wave at us from the main stand. Everyone was singing and dancing, then we headed for Wimbledon town centre, marching down Queens Road, chanting all the way and holding up the traffic.

Wimbledon should have been allowed into the English Football League there and then, but in those days there was no such thing as automatic promotion. Instead, Football League club chairmen voted: they could either let a new club in – and demote one of the four clubs that finished bottom of the old Fourth Division – or they could close ranks and spare the basement clubs. Nearly always they closed ranks. It was only when Wimbledon won the Southern League for three consecutive years that we were begrudgingly allowed in. Even then, it took an extraordinary campaign by our then chairman, Ron Noades, to persuade them. He came up with the slogan Dons4Div4, the words stuck and Workington dropped out.

Looking back now, I have absolutely no doubt that all these experiences were what motivated me to fight for my club in 2002.

The 1974–75 season sowed the seeds. When we started AFC Wimbledon, I gleefully told everyone that we would 'win things' and that we'd have a 'lot of fun' along the way. But fans who had got used to Wimbledon playing the likes of Manchester United and Liverpool in the Premier League looked at me like I was mad.

'What do you mean?' they asked.

'We'll win the London Senior Cup again and we'll probably win the Surrey Cup and a league trophy for sure. We will win things and it will be an incredible journey – one you'll never forget,' I explained. The 1974–75 season had taught me that it didn't matter what the level was. It would happen again, history would repeat itself – of that I was certain. That's what I would promise the fans in 2002.

Chapter 8
WINNING THE CUP

I LOOKED at their faces as I clambered on to the double-decker bus. It was like we'd been waiting all our lives for this journey. Everyone was on board – Steve Elson, Dickie Mason, Martin Newton, Russell Smith, John Hyam, Jonesy, Dave Snowdon, Bob Walsh. Then there was Ian 'Woody' Wood, Tommy Woolgar and Richard Pope. We called ourselves the Batsford Boys in honour of the manager we all worshipped. Everyone on that bus had done the hard yards, had seen us lose horribly at godforsaken places up and down the country. But we'd kept coming back until we'd witnessed the club's rise from non-league to the First Division – and now to the FA Cup final.

We were little old Wimbledon, pariahs, renowned underdogs with a tinpot ground and players who respected nobody and relished a punch-up. I suspected half the country thought we were still a non-league club. But everyone on that bus knew something the country didn't know. We weren't scared of Liverpool. Along with the players, we were probably the only people in the world who believed we would win the cup that day.

We set off at 8.30 a.m. exactly from the Lord Palmerston pub in Merton Road. I'd never seen so much booze on a bus before: crates packed with cans, stuffed under seats and piled high on baggage racks. Cliff Jackson, doorman at Plough Lane's pub, The Sportsman, had organised it all. Everyone was battered by the time we reached Wembley, singing manically and ready for a laugh. The comedian Harry Enfield was huge on TV at the time, particularly his Loadsamoney character. One of our gang had photocopied piles of £20 notes and every time we saw some Scousers, we'd wave the fake notes at them and chant 'loadsamoney'. We all found this hilarious. Most of the Scousers laughed, but some really didn't like it. We were beyond caring by then: we kept going up and down Wembley Way, soaking it all up – the scarves, the banners, the burger vans and the sheer incredulousness of us, little ol' Wimbledon, outside Wembley for an FA Cup final. And we kept waving our £20 notes.

We were heavily outnumbered inside the stadium – our ticket allocation had definitely sold out, but many had slipped into Liverpool hands. Out of 100,000 fans, I'd say there were 20,000 who truly wanted Wimbledon to win. Nothing could have diminished the day for us, though, and I felt goosebumps when the traditional cup final anthem, 'Abide with Me', swept over the stadium, followed next by a volcanic roar as the two teams emerged from the players' tunnel.

Then it started. Just six minutes into the game, Vinnie scythed down their most influential player, Steve McMahon. We roared our approval because that tackle, as ugly as it was, literally terrified the whole of Liverpool.

Then we scored, Lawrie Sanchez's looping header, right below us, soaring high into the net. Then we roared even louder. Then big Dave Beasant became the first goalkeeper to save a cup final penalty and we roared again and I distinctly remember thinking: 'Bloody hell. We're actually going to win this.'

Then the ref blew the whistle. Then we were grabbing each other and jumping up and down and screaming, 'We've won the fucking cup.' It was sheer pandemonium, sheer disbelief and sheer joy. It was undoubtedly the pinnacle of everything I had seen and experienced with Wimbledon FC. I was delirious.

Then Lady Di – *bloody hell, Lady Di* – coyishly handed the cup to big Dave Beasant, and he thrust it our way, like it was for us, ours to keep for ever. I remember watching the players dancing and jigging their way round the pitch for their lap of honour. I'd seen so many cup finals on the telly, but there seemed to be something more intense about the way we were celebrating. It bordered insanity. Wimbledon beating Liverpool at Wembley in the FA Cup final was pretty insane, after all.

We eventually got back to the bus but we never stopped celebrating. There was ceaseless singing on the top deck and all along the roads people were tooting their car horns at us, and we were waving and cheering and laughing and, best of all, pointing at any groups of deflated Scousers trudging home.

Then we got back to Wimbledon and I'd never seen anything like that. Unbelievable. The main road from the town centre all the way up to posh Wimbledon Village was rammed, and people were walking around like zombies, totally pissed. Anyone who hadn't made the final had come out for the street party and the crowd kept getting bigger and bigger.

Every pub and off-licence in the area ran out of booze that night. I don't know how or when I got home, but I went back to Plough Lane pretty early the next morning so I could follow the team parading the cup on their own double-decker bus through the town centre. I walked ahead of the bus as it was driven up to the town hall, and then I stood right at the front as the players waved to the fans from the balcony above.

We kept on partying, long after the crowds eventually headed home that Sunday. Even on Monday night you could hear car horns going off and see human beings slumped in doorways, fast asleep. It was euphoric, it was unbelievable, and it was incredibly drunken. I don't know how I survived it, but I do know it was the best four-day party of my life.

Chapter 9
BEREAVEMENT

I SEE the exact spot where we once stood behind the goal: me, Steve, Russell and Dave, laughing and joking and being a bunch of lads at a football match. Dickie's turning round to smile at us and then I hear an almighty roar as Cookey rifles the ball home down the other end. We all go mental. Then I look again. There's nothing there, just shattering silence and a car horn going off somewhere in the distance.

It's a grey, dull, London morning, a faint mist hanging in the air, not quite rain but dank and annoying. I press my head closer to the gap in the gate grille and see the reality: the rotting carcass of an abandoned football ground I once considered more precious than my own home. Uncontrollable clumps of weeds and knee-high undergrowth have invaded everywhere, sprouting wildly from the crumbling concrete steps where we used to stand. The pitch has vanished, in its place an ugly wasteland, strewn with builders' rubble and sheets of sodden plasterboard and what looks like old kitchen worktops.

I feel myself reminiscing once again and swear I can see Vinnie grabbing Gazza by the balls and hear the crowd erupting in delight. My eyes move over to the South Stand and I can just about see the fading words WELCOME TO WIMBLEDON FC running along the front edge of the rotting roof. Then I switch over to the North Stand. It looks so much smaller than I remembered, barely covering half the length of the pitch and yet this was our main stand. Corrugated-iron panels dangle precariously off the sides now and I wonder if the main support posts are going to crumble at any moment and bring the whole derelict structure crashing down. The players' tunnel has all but disappeared – blocked out by the grotesque shrubs and bramble shoots that have spread so disrespectfully over my sacred arena. Everywhere is depressingly derelict, like a Wild West ghost town, and although it triggers fleeting memories of what we once were, that's all they are – memories.

The FA weren't the first to strip us. Just three years after winning the FA Cup, we lost our home while we were still in English football's top division playing the best teams in the country every week. In 1991, our club's then owner, Sam Hammam, announced we'd be ground sharing with Crystal Palace at Selhurst Park. My beloved Plough Lane would only be used for reserve team games. We begged and hollered and demanded to go back, but we never did. Instead, Hammam secretly sold our home to the Safeway supermarket chain and pocketed the money.

I hadn't the faintest idea this was going to happen – until it did. In fact, I'd just moved into a new flat with my then girlfriend, Claire, in nearby Leopold Road, purely because it was a short walk from the ground. Ironically, we played Palace on the last day of the season; Ian Wright scored a hat-trick as we lost 3-0. After the game, I got outrageously drunk – so much so, I stripped off all my clothes and, stark bollock naked, gleefully scored a goal in front of the West Bank in an impromptu game on the Plough Lane pitch. I've no idea why I was naked; it must have been a bet. I was so hammered that I attempted all sorts of somersaults to celebrate my goal, never once suspecting everything was about to go bottoms up the next day.

I woke up the following morning, feeling groggy, and turned on my radio, only to hear: 'And now some breaking news: Wimbledon Football Club will no longer be playing at their famous old ground, Plough Lane. It's been confirmed this morning that the club will ground share with Crystal Palace at Selhurst Park.'

What the fuck.

The most crushing, sick-to-the-pit-of-my-stomach nausea overwhelmed me. I grabbed my phone and called Steve Elson. I'd never felt so completely out of the loop and panic-stricken.

'Ivor, what planet have you been on, mate? The rumours have been flying around for ages. It's all true; we're off to Crystal Palace next season,' he confirmed. 'But even if you'd known, what could you have done about it?'

And that made me think. The club I considered mine, the ground I considered home, wasn't mine or home at all. I was utterly invested in Wimbledon Football Club – heart, soul, wallet

– yet that entitled me to nothing. I had no say over its destiny. If Sam Hammam chose to sell it, then that was his right. Us fans could go do one. I'll never forget the empty, hollow feeling that engulfed me. Then came real anger: I hated Hammam, I hated Palace, I hated the world. I even hated myself – I'd taken my eye off the ball; I'd never seen it coming.

Fucking hell, I've only just moved into this poxy flat.

I'd actually mapped out my drive to work so that I'd go past the ground every day and know it was there and everything was okay. The thought of never going to Plough Lane again to watch a match was inconceivable, incomprehensible. It felt like a bereavement to me. Losing the ground felt like we'd lost the whole club. It was heartbreaking and I felt deeply betrayed. I even started taking detours in my car, driving a much longer, circuitous route to work so I didn't have to endure the agony of seeing the ground. It was too upsetting.

Selhurst fucking Park. They can fuck right off.

My anger simmered all through the summer and, just as the next season came into sight, I told Steve: 'I've been thinking long and hard about this. I won't be going to any of our home games.'

'What the fuck do you mean, Ivor?'

'I'll go to a few away ones but I'm not going to Selhurst Park. I'll feel dirty going there.'

That was how I felt. So I didn't go. And I didn't go for the next three seasons, even though they were some of the best years Wimbledon enjoyed in the Premier League. They finished sixth in the Premier League's inaugural season – beating Arsenal, Liverpool, Leeds and Forest. I missed all that. This was a matter of principle.

There were anguished moments when I almost caved in: several times I got in my car to go to Selhurst Park but then I'd reach Plough Lane and turn right back round again. I'd literally see the ground and think: 'Fucking hell, I now have to drive another hour to Selhurst Park. Why should I be forced to do that when – right in front of me – is the football ground we should be playing in. Our real home, just standing there, empty.'

I genuinely had no sympathy for what Hammam did. At the time, he blamed it all on the Taylor Report, which demanded all-seater football stadiums after the awful Hillsborough Disaster when 96 Liverpool fans died, crushed on overpacked terraces. None of us could argue with the Taylor recommendations. I'd been to games when I'd thought, 'This is dangerous.'

In 1989, the same year as Hillsborough, we were drawn away to Aston Villa in the FA Cup fourth round. We were defending the cup and we all hit the pubs beforehand, getting to Villa Park about 20 minutes before kick-off. As usual, we were directly opposite the Holte End in a stand that had been subdivided into pens – like cattle pens really – with prison-style fencing separating each section from the next. It started to get extremely uncomfortable very quickly. My height hardly helped: I was increasingly getting pushed up against a fence as more and more fans got shovelled into our pen. Anxiety quickly turned to panic. My body was trapped against the metal barrier by the sheer force of fans crammed into our section, my face squashed against the stanchions. I saw a steward and started yelling: 'I can't breathe, I can't breathe, get me out of here.' Fortunately, he heard me and one of the gates into the adjoining pen was opened so fans could pour straight into that.

When Hillsborough happened, I flashed back to that Villa Park moment. When the Taylor Report called for all-seater stadiums, I knew it was for the right reasons. But that didn't mean Plough Lane had to close. Hammam insisted the site wasn't big enough to house an all-seater, but that was bollocks. In fact, I later discovered that his brother, Ned, owned an adjacent piece of land where an office block stood surrounded by car parking spaces.

If that site was combined with the football ground, there would have been plenty of room for at least a 20,000-capacity stadium. That would have been way bigger than Bournemouth's current ground – and they've managed to thrive in the Premier League.

We'll never know what Hammam's true motives were, but they killed me. How could the people who gave themselves so completely to a football club, who built their lives and dreams around it, who gave it heart and soul and love and loyalty, be so utterly uninvolved in determining its future? Was it right that one man had the power to switch off the lights, just like that? Did we count for nothing? Was the club we thought was ours never ours at all? Were we just mugs? I never felt so low and I quietly vowed that nobody would ever do this to me again. And here's the thing. Selhurst Park was barely seven miles from Plough Lane. Milton fucking Keynes was 70.

Chapter 10
MUTINY

IT WAS the moment I crossed the divide. It was the moment I literally stuck two fingers up to the suits and power brokers in the boardroom – and began the battle to save my club. My career was soaring, I owned my own print company and we did a load of work for the club – as well as some major blue-riband clients like Samsung, Liberty's and J&B Whisky.

I ended my one-man protest against Selhurst Park in 1994, largely thanks to Ken Budgen, a business colleague and dear friend. He had the best four seats at Arsenal's old ground, Highbury, and whenever we played the Gunners, he invited me into their executive suite. I learned so much about hospitality from those trips and he persuaded me to book four really good hospitality tickets at Selhurst Park so I could return the favour. I remember having lunch in the ground-floor restaurant ahead of the game when two faces suddenly appeared at the window: Jonesy and Steve Elson. I went out to see them, we had a giggle and – in that moment – I realised I didn't want to miss any more home matches.

Ken had changed the way I wanted to go to football: he'd introduced me to the world of hospitality and I soon took up the sponsorship opportunity to become a Wimbledon vice-president, in exchange for a reasonable fee, so I could take business clients and friends to matches. I'm eternally grateful to Ken for that. Everything was rosy, and the team were doing well under manager Joe Kinnear. Selhurst Park was almost bearable. What could possibly go wrong? Plenty as it turned out.

Rumours that we might leave Selhurst Park were flying around thick and fast. Places like Beddington Lane were mentioned – that was close enough to Wimbledon to actually make sense. Less appealing were locations like Gatwick. The words Milton Keynes sprang up but, far more alarming, was the very real possibility we might move to Dublin, be renamed the Dublin Dons and football-crazy Ireland would get their very own Premier League football club. As much as I hated the idea, I could begrudgingly see the business sense. I suspect the Dublin Dons would still be in the Premier League today if it had actually happened.

Then Hammam took us by surprise all over again – this time selling the club in 1997 to two mega-wealthy Norwegians: Kjell Inge Røkke and Bjørn Rune Gjelsten. They inexplicably paid an eye-watering £26 million for a club that had no ground, just a bunch of players who could leave at any moment because they were so poorly paid and had new freedoms thanks to the Bosman ruling.

I was a lot more political by then. Not having a clue that Hammam had sold Plough Lane had taught me a valuable lesson: if someone was fucking up my club, I wanted to know about it. Many fans felt the same way and the Wimbledon Independent Supporters' Association (WISA) grew in strength.

Not long after the Norwegians took over, I was one of a group of fans invited to a presentation on the club's future. Gjelsten was there, and we were all shown wonderful artist impressions of a new stadium. There was only one thing missing, so I stood up and said:

'That looks fantastic, but where's it going to be? Is that Beddington Lane?'

'Could be,' Gjelsten responded.

I looked at him and instantly knew we inhabited different planets. He'd tried to dress down a bit, smart casual, no tie – man of the people. To me, though, he looked like a rich investor who'd suddenly realised he'd been sold a £26 million pup and wanted his money back – quick. Gjelsten had as much connection to me as I did to the Norwegian fjords. 'We know this is where we belong – in Merton,' he added.

Yeah, mate, you just love Merton, I bet.

'So we will keep circling the area but slowly push the circles further and further out until we find a home.'

'Do those circles go all the way out to Milton Keynes?' I snapped back.

'If there's nowhere between Merton and Milton Keynes, then yes.'

And there it was. That's when I got the bit between my teeth. That's when I thought, 'I've got to do something.' We were about to play Southampton live on Sky in the Premier League on 8 May 1999. It was our last home game of the season, and we'd be seen on national television, so I decided to print a load of posters and banners on my company's printing press.

We came up with two slogans: Dublin = Death (with a skull and crossbones) and: MK NO WAY. They were mainly A3 size, some with blue lettering on a yellow background, the rest the other way round. We also did some much bigger banners, with the same messaging. I wanted us to be seen. I churned out 4,000 of each and started spreading the word. The internet was becoming far more prominent in all our lives and WISA got involved, too.

We were going to show the nation that something was wrong at Wimbledon. We were going to protest in a way that, I'm pretty sure, had never been seen at a televised football game before. Claire and I drove to the Foley Arms pub, where hundreds of fans would congregate, and we started handing out posters there. 'Take them to the game and when the players come out, hold your poster as high as you can. We want the TV cameras to see them.'

Then we headed for Selhurst Park and carried on handing out posters to supporters as they entered the ground. 'This is all very well, Claire, but they'll just screw them up and chuck them on the floor once they're inside,' I groaned. That was my biggest fear – and hers, too. The whole thing could easily backfire. We had no idea what to expect.

Claire and I headed up to the vice-presidents' lounge next and took a load more posters in there with us. And that's where I first started to clash with the hobnobs in the inner sanctum. A lot of them thought it wasn't my place to bring protests and posters into their privileged little bubble.

'This isn't the place for nonsense like this,' they complained.

'So you're happy for our club to end up in Dublin or Milton Keynes,' I argued back.

'Well, it'll probably never happen.'

'But they're talking about it. Are we meant to shut up and keep quiet? I'm not making that mistake again. I don't trust any of them.'

The Norwegians were in the boardroom with around 75 vice-presidents and their guests and they heard every word of what was going on. I tried to give posters to them but stewards intercepted me each time. Instead, Claire and I headed out to our seats early.

As we got to our row, another steward blocked my way and whispered: 'We don't want any funny business in here.'

I looked at him contemptuously. He was taller and heftier and more menacing than me, the sort you see working as a bouncer outside nightclubs. He'd no doubt been told to keep an eye out for me.

'What do you call funny business?' I snapped back. 'If you're telling me a poster is funny business then you're going to have to throw me out.'

'No, no. I'm sure that won't be necessary,' he replied, clearly biting his lip. I didn't like the way he'd tried to handle me. Was this a sign of things to come?

My seats were directly behind the visiting dignitaries, right in the heart of the directors' box. To our right was where all our main execs went, including the Norwegians and even Hammam, who still had a role at the club even though he'd sold 80 per cent of it. Claire and I sat there and watched the fans starting to file in. We still had our posters with us but we couldn't see much sign of the ones we'd handed out.

Fuck, they've binned them.

Then, as the two teams emerged from the tunnel, arms were universally thrust upwards into the floodlit night and thousands of posters were suddenly held aloft, all round the stadium. It was beyond my wildest expectations: the Holmesdale End, where our hard-core fans went, was completely covered, everyone holding my posters high.

The Norwegians and the directors and all the arseholes came out at that point, all trying to look pompous and important, and Claire and I immediately turned round to thrust our posters right at them. I remember the feeling so vividly as we waved our posters high. You don't get that sensation often in life, but I felt an electric surge of defiance, a real adrenalin rush. We were being heard, the cameras were recording it all and the enemy within – the people plotting to dispose of our club – visibly had fear in their eyes. It was exhilarating and, in that sweet moment, it felt like winning.

I felt real anger that day, I can't deny it. Nobody tried to say, 'Listen, this is a massive overreaction. This will never happen, put your posters down, calm down, everything is going to be okay.' They probably thought we'd all bugger off home once the game ended. Instead, Claire and I stayed in our seats in the directors' box. We were joining a sit-in organised by WISA and that really pissed off the hierarchy.

We were eventually ordered to leave and were escorted down the stairs and along the side of the pitch. When fans realised what was happening, we got applauded and cheered. I was visibly crossing the line. I was letting the directors know I was not one of them. I didn't want to be in their company; I wanted to go to the people I trusted most. The people who truly held the club's best interests closest to their hearts. As we clambered over seats, people continued clapping and cheering, willing us to stand shoulder to shoulder with them. As we got closer I could hear random shouts: 'Come on, Ivor, fuck that lot, you're one of us.'

Yes, I am.

It was a defining moment. I felt empowered and I also felt exhilarated to be joining a fight for something I truly believed in. It's always easy to have a go from a distance, to hide behind someone's back while you're slagging somebody else off. This was different – there was no hiding place for Ivor Heller now. I was protesting up close and personal and it felt good. I was also showing the Norwegians and Hammam and everyone else in their cosseted little bubble that I was rebelling.

That was the start of it for me. Everyone knew where I stood. I came alive that night. Claire was on the same page as well. We shared the same belief. When we eventually got home, we watched the game on telly and saw the protest broadcast for the first time. It was getting huge exposure because nothing quite like it had ever been seen in the Premier League before. That alone felt like vindication.

What we had done had been worthwhile, even though we didn't know precisely what we were protesting against. The full horror of what was up their sleeves hadn't yet been confirmed. We were just a lot of people with a lot of suspicions that these bastards were trying to do something none of us wanted to our club. So we were laying down a marker.

We were showing them we were a force they couldn't contemptuously brush aside. They had a problem on their hands – and the problem was us.

Chapter 11
A UNIQUE ENEMY

CHARLES Koppel was the most reptilian man I ever knew. He made my skin crawl. He had such a supercilious face. What a twerp. I only ever saw him in a dark suit, white shirt and tie, the arrogant public schoolboy demeanour completed by a pompous 'I'm superior to you, Heller' sneer.

Who was Charles Koppel? He was Wimbledon's chairman when the sinister plan to take my club away became reality. At the start of the 2001–02 season, he produced an appallingly titled brochure called 'A Unique Solution to a Unique Problem'. How could any intelligent human being come up with such a title? Did Koppel not see the obvious parallel with the Nazis' Final Solution for starters? I'm not religious at all – I'm Jewish by birth and that's all – but my sense of revulsion was overwhelming, and that was before I even read the brochure to see what it was saying.

I'll assume he did it without thinking because everything inside the brochure clearly hadn't been thought out, either. I can't deny the club was floundering when his diabolical brochure appeared. The Dublin proposal had withered and died, finally killed off by the Irish FA who didn't want us on their turf. That was good. Then came a real hammer blow: the loss of our exceptional manager, Joe Kinnear, who tragically suffered a heart attack in March 1999. The Norwegians replaced him three months later with their fellow countryman Egil Olsen.

Whereas Kinnear had made us a force to be reckoned with in the Premier League, Olsen turned us into a laughing stock. Eccentric to put it mildly, he was widely lambasted for wearing wellington boots on the touchline and became known as the Wally in the Wellies. Olsen was obsessed with zonal marking, something totally alien to our players. Players who would run through brick walls for us – like Robbie Earle and Neal Ardley – were suddenly dropped and replaced by ones we'd never heard of, and who hadn't an ounce of steel in them. We plummeted down the table and although Olsen left in May, replaced by Dons thoroughbred Terry Burton, it was too late. We were relegated in the year 2000, after eight consecutive seasons in the Premier League.

By then, the Norwegians wanted out big time. Their escape route was 70 miles away, where music mogul Peter Winkelman dreamed of running a Football League club in Milton Keynes. But instead of starting at grass roots and rising up through the leagues, he wanted to buy one straight off the shelf.

Koppel's vile brochure made it official: a statement of intent, unequivocal proof that we were the key to making Winkelman's dream come true. Wimbledon would be moved lock, stock and barrel to Buckinghamshire. Patronising and packed with lies, the brochure was sent to every Wimbledon season ticket holder and did everything it could to talk them into it. Our club was sinking under a mountain of debt, it argued, and we would go under if something wasn't done, but – praise the Lord – salvation was just 70 miles down the road. Even better, the brochure rejoiced, we'd still be allowed to call ourselves Wimbledon. Koppel actually wrote: 'There will be some people upset over this but there will be no rebranding of the club. It will remain Wimbledon FC and play in the same colours. We aim to take our history and heritage and build upon it further.'

What really stung was the way he used the word 'our'. That sickened me to the core. The word 'our' had to be earned: it could only be used by the people who had built Wimbledon and taken it to the top, or supported it through thick and thin. Allen Batsford could use the word 'our'. So could Dickie Guy and Ian Cooke and Dave Bassett and Wally Downes and Vinnie Jones and the Crazy Gang and Joe Kinnear. The fans could say it's 'our' club. But Charles Koppel couldn't. He besmirched and polluted that word.

He was the anthesis of everything Wimbledon stood for, everything we had become thanks to the legends who served our club so heroically over the decades. Koppel hadn't built or contributed anything. In fact, he was the exact opposite: a destroyer, here to disfigure and dismantle. He didn't *love* the club like we did. His blood wasn't yellow and blue. Wimbledon was a payslip for him and nothing else.

I hate you, Koppel.

His brochure took us for idiots, stupid irrelevant football fans with no principles and even less intelligence. It also confirmed everything we had feared. We all reacted the same way. Koppel had declared war and, with the 2001–02 season about to kick off, WISA planned a year of protest. I resigned as a vice-president and decided I wouldn't spend another penny at the club. I still went to every home game but got tickets mainly from players and mates.

Our first home game was against Birmingham when we let off a barrage of black balloons. We had sit-ins and we picketed at every single match after that, and I made a solemn pledge to always be the last one to leave the picket line. I'm proud to say I kept my word. We surrounded the directors' box and we printed thousands of T-shirts with a motif that said: 'Wanted for the Attempted Murder of Wimbledon Football Club'. Slap bang in the middle was a huge headshot with a caption saying: Charles 'Club Killer' Koppel.

We campaigned ceaselessly and did countless newspaper, TV and radio interviews with local, national and even international press. We never stopped getting talked about – and got incredible coverage on 9 September when we played away at Watford. The game was being televised live. Thousands of us went to Vicarage Road, all wearing black T-shirts with Koppel's face on the front alongside our 'wanted for the attempted murder' slogan. We then released more black balloons and, as everyone was looking up to the sky, a small plane flew over, trailing a banner that read: Dons Fans Say Koppel Out. The sound of its engine was completely wiped out by the thunderous roar that erupted from the entire stadium below – including the Watford fans, who broke out into applause.

We weren't just uniting our fans, we were uniting fans everywhere who realised what was happening to us could also happen to them one day. Moments like that were energising; they lifted our spirits immeasurably. We were fighting for something that was vital, that struck to the core of what football fans wanted from their national game. It felt so good to know we weren't alone. At the televised game against Nottingham Forest on 16 December, we held a 'fans united' protest and supporters from Brighton to Barcelona came to the game wearing their own club shirts.

One of our best demonstrations was triggered by one of the club's directors, Peter Miller, who was also a fellow mutineer. He secretly tipped us off that a board meeting was being held in London in the basement of a converted Georgian house, and gave us the exact address and exact time. All the slimy bigwigs were there – Hammam, Koppel, the lot. It was an amazing coup: fans started quietly gathering outside, including many who had spent all day working in the city and were still dressed in their smart suits and overcoats. Once everyone had gathered, we unfurled an enormous banner that read: 'Dons fans want Koppel out' and we didn't leave until the cowering directors emerged, sheer horror spread across their duplicitous faces.

Our protests were always peaceful, they never became abusive, but they were extremely well organised. A group of fans, led by WISA, successfully boycotted club merchandise and launched an alternative matchday programme, Yellow and Blue, which sold thousands while the club's programme was left untouched. That was masterminded by Niall Couper – who, much later, would make that emergency dash to the London FA to pick up the form we needed to make AFC Wimbledon official.

One of our most intelligent campaigns was called 'It's a Community Thing'. Marc Jones created a series of six postcards which we printed and then sent to MPs. Each one had a different photograph that depicted what the football club meant to its local community. For example, there was one of a child (Marc's son, Tom) with his Wimbledon hat on walking to the game. Underneath ran the slogan 'It's a Community Thing'. On the back of the card was a message simply saying: 'When you rip a club from its community, it's the community that suffers'. Tom remains a staunch fan to this day. We printed 20,000 of all six cards, all with similar images, all with the same slogan. Those cards took our campaign to the next level: we were being professional and thought-provoking and creative. Everything Koppel and Co thought we could never be.

I decided to hire an open-top bus and go round the entire borough with a microphone and leafleteers on board. We'd pull up at busy places, get out, distribute our leaflets and postcards, and tell people what was happening. I'd got the bus done up in our yellow and blue colours and, as it drove through the town centre, then Morden and Raynes Park, I stood on the top floor with the mic, telling everyone below: 'We're battling to save our football club, to keep it here – in our community – and we need your help.'

Everywhere we went, the reaction was always the same: 'How can we possibly let our football club go?' We were raising awareness so people would start talking about it in their homes, then in the pubs and then – hopefully – they'd join our protests or write letters to our local MPs and councillors. Ultimately, we hoped to build a political momentum to block the move.

Everything we did, we did with dignity. We never crossed the thin line into thuggery, although I'll never forget going to one match and, as I chatted to another fan, I heard security guards on the radio say: 'Activist One and Activist Two have just entered.' What did the fucking idiots think – we had bombs or something?

There was no doubt we were getting heard and we all thought it was working when the English Football League (EFL) announced they would not approve the move. They had a rule that barred clubs from going more than 25 miles from their historic heartland. I was euphoric and felt victory was in sight. 'This is the breakthrough, they're fucked now,' I told Claire. But Koppel appealed – and that's when the FA passed the buck and set up their three-man commission to make a final, binding decision.

Chapter 12
NO TURNING BACK

IT WAS an abhorrent thing to do but we needed to show the world the depth of our pain. As soon as the referee's whistle signalled the start of the game – our last of the season – we all turned our backs on the team and never looked round for the next 90 minutes. Instead, we humiliated and harangued and stared threateningly at the very people destroying our club as they sat in the directors' box, indifferent to what they were doing to us. We hurled abuse – vile, venomous and personal. It was a ferocious never-ending torrent and, for once, the directors had good reason to be cowering in their crumbling little empire.

The entire protest was orchestrated by WISA and thousands of T-shirts were produced with the slogan: 'Turn Your Back on the Game'. We were playing Barnsley and, when kick-off came, it looked like absolutely everyone inside Selhurst Park was wearing one of those shirts – except the snivelling directors about to betray us.

As usual, everyone congregated at the Foley, then we marched in unison to the ground. I'd seen anger before, but this day felt so much more acute. As we marched towards the ground, I saw people with burning defiance in their faces. Even the way they walked looked menacing, like they were spoiling for a fight. I think deep down we all felt this was probably the last time we'd see Wimbledon again. We prayed, of course, that the commission would see sense. But we also knew that money talked – Winkelman and the Norwegians had it, we didn't. The chances were high that we were fucked.

I had fire in my belly as I walked along, thinking: 'This is the most diabolical thing that's ever happened to me.' Nobody else faced losing their football club like this. Some had gone bust and gone down the divisions – but they still existed. Workington, whom we'd replaced in the Football League, were still going, and so were Barrow and Aldershot.

But we were about to lose ours completely and yet we were still in the Championship. In fact, we'd gone close to reaching the play-offs that season – which would have fucked up Milton Keynes completely. If we'd bounced straight back into the Premier League, the commission would have never believed Wimbledon was a club in crisis.

More and more fans started pouring in, chanting against the board. The atmosphere was ugly, to put it mildly. Then the team came out and I saw the directors and Koppel, surrounded by security, emerge from their protected little lounge within the main stand. A fence separated us and I rushed straight up to it, yelling loudly: 'Come and face us, tell us the truth, you liars.' I could see the police were circling so I very deliberately didn't swear.

They were liars, too. They'd lied about trying to keep us in Merton and they'd lied about their fucking circles slowly spreading out until they found a home. They never had any intention of keeping us in the area. Once again, they couldn't look at me. 'Look at me you snivelling cowards,' I yelled.

Then the police moved in and one of them said: 'Ivor, we're going to lift you.'

'Good, do it, go on – lift me. But you'll have to carry me out because I've done nothing wrong. If I swear then arrest me, but if I don't, then I suggest you stay away.'

Then the referee's whistle cut through the tension and triggered what we'd all been planning. Everyone turned their backs.

It was unbelievable. I looked over to the Holmesdale End and there wasn't a single fan watching the game. Even in the main stand, I'd say a good 70 per cent turned round. Some were complaining, 'Sit down, we want to watch the match.' That was instantly met by choruses of: 'Fuck off and fuck off to Milton Keynes while you're at it.'

I kept my back turned the entire match but it wasn't as easy as it sounds. All of us instinctively wanted to roar on our players and watch the game. Why else do you follow a football team? I was so angry, though; the police and stewards never left my side even though I never did anything illegal. I just looked and sounded like I might. People still come up to me today and say, 'I remember you up against that fence at Selhurst Park, you never stopped, shouting and cursing. We thought you'd explode.'

The protest that day had come right from the heart. It was our last throw of the dice and our last chance to expose the board for what they were – liars – and for the world, but especially the FA and their fucking commission, to sense the pain they were inflicting on us. The owners didn't give a damn, but surely the FA would . . .

Chapter 13
TRUST IN US

ON 10 FEBRUARY 2002, Wimbledon Theatre staged the greatest show on earth as far as I was concerned. Packed to the rafters, there was barely a dry eye in the house as we took a historic step forward. Our seismic year of protests had shown us that, united, we were a force to be reckoned with and could pull off some incredible stunts and campaigns. But there was still an overriding sense that we needed to appeal to an even bigger audience.

We had no firm idea, yet, what would happen to our club other than it was in the hands of people who were trying their best to rip it away from us. Emotionally, Wimbledon FC was *our* club; unemotionally, it belonged to the Norwegians and they didn't give a fuck about us. Was there a way, maybe, that we – the fans who truly loved the club – could take over and steer the ship away from Milton Keynes?

Deep down, we all fantasised about owning the club. That was the only sure-fire way of safeguarding its future. But we didn't have the organisation or structure or funding or people to realistically make that happen. Our only fans' body was WISA, which had done a magnificent job organising the protests and rallying fans on matchdays.

But WISA had its limitations. Although it seems absurd now, back then it was considered a bit of an extreme, almost political organisation – a bit too disruptive to attract moderate fans, or intellectuals like lawyers and business strategists. We needed an alternative to WISA to bring everyone on to the same page. To be a real force, capable of being taken seriously; we needed clever people with real experience of finance and running organisations. So long as their blood was yellow and blue.

So we looked towards Northampton, barely half an hour's drive from Milton Keynes, where The Cobblers Trust had been formed by a fan who, like us, believed there was a better way to run a football club. Brian Lomax, who sadly died in 2015 aged just 67, pioneered the idea of getting fans involved in the running of their clubs. The recently installed Prime Minister, Andy Burnham, was a pall-bearer at Brian's funeral and said: 'He was a true father figure to many of us. He changed our lives when we were young, radical men, who wanted football to change for the better. Brian offered a vision of how that could be done.'

In 2000, Brian became the first managing director of Supporters Direct, set up by the Government to help fans secure a bigger say in how their clubs were being run. WISA's vice chair, Lou

Carton-Kelly, had already spoken to him but I also gave him a call, wanting to know more about supporters' trusts and whether they were something we should be looking at. I really liked what he told me.

I remember him saying: 'Fans want to know their club will be run properly so it is protected and doesn't become a toy for some rich owner who might suddenly get bored of the whole thing. A trust is a way of saying to fans, 'We will always put your club's best interests first. We will run it in a certain way so it is capable of doing what we all want to see. In our case, that was rescuing Northampton Town.' I was hooked and listened attentively as he explained the template he had created. Everything seemed so relevant to the position we were in. 'This is exactly what we need,' I purred.

Various meetings followed: first, a steering committee was formed, and I was vice-chair of that, and then – in October 2001 – we established a board which included me, Nigel Higgs, Heather Jackson, Richard Faulkner, Lou Carton-Kelly, Tom Adam (RIP), Colin Dench, Roger Dennis, Ray Downham and Ron Trayhorn. I eventually became the trust's vice-chair and we adopted a constitution that spelt out our guiding principles. These included:

- Owning, or having a substantial stake, in our club;
- Being a democratic voice for all our fans;
- Strengthening the bonds between our club and the surrounding community;
- Achieving greater financial accountability and transparency so that everyone can see how the club is being run and where money is being spent.

Now we needed to spread the word and physically enrol new members – and that's when we decided to launch the Dons Trust at Wimbledon Theatre. But would anyone actually turn up? Did our fans really want to become football club owners? We put a lot of effort into publicising the event. My company printed thousands of leaflets and posters telling everyone what was happening, where it was happening and why we needed them there.

Given we'd be in a theatre, we put together a star cast of Wimbledon legends – the sort our fans would love to see like Allen Batsford, Dickie Guy, Ian Cooke, Roy Law and Carl Leaburn. But there was always that nagging thought: it's a Sunday afternoon and what if people can't be arsed to show? What if the thought of roast beef and Yorkshire pudding is more appealing? I should have known better.

I remember walking on to the stage to do the compering and there was practically a football crowd rammed into the theatre – almost 1,300, either in the stalls or up in the gods, waving their scarves and turning the grand old arena into a yellow and blue spectacular. The memory still gives me goosebumps. I'm pretty sure they'd never had a football crowd in there before. But it somehow felt we were in the right place, at the right time. We were doing something important. We were about to change the world.

All our star guests were applauded thunderously as they walked on to the stage, then our fans listened and cheered as they heard speeches from Brian Lomax and the Supporters Direct chief executive, Dave Boyle. Their messages were straight to the point: you need to save your football club and this is the way to do it.

Everyone in that theatre was as hooked as I had been when I first spoke to Brian over the phone. 'Trusts are a body that can take over a football club – by either buying it, owning a stake in it, or even taking it out of administration,' they were told. 'If you all line up behind a trust, and that includes everyone from the most active of fans to those who just want to lend their names to something they believe in, then it becomes easier to secure funding. Do that, and you can start to think seriously about buying the club yourselves.'

There was no doubt we needed money and so we asked everyone in the theatre to sign up to the trust for £25 a pop. By the end of the afternoon, a phenomenal 750 fans had joined.

I'd suggested we held an auction and so I donated one of my prized possessions – a giant TV-sized photo of Lawrie Sanchez scoring our FA Cup final-winning goal against Liverpool, signed and framed. Hands shot up left, right and centre and it finally went for £3,850.

The launch was a colossal success – way beyond our wildest dreams – and when I eventually left the theatre, I genuinely felt we had a chance. The mood had been so upbeat and everyone was visibly united and on the same page. We were properly organised, our fans had backed us and funds had started to pour in.

We can save our club.

Chapter 14
WE WILL PLAY IN YELLOW AND BLUE

I FIRST mentioned the idea of starting a new club in November 2001, when I talked to Kris Stewart, Steve Elson and Marc Jones. The four of us were at Selhurst Park: Charles Koppel had asked me to arrange a meeting and bring along some concerned fans. He was trying to find people he could convince about moving to Milton Keynes but it was extremely hard not to punch him when he proclaimed: 'This move is to save the club.' It was the first time I seriously thought we might not win this, and they might take our club away.

He eventually left, leaving us more anxious about the future than ever before – and that's when I said to them: 'Fuck it, if they decide they're going to Milton Keynes, or anywhere else, then we will just restart our club. If we have to play in a park, then we'll play in a bloody park. But here's the thing: if that happens, we will play in yellow and blue. We will be the team that represents Wimbledon – and nobody else.'

I remember all this so vividly because two weeks later Kris rang me and said: 'You were serious, weren't you?'

He didn't have to explain what he was talking about – I instantly knew. 'You're goddamned right I was.'

It was one of the most profound moments amid everything that had happened and everything that was about to happen to us over the days, weeks, months and years ahead. I knew Kris fancied it. I wasn't alone.

Without me realising it, that thought – *we'll restart our club* – subconsciously prepared me for the moment when they took Wimbledon away from us. As much as I prayed it would never happen, I knew what we'd do if it did.

The extra day we gained by not going to Soho Square and floundering about and getting pissed and crying, we spent putting ourselves in a position to start again – and quickly. I'd been agitated and angry while the commission was happening, but that was down to the 'not knowing for sure what these tossers will decide' of it all. It felt like someone had pressed the pause button on our lives, and nobody could say whether it would pick up again in the same place. In fact, had the commission gone our way, I believe the trust would have put forward a plan to run the club in the absence of a new owner stepping in. But none of us were getting any real intel. There was no reassuring pitter-patter coming out and that made us all even more nervous.

I was surrounded by Dons fans at work and most of them were saying, 'They'll never let this happen.' But the more it went on, the more I was thinking and verbalising, 'Don't worry – if we lose this, we will start again.' And I repeated that mantra regularly while we were still waiting. 'If this decision goes against us, we start again – and we'll have a riot along the way.'

When the decision was finally confirmed, I'd say 99.9 per cent of our fan base were totally devastated. To some, it meant they'd turn their backs on football for ever, permanently disillusioned and incapable of finding another club to support. But the thought of starting again definitely didn't scare me. In fact, to be honest, it excited me because it meant we would have something untarnished to support. Something that no longer needed demonstrating and fighting over, something not owned or run by bad people. Our only fight would be to go forward. Our motives would be pure, the polar opposites of everyone who had conspired and united to destroy Wimbledon FC. Yes, I was devastated by the decision but, paradoxically, I was also invigorated by it.

Why? Because, I thought, if we got our reaction right then my club would return to me. The feeling, the depth of feeling, the matchdays, the cup runs, the euphoria, the heartbreak and the frustration and the ecstasies and all those exhilarating, all-encompassing feelings that go with a football club would come back to us. We would be free of all the badness that had drowned Wimbledon FC. All that mattered was that we started again. How ironic: the commission's real legacy, the one they desperately wanted to avoid, was to actually push us into creating AFC Wimbledon. That makes me smile.

Chapter 15

YOU HAVE 12 DAYS TO SAVE THE CLUB

I HEARD him long before he stepped through the door: heavy-footed, he clumped, clumped up the fire exit steps outside, almost drowning out the clunking and clanging of the printing presses below. Less than 48 hours after our club was wiped off the map, a man I'd never met was about to walk into a first-floor office above the small printing business I owned in Wimbledon. He would change everything.

There was no uncertain knock. Instead, the door was confidently pushed open and in he walked, purposefully, like a man on a mission. I clocked his narrow handlebar moustache instantly, then the blue blazer, the classic white shirt, striped tie in a perfect York knot and the black Farah trousers.

I glanced to the floor: his shoes – black – were so highly polished I could almost see my entire office reflected in their toecaps. Each foot was splayed outwards – together they looked like ten to two on a clock. He must have been in his late fifties, tall and powerfully built. He was every inch the embodiment of an archetypal English bureaucrat. What a beautiful man.

'You must be Ivor,' he declared confidently, thrusting out his right hand, which almost crushed mine to dust as we shook hands vigorously. 'Very nice to meet you.'

He then pulled out the only chair on the other side of my desk, sat down in a 'let's get down to business because there's no time to waste' manner, and added: 'I've just one thing to say. I think it's an absolutely disgusting decision and I will do everything I can to help you get restarted.'

Fucking brilliant.

David Fowkes had entered the building and nothing would ever be the same again.

There were already millions of 'how-do-we-do-its' cascading through my head before David walked in. I instinctively knew we needed to make things happen quickly – but I didn't know how. None of us did. Who could push us in the right direction? If we were somehow going to start again, then we had to be up and running for the forthcoming season or we would lose momentum. I knew that much. I deep down believed people wanted to support us but we had to harness that before they all splintered and found other clubs to support.

I barely slept the night before the decision. Claire and I talked for hours, especially about fan ownership, which very much appealed to her staunch socialist principles. 'If we restart this club, we will never let it slip into the hands of a single owner ever again,' I told her. 'We will always be fan owned.'

I drove to the office very early the next morning – the day of the announcement. Marc turned up early, too, closely followed by

Trevor. It must have been 7.30 a.m. and the three of us looked bleary-eyed at each other. Almost in unison we said: 'Now what do we do?'

The decision was confirmed at 11 a.m. The FA's headquarters in Soho Square immediately got pelted with eggs by a group of our fans outside and some even broke into the building. I wanted to lash out just like them, but the way to really strike back was to restart the club and show them what we could do.

We were already hitting the phones by then, desperately seeking advice, and got told to phone the London FA, which I did around 2 p.m. that day. And that's when I got through to their head – David Fowkes. 'David, we don't know each other but my name is Ivor Heller. You've probably heard that the FA are going to let my club, Wimbledon, be moved to Milton Keynes.'

'Yes, how can I help?'

That sounded hopeful.

'I'm one of four Wimbledon fans who are determined to keep our club alive. But we need to move quickly so it can be relaunched in time for next season. We want it to be the rightful continuation of Wimbledon Football Club because that's who we are.'

And before I could continue he interjected with one word that meant so much in the anxiety of that moment: 'Brilliant.'

He just said, 'Brilliant.'

I took a massive intake of breath but before I could respond, he added: 'I think the decision is diabolical and I really want to help you. But if you want to start again then you need to fill in a form very quickly and then we can get things moving. I can come to you tomorrow to help out.'

Fucking hell.

There was more, though. 'You'll need to get into a senior league – one that's in the football pyramid. The most obvious candidate is the Ryman League. But you've only got 12 working days left to get senior status if you want to be playing next season.'

'But how do we get senior status?' I blurted. It sounded an impossibility.

Then he spelt it out. The enormity of what lay ahead: 'For starters, you'll need a groundshare deal that guarantees you've got a home ground for the next three years – minimum. And we're not talking any old ground, Ivor. It must have some basic facilities – such as a fence around the pitch, floodlights, changing rooms and a bar. You can't play senior football without a clubhouse and somewhere for the referees, match officials and the teams to change.'

I remember putting the phone down – I wasn't surprised by what we needed, but the 12-day deadline felt hopelessly impossible. How the fuck were we going to get a ground in less than two weeks? I repeated everything Fowkes had said to Marc and Trevor. Then came the added bombshell we hadn't anticipated. Kris, who had gone to hear the announcement at Soho Square, phoned in and told us what the FA had added about us starting again. About it not being in the game's 'wider interests'.

When we heard that, an overwhelming sense of righteous indignation kicked in. In fact, that one sentence fuelled everything from then on: it resonated even more than the decision itself. I hated the FA.

We'll go again and we'll call our club Wimbledon, you fucking idiots.

I carried on talking to Marc and Trevor. 'Let's get that form Fowkes said we need to fill in – quickly.'

The London FA were based in Lewisham. I knew one Wimbledon fan who lived there – Niall Couper – so I got on the phone. 'Niall, mate, we need a favour. Could you go to the London FA offices near you, pick up a form and get it over to us first thing tomorrow because we need to get it filled in, ASAP.'

Next, we phoned Terry Eames and asked him to come and help us. Terry was a football man, a former Wimbledon player who had managed at non-league level and understood the game better than any of us. I'm pretty sure he told us to get in touch with Nick

Robinson from the Ryman League, which we did, and later that afternoon they both turned up at my office. I remember Nick saying: 'There shouldn't be any problem getting you into Ryman 3 – so long as you have senior status.'

Meanwhile, the rest of the football world was absorbing the FA's ruling – and were clearly horrified. There was pretty much universal condemnation and we started to hear that a crowd was congregating at the Fox and Grapes pub in Wimbledon. More and more calls came in about the gathering so I said to Marc: 'Why don't you go to the pub and tell everyone there that we are going to restart our club.' Jonesy was the perfect man for that job, so off he went.

Kris also joined Marc at the Fox and Grapes later on and word quickly spread from there: mates told their mates, who told their mates as the beer flowed. Social media was becoming an increasing force and it wasn't long before we were getting phone calls from newspaper and TV reporters who wanted confirmation and quotes. Many years later that spawned a fallacy that all of us – me, Marc, Trevor and Kris – actually planned the club's rebirth in a corner of the pub that day. I'm afraid that's not true – we had already set the ball rolling by then. Besides, I never went there. Nor did Trevor.

But the story of us starting again was soon widespread. When I eventually went home that night, I said to Claire: 'I think we've started something pretty big.'

Kris came into my office early the next morning and Niall appeared shortly afterwards with the London FA form. Kris and I started reading through it but within seconds we'd both fallen silent: there was barely one question we could answer. Top of the pile was the most basic one of all: name of the club? We had ideas of what we wanted to write down, but no idea whether it would be accepted. It was the same problem with 'date formed?' We didn't want to waste time by putting in the wrong answers.

And that's when David Fowkes walked in. True to his word, he marched into my office that afternoon. What followed was one of the most pivotal moments in the history of our club.

'Right, let's get this form done,' he said.

With that, he sat down and pulled out a silver, expensive-looking ballpoint pen from his blazer pocket. Holding it a hair's breadth above the first question, and without looking up once, he demanded:

'Name?'

We'd already agreed on two contenders – one we thought might be OK, the other we kind of knew wouldn't be, but wanted to try just in case.

'Real Wimbledon,' and we all exchanged furtive glances with the hint of a smirk on our faces.

'No.'

He didn't flinch and he didn't look up. We all sensed it wasn't up for debate.

'FC Wimbledon?'

'No.'

'Why not?' I asked courageously. We'd been hopeful that one would fly.

'Too close to Wimbledon FC.' And still he didn't look up. That was obviously not for debate, either.

He'd clearly done his homework and wasn't going to waste time justifying his rulings. But we hadn't got any other names to suggest. We all looked a bit bereft so I broke the silence and said: 'I've been looking at non-league football and there's one team doing quite well at the moment: AFC Sudbury.'

'Yes . . . yes . . . AFC Wimbledon,' he ruled. 'Yes. That would be acceptable.'

Silence. Then we all started nodding slowly as the name began circulating through our brains and we watched, wide-eyed, as he began writing AFC Wimbledon next to 'name of club'. Wow. I remember feeling goosebumps – there it was, AFC Wimbledon, our club, the club the FA had ordered us not to resurrect.

There was something official about seeing it on that form. Suddenly it felt like we had an identity and that felt incredible.

'I've just one question, though,' I said.

'Yes, Ivor?'

'What does the AFC stand for?'

'Absolutely fuck all!' he replied.

The tension disintegrated there and then and we all burst into laughter. 'Doesn't it stand for Association Football Club or Affiliated Football Club or something like that?'

'Nope, it's a straight prefix and nothing else. It's got absolutely no meaning,' he answered.

And still he hadn't looked up.

'Colours?'

'Yellow and blue.' On that, we had no doubt whatsoever.

And then came the most profound moment of them all.

'Year formed?' and to a man we all said in unison, without a second's pause: '1889.'

And David Fowkes wrote down 1889 without hesitating. And without looking up.

That was the closest I came to tears. By doing that, Fowkes was confirming that the history of the club we all loved still belonged to the club we were creating. The two were inseparable. AFC Wimbledon was not a new club being started from scratch. It was the continuation of our heritage and all the dramas and heroics and the ups and the downs that defined everything about Wimbledon FC.

When Fowkes wrote down that date, the 1988 Cup triumph instantly belonged to AFC Wimbledon. The Crazy Gang and the 1963 Amateur Cup final heroes were our heroes; Allen Batsford and Harry Bassett and Joe Kinnear were our former managers; Vinnie Jones and Lawrie Sanchez and Dickie Guy and Eddie Reynolds were our former players and all the promotions and the cup wins and the trophies that came with them were all ours.

All that now defined AFC Wimbledon and none of it – not one single bit of it – could ever be claimed by a fucking franchise abomination about to be launched in Milton fucking Keynes. They were the club with no history, not us.

AFC Wimbledon had no players, no manager, no ground, no balls, no bibs, no cones – but my God, it had a glorious history. In that moment we felt vindicated and it was a gigantic leap forward. Having ownership of that history meant everything. Some people might argue, 'Well how can it be yours? It's a different name altogether.' But Wimbledon's name had already changed three times since 1889 – this wouldn't be the first time at all. We'd been Old Centrals, then we were Wimbledon Old Centrals and Wimbledon Borough – as well as Wimbledon FC. Yes, AFC Wimbledon was another new name, but the story remained the same.

What made that moment even more beautiful was knowing that a London FA officer had written this down on an official document. By doing that, he'd effectively rubber-stamped our legitimacy, made it real and indisputable. It was also a gigantic two fingers to the FA and their poisonous attempt to stop us doing exactly what we were doing.

Those four numbers, 1-8-8-9, felt like four gigantic sledgehammers smashing into the monstrous wall the FA had tried to build round us. It had always been in Wimbledon's DNA to stand up to bullies and refuse to lie down. The players and the managers had been doing it for generations. Now it was our turn. The FA's threat was exactly what Wimbledon had been standing up to for decades. We were telling the world, but mainly the FA, that a club in Wimbledon was being resurrected and it was carrying the same DNA of all its previous incarnations – the never-say-die spirit, the Crazy Gang solidarity, the sheer bloody-minded refusal to surrender.

We're alive you bastards, we're breathing, we're the resurrection of a light you'll never extinguish. And the history of Wimbledon football club belongs to us. It's written on one of your fucking forms.

All of this was there in that room at that moment – unspoken but as loud as any football crowd could ever be. And still Fowkes never looked up.

Chapter 16
FIT FOR KINGS

THE Ryman League chairman, Nick Robinson, had left by now, but his words were still echoing. 'I don't think there'll be any problem getting you into Ryman 3,' he'd said, 'so long as you have senior status.'

We had a name, that was good – but we didn't have any players, coaches, kit, boots, training ground, cones, footballs, bibs or money. And now we needed a ground, quickly, or all bets would be off. Terry Eames and I were left in my office. He'd already phoned round mates and contacts, asking for favours and looking for advice, but my blood ran cold when he looked me squarely in the eyes and said: 'Listen, I'm telling you, we can go to Dulwich easily.' I nodded, pretending that was good to know, when I was really thinking: 'What the fuck do we want to go to Dulwich for? It's miles away.'

But I played it diplomatic and simply said: 'That's interesting, thanks, Terry.'

Then he mentioned Ron Dixon, a director at Leatherhead. 'He'd take you as well.' That sounded marginally better as we had fans who lived in that area. But it didn't feel ideal. I wasn't sure their ground could cope with the amount of supporters we might attract. For me, there were only three geographical possibilities – and two of those would never work. Someone had suggested Tooting and Mitcham, our fiercest local rivals in our non-league days. That rivalry might have been historical, but it still burned too strong for us to suddenly become housemates. The other possibility was Sutton. They were on the mainline from

Wimbledon, a lot of our fans lived there and their ground was big enough. I just didn't believe they'd want us.

It was option number three that most appealed to me. Kingsmeadow, on the outer edges of Kingston, was home to Kingstonian Football Club and only a mile and a half from Merton's border. There was a frequent train and bus service, the ground had a 4,000 capacity and would meet all the Ryman League rules and regulations. The only problems? There were already four teams sharing there and the ground's owner, Rajesh Khosla, had a fearsome reputation for being a tough negotiator who would put money before sentiment. And we had no money.

That night my mind was obsessed with one thought: would they, could they, take us at Kingsmeadow? The more I thought about it, the more impossible it seemed. Not only did we need a ground, we needed it overnight; there wasn't enough time for lawyers to draw up complex contracts and then squabble over intricate subclauses.

We needed someone who would agree a deal on the strength of a handshake. That sobering thought kept me awake most of the night. Footballs and cones could wait – we'd get that stuff somehow – but getting a groundshare deal on the strength of a 'my word is my bond' promise was surely out of the question?

We were all in my office by 8 a.m. the next morning. I grabbed a Yellow Pages phone directory and found a number for Kingstonian. I didn't know a soul there and nobody answered, but I left a message: 'Good morning. My name is Ivor Heller and I'm ringing from Wimbledon. You probably know the FA are letting our club be moved to Milton Keynes. We're not accepting that and need to find a local ground urgently so we can start again. Kingsmeadow could be ideal for us and we wondered whether you'd consider a possible groundshare? If so, could someone please call us back urgently to discuss this further.'

My eyes were glued to the phone on my desk for the next hour. Calls came in but they were all bloody customers chasing up print orders.

Go away, you bastards.

And then it happened. 'Ivor, there's someone called Anup Khosla on line three for you,' my PA yelled out and it felt like the entire printing press instantly ground to a halt. I had around 15 employees and they all wanted us to succeed. Anup explained that he was Rajesh's son and that his father – who had taken Kingstonian out of administration and who owned Kingsmeadow – had heard my message.

'Thanks for calling back, Anup,' I replied. 'This is the situation: we want to get into the Ryman League but to do that, we urgently need a three-year groundshare deal or else they won't accept us. Can you help?'

'It's not really up to me, it's up to my dad,' he explained. 'I'll speak to him and he'll come back to you.'

And he did. Within minutes. I was repeating every word Anup had said back to Marc, Kris and Trevor when my mobile phone suddenly burst into its familiar ringtone – cricket's *Test Match Special* theme tune – but I didn't recognise the incoming number.

This must be him.

I mouthed 'stay quiet' at the other three, pressed the green button to accept the call and instantly heard: 'This is Rajesh Khosla. Is that Mr Ivor Heller?'

I liked him there and then. I could just tell from his tone. It was can-do, positive. I knew from the moment I heard his voice that there was a chance this could happen – even though I'd never met him in my life.

'Could we have a meeting, Mr Khosla? I'm sorry but we need to move really fast.'

'Sure, when do you want to come and see us?' he replied.

Kris and I were there the next day. We had no targets, no projections, no preconceptions. Not then. We needed to start a football club quickly and see how far we could go. We got to the ground nice and early, so we could check out the nearest train station (Norbiton) and see how big the car park was. *Plenty big enough.* I instantly liked the set-up. Then we met Rajesh. He was only a tiny bit taller than me, but stockily built. His handshake was one of those that instantly said, 'Don't even think about fucking with me.'

Born in India, he was now in his fifties and looked every inch a self-assured businessman who could do a deal – so long as it was on his terms. His full head of black hair was immaculately cropped, with his dark moustache perfectly spanning the full width of his upper lip. His eyes were black like his hair and deeply penetrating. But there was also mischief in those eyes and that gave me hope.

'Come, follow me, let me show you round,' and he waved us enthusiastically towards the players' entrance. Then he took us on a walk round the entire ground and bars.

Fuck me, this is perfect. This is proper.

I started to get excited. 'Your tills will be clicking like you can't believe if we do this deal, Mr Khosla. Our lot like a drink and people will come here and they will drink an awful lot.'

'How many do you think will come here then?' he asked.

'Minimum a thousand – I can guarantee that,' I replied. I absolutely couldn't guarantee that at all; I had no idea what I was talking about but I could see the cash till signs kerchinging in those dark eyes.

'How many matches?'

'Well, there's 16 teams in the Ryman League – add a couple of cup matches plus a pre-season friendly, so 17 to 18 matches at least, Mr Khosla. And if we have to pay for extra cup matches on top, then we will.'

'Let me have a think,' he replied and then wandered off with his son for a short while.

I immediately turned to Kris and said: 'We've got this.'

'Don't count your chickens, Ivor,' he replied.

'No, we've got it, I'm telling you. He can hear his tills clicking, and this is the perfect spot for us. Nothing will persuade me there's anywhere better.' Kris fell silent for a few seconds and then said: 'Okay, I agree, you're right. This is the place.'

Khosla soon came back into sight and, as he walked towards us, I was pretty sure I saw a slight grin breaking his businessman facade. 'Right then, we can do this,' he said.

'But what's the deal, Mr Khosla?' I asked nervously.

'Twenty grand.'

We haven't got a penny to our names.

'Does that include everything, Mr Khosla?' I asked.

'Yes, pretty much everything – there'll be some other bits and bobs like stewards but basically, yeah, that's everything.'

I looked at Kris and could tell he wanted to have a think about it. 'Could you please excuse us, Mr Khosla. We just need a moment to have a chat with each other.'

'Let's not fuck about, Kris,' I immediately blurted. 'Let's not give anyone a chance to say, "Leatherhead or Dulwich might be better." There's nowhere better for us, end of, and we can get this deal done right now.'

I knew we were in the right place. We had a home. At this stage, Kris and I each owned 50 per cent of AFC Wimbledon, which we'd set up as a limited company the moment David Fowkes let us use that name. Although the registered office was my office – 297 Haydons Road – neither of us had any intention of remaining the club's owners. We'd set up the company as an act of expediency so it could theoretically start trading straight away. It was essential we could make key decisions quickly: there wouldn't be time for committee meetings and debates at this crucial moment in our genesis. But Kris and I also passionately agreed that we'd hand over the company to a supporters' trust as soon as we practically could – for the same amount we'd paid for it: £1 each.

Until then, we had to be able to make decisions in the heat of the moment. And this was one of those moments. 'Let's get on with it, Kris; let's do this deal,' I said as Khosla disappeared from sight. So we did. There and then.

There was, however, a pretty big problem. Khosla wanted the 20 grand up front and we were penniless. 'We'll sell season tickets,' I proclaimed. And we both agreed that was a brilliant idea – except for one thing. Our club only existed on paper: it had no players, no manager and, technically at least, no ground until we handed over £20,000.

'It almost makes sense,' Kris smiled.

We verbally agreed the deal with Khosla there and then. He'd take all the food and beverage income (even from AFC Wimbledon matches) but we would keep the gate money – so long as we manned the turnstiles ourselves.

'I will supply all the food and all the drinks,' he insisted. 'What about the players' energy drinks?' I replied. 'You're free to provide those – but absolutely nothing else.'

'That's completely reasonable, Mr Khosla. I have no issue with that.'

He also insisted that we drew up the lease, which actually was a blessing. We were lucky that a property lawyer, Dan Norris, was a fan (he still does club legals today) and he agreed to oversee the paperwork for us, pro bono. The decision to start again wasn't a dark moment – in fact that's when the lights started to go on. There was a future.

Chapter 17
CAN YOU HEAR US?

IT STARTED like an insecure murmur, barely audible, a few scattered voices in the room nervously daring to chant something unprepared and unrehearsed.

What the fuck are they saying?

Then a few more voices joined in, and a few more until suddenly people picked up a rhythm and the scattered voices became a heaving chorus. There must have been at least 1,000 fans in the room – Wimbledon's Community Centre – and the doors had been left open so many more on the streets outside could hear what was going on. The chant quickly reached them and they, too, joined in spontaneously. It was like someone turning the volume up to maximum on a gigantic ghetto blaster.

I looked at Kris and Jonesy, standing smiling beside me on the stage. We knew by now what they were chanting, even though we'd never heard the words ever said like this before.

'A . . . F . . . C . . . Wim-ble-don', getting louder, 'A . . . F . . . C . . . Wim-ble-don,' getting confident, 'A . . . F . . . C . . . Wim-ble-don', no holds barred: A . . . F . . . C . . . Wimbledon.'

It seemed like the individual letters and words were being played with and experimented with, voices working out the gaps between the 'A' and the 'F' and the 'Wim' and the 'ble'. The repetition grew louder and louder with each cycle until it reached a crescendo, over a thousand voices in harmony and unison belting out a chant that has become the bedrock of our club to this day.

It wasn't just a chant, though. It was a message. It was our defiance bursting out of us and it kept rising and rising until it was heading down the streets and snaking all over the borough and then bombarding the tunnels of the district line until it made its deafening way to Soho Square, where no double glazing could stop it invading the FA's cosseted headquarters. Are you listening? Can you hear us? 'A . . . F . . . C . . . WIM-BLE-DON'

Take that, you bastards.

Jonesy and I had been working overtime on a presentation we wanted to make to the WISA annual meeting. We had already achieved so much – agreeing on a name, getting it accepted and registered, filling in the London FA paperwork and securing a groundshare deal in principle. But only a few of us knew what had been going on. It was time to tell as many fans as physically possible and WISA's annual meeting seemed the ideal opportunity to do it. We needed to talk directly to the fans ourselves and show them what their new club might look like. We needed to know they were with us.

I spent a lot of time with Jonesy coming up with ideas. Marc was a professional designer, working in my printing company's studio, so everything we did looked really polished. We prioritised a new kit and Marc did what Marc does best, coming up with a brilliantly evocative design – and also a new badge. That was basically the Merton badge, which had been Wimbledon's original one. Perfect.

We had big screen-printing presses at the factory and I said: 'Let's do something we can hand out at the AGM, something people can take home with them.' So we came up with the tag line 'Follow The Dons'. Marc then designed car stickers with that slogan in yellow lettering and a white outline, all on a blue background. He added the new badge at each end and we printed over 1,000 of them. We even vowed that if AFC Wimbledon really got going, the stickers would always be stocked in the club shop. I think they still are to this day.

We then wanted to print massive backboards displaying Marc's new shirt and badge, but the bloody presses started playing up, big time. The printer would run out a line, painfully slowly, then stop like it needed a rest. In the end, the two of us spent all night in the factory and never went home. We knew it was vital that we presented something that would make fans go, 'Fucking hell.' In a good way.

Next, we produced leaflets that mapped out who we were and what our aims were going to be. It was like a brief manifesto: we'll be fan-owned and we'll play in our locality in yellow and blue. That sort of thing.

When the day of the annual meeting came round, we took all the stuff we'd designed and printed to the Wimbledon Community Centre and went in via the side entrance. Nobody had a clue what was going on, which was what we wanted. I was the Dons Trust vice-chair by then and sat on the top table so I could explain everything to everyone – and show them how far we'd got.

The place was rammed to overflowing. At least 1,000 were squeezed into a room designed for 400. There were people hanging on to the rafters in the entrance hall and many more on the street outside. And somehow TV crews managed to squeeze in as well. There was anger in the room, though. Some fans were agitating and yelling, 'We need to keep on fighting.' They didn't want us to give up on Wimbledon FC by starting afresh. But we'd exhausted all that: it was a dead-end battle we knew we could never win.

Then came an iconic moment that is still talked about today. With feelings still raw in the room, Kris stood up boldly, pushed his chair aside, walked to the front of the stage and simply said: 'I just want to watch some football.' For a nanosecond, the Wimbledon Community Centre fell completely quiet as his words were absorbed by everyone inside – and those out on the streets. Kris stood frozen to the spot.

Which way is this going to go?

And then, like there'd been a universal awakening, an enormous roar tornado-ed round the room before shooting straight outside. Kris had nailed it. He'd said the very words everyone was feeling deep within their hearts and souls but hadn't been able to articulate.

It totally won the room. I leant over and whispered to him: 'Fucking hell, Kris, we have to strike right now.' Then I grabbed the mic and said: 'Right, just so you know, this is what we have been doing. Marc . . . bring out the badge.'

It was like we had won the World Cup there and then. Pandemonium. I wish the FA could have seen it. Not in the wider interests of football? We were, in that moment, the life and soul of football, the very reason why the game has survived and flourished for centuries.

We were everything the FA couldn't comprehend. I'd never expected Koppel or Winkelman or the Norwegians to understand it – but the FA? Weren't they meant to be our protectors, guardians of the game serving our best interests because they had their fingers on the pulse of everything we felt, wanted and strived for? They just didn't get us – and they still don't. Theirs was the dereliction of duty. They should have been savouring moments like that because it was the definition of what football means to fans and the wider community.

'Now bring out the kit,' I roared after the badge had been studied and approved by one and all. It felt like the roof was about to take off. Out came Marc with Wimbledon's original 1970s kit and, I swear, there were people with tears in their eyes.

'Bring out the car stickers.' Uproar.

'Bring out the leaflets.' Bedlam.

And then the chant started: 'A . . . F . . . C . . . Wim-ble-don'. All together now: 'A . . . F . . . C . . . Wim-ble-don.' It felt like we were alive: we were kicking, we were fighting back. AFC Wimbledon came to life in that room that night and it sent a gigantic shiver down my spine – whoosh, like a million-vault electric current.

I'd no doubt this was all going to work out until somebody piped up: 'How the fuck are we going to pay for it?' Fair question, although not exactly in keeping with the spirit in the room. Frustratingly, we couldn't tell them about Kingsmeadow because nothing had been physically signed yet.

However, we still explained that we were looking at potential groundshare deals, and Kingsmeadow was one of the options. Then we added: 'We will need everyone to buy season tickets for a club that, admittedly, doesn't technically exist yet.

'If you do, we will then be able to fund a groundshare deal. And – we promise – if it doesn't happen, then we will give you your money back. Every penny. But we need you to back us – and we need you to tell your mates to back us as well.'

The room took it. Heads were nodding. We set a price of £200 for a season ticket with an optional but preferrable £50 donation.

To be honest, we had them in the palm of our hands by then: everything we said was being accepted. Nobody knew the £200 was a total fucking guess. We hadn't a clue what price to charge. We just knew we had to cover the £20,000 Khosla wanted up front for the groundshare.

The response over the next few days, though, was unbelievable. The postman started appearing at my factory with sacks full of mail and almost none of it was to do with my business. Remember, there was no internet banking in those days. The only way to send us money was via cheques through the post – or even cash stuffed into envelopes. People were sending all sorts to us. Good luck messages were landing from all over the world – Australia, the USA, Outer Mongolia, you name it, just about everywhere that had footballs. 'Good luck to the real Dons' – 'Show the FA what football's all about' – 'You're the heartbeat of the game'. We had struck a chord with everyone who understood.

More importantly, there were an awful lot of cheques – some even from people in Africa, who'd never see a game but had heard our story and wanted to be part of it. Football fans in the USA were buying season tickets and there were others from France, Spain, Switzerland and across Europe. It was incredible and it was inspiring.

Within a matter of days we had raised £80,000. The trust already had a bank account with the Co-op and then they opened a new one in the name of AFC Wimbledon Ltd. About six weeks after we started, Kris and I formally handed the club over to the trust as we had always promised to do. For £1 each. Now it truly belonged to the fans.

The clock was still ticking, though, on our application with the London FA. We urgently needed a written agreement with Khosla – and there was less than a week to get it done. We still had no idea which league we'd be in, but we couldn't secure that until we had an indisputable groundshare contract.

We'd been pushed, though, towards the Ryman League, so we got in touch with their execs to find out what they needed from us and when their annual meeting would be held to vote in new clubs.

Chapter 18
OUR FIRST FIXTURE

WE HADN'T got players or a manager, or even a league to play in, so what did we do? We arranged our first-ever game . . . even though we didn't have a team to play in it. I guess we were flushed by the WISA meeting and the groundshare agreement, although that hadn't yet been signed. Theoretically, Khosla could still pull the plug on Kingsmeadow. We were itching, though. We were men in a hurry and having a real-life fixture in the bag would only make AFC Wimbledon seem even more real.

'Who shall we play first?' I asked Kris, Jonesy and Trevor as we made plans in my factory office. Some names were bandied around but, to be honest, I'd already made my mind up. I wanted our first game to be against one of our biggest rivals during the club's amateur era – our nearest neighbours, Sutton United.

We had famously beaten them 4-2 in the 1963 FA Amateur Cup final at Wembley, a match that became historic because all four of our goals were headers scored by Eddie Reynolds. That had never been done at Wembley before.

But would Sutton commit to playing a club that had no players? There was only one way to find out so I phoned their supremo, Bruce Elliott, whom I didn't yet know. Someone told me he had a droll, dry sense of humour and I already knew he was an old hand around football. Which we certainly weren't.

'Bruce – it's Ivor Heller here from AFC Wimbledon. You've probably read what's happened but we are determined to start the club again and I just thought – given our clubs' great historic rivalry – that our very first game should be against Sutton.'

'Really. Why should we play you?' came back the reply, instantly. I wasn't detecting any humour.

'Well, er . . . we'll bring a lot of people, that's for sure,' I replied, hoping to appeal to his bottom line. Money.

'How many?'

Fuck. How the hell do I know?

'At least a thousand.' I immediately looked at Kris, Jonesy and Trevor. In unison they were mouthing, 'You can't promise him that!'

'Fuck off, it's too late – I've already said it,' I mouthed back.

'We will definitely bring at least a thousand, Bruce,' I repeated, this time with a bit more bravado. And, just like Khosla, I could sense the cash tills kerchinging in Bruce's head.

'Well, mmm, that's certainly quite a lot for a pre-season friendly. Unfortunately, we've already got a packed diary and all our summer dates are booked up.

'I wish you the best of luck, though. Goodbye!' And with that he hung up.

The others could guess what had happened, but I was pretty sure this was just the beginning of the negotiations. 'Don't worry, he'll ring back – you mark my words. A thousand fans for a pre-season friendly at Sutton will be irresistible.'

'But how do you know we'll take a thousand, Ivor?' asked Jonesy, not unreasonably.

I was feeling bullish by now. 'You know what – I reckon we'll take way more than that,' I insisted. 'We'll attract so much news by the time the game comes round. People will come because it'll be historic.'

Sure enough, 10 minutes later, the phone rang: 'Hello, Bruce.'

It was straight to business, no small talk. 'How many did you say you'd bring – at least a thousand?' he asked.

'Nah, forget that Bruce, I was wrong. It'll be at least double that.' The others were now looking at me like I'd completely lost my marbles.

'Really – so now you're saying 2,000. You sure of that?' he replied.

'Yeah, all day long. We'll bring 2,000.'

'Right, 10 July. Kick-off 7.30 p.m.'

'Done.'

And there it was. We had a pre-season friendly. I didn't tell him we didn't actually have a team, or indeed anything a football club should have before it arranges a fixture. I flicked through my diary and noted that 10 July would be just six weeks after the FA had taken our club away and told us to disappear. We announced the game two days later. I quickly learned Bruce was no fool – the entrance fee would be £10 but we'd only keep £1 of that. Plus, they'd keep all the food and drink revenue, which would be colossal. We'd be allowed to produce the matchday programme and keep the proceeds from that.

Chapter 19
TELL US IT'S NOT TRUE

THERE were hundreds of fans there, most of them drunk, scarves tied round wrists or draped round shoulders. They were all outside the Fox and Grapes pub – where Wimbledon Old Centrals' players used to change when our club first formed in 1889 – soaking up the barmy evening air.

I could hear the clinking of glasses and bursts of laughter as I slowly pulled up in my car. Kris and Trevor were with me. The light had faded but it was a bright, starlit night and a group spotted me as I got out and slammed the door shut. 'They're here' – 'This is it everyone' – 'Get another round in' – 'Come on you two, give us the news.'

Shit.

I knew so many of the people there: Dave, Jim and his brother Alex, Steve, Lee, Russ, Simon, Joe, Mark – and on and on. We all shared the same bond and the same dream. Everyone expected us to deliver the news we'd all been excitedly waiting for. It was meant to be a formality. This was the night when AFC Wimbledon would be welcomed into the Ryman League and the long haul back through the football pyramid could officially begin.

Instead, we were about to leave them crushed. We were about to stop pints in mid-air, we were about to spoil the party and tell them something that would persuade many fans to walk away there and then, some in tears – utterly convinced the AFC Wimbledon dream was dead. It was certainly not the ending to a day that I had anticipated. Everything had been falling beautifully into place.

With 24 hours remaining to submit our paperwork to the London FA, our property lawyer, Dan Norris, had reached agreement with Khosla after much toing and froing over terms and conditions. In fact, I'll never forget the moment Kris and I signed the contracts. We were at a second public meeting in the Wimbledon Community Centre to give a progress report on the club.

Both of us were anxious that the Kingsmeadow contract still hadn't materialised, acutely aware the London FA wouldn't accept us if we didn't get it signed. Suddenly we heard a knock on the side door. We both jumped up and there was Dan, standing directly under the fire escape, looking a bit dishevelled and sounding breathless. 'I've got it – the lease – and it's ready to sign. It's okay, it's not perfect, but it's definitely okay. This gets us in,' he said. And that's where Kris and I signed our first lease – underneath the fire escape at Wimbledon Community Centre.

Then we went back in and told everyone. It was a big moment: we had a home and that meant we'd be accepted by the London FA. We were up and running. Now we could concentrate on getting into the Ryman League. We'd already been told they would want to see a proper document that mapped out who we were, and how we were going to run our club.

Putting that together was really tough and took up a lot of time and effort. They were expecting a proper, professional business plan, something we had little experience of. We'd already had 450 people buying season tickets by then – which was considerably more than any other Ryman club could ever dream of. And the cheques were still pouring in. Kris and I worked round the clock to put the presentation together and in the end it covered everything we could think of, from funding and expected crowds to how we'd find players and how we'd get balls and cones and kit.

Mercifully, there was someone already working with the Dons Trust who knew exactly what was required. I vaguely knew Erik Samuelson, but it was only then, as he pored over our figures and projections, that I saw first-hand just how invaluable he truly was. Erik was a senior partner at PricewaterhouseCoopers and not many organisations have access to someone of that calibre. When he spoke, you instinctively listened because if you didn't, you'd be an idiot. I liked him straight away. He knew exactly what the Ryman expected to see and he was all over our presentation, advising us on just about everything. Over the ensuing years, he became the reason why our club went on to realise so many impossible dreams.

We all felt extremely confident about getting into the Ryman. Although it was the lowest rung of senior football (step nine, the Premier League being step one), it was part of the pyramid. That meant, theoretically, we could climb our way back into the Football League and, heaven forbid, one day return to the Prem itself. It looked like a shoe-in. We'd be bringing a level of support – and therefore revenue – never experienced before in the Ryman, where average attendances usually hovered between 50 and 100. Plus a few dogs. Their league secretary, Nick Robinson, had already told us it was a simple majority vote. It was inconceivable we wouldn't be accepted.

Our fate would be decided at their annual meeting on 17 June 2002. Kris, Trevor and I went to a hotel just outside Gatwick and got greeted by everyone. The atmosphere was jovial and Nick said: 'You'll be called in after 20 minutes or so.' But 20 minutes turned into 30, which turned into 45 and then an hour. 'Something's not right here,' I said – as much to myself as the others. About 20 minutes later, we heard a little mumble from the room and then Nick walked out. He was ashen-faced. 'Boys, I don't know how to tell you this, but I made a mistake. I thought it was a simple majority vote but it wasn't. You needed 95 per cent support from the 67 clubs eligible to vote – and six have gone against you.'

Fuck.

My mind shot to the Fox and Grapes where I knew fans were congregating and partying, waiting to be told AFC Wimbledon had a league to play in. Then we drove back to tell them we didn't. 'It's not what we expected. It's not gone our way,' I confessed. Expletives filled the air, glasses were thumped down, and everyone universally yelled, 'Why, what the fuck?' I saw some wipe away tears, while others were saying, 'That's it, we give up; no more football for me.' Then came, 'There must be a way out of this,' and I desperately wanted to say, 'Yes, Kris and I have come up with a plan that might just work.' But we hadn't. It really felt like the end of the road. Then someone said, 'Ivor, let it go,' and that really stung. 'No. I don't want to do that. No.' But, truthfully, I didn't know what we could do.

People started heading home dejectedly then, around 11 p.m., my phone went. It was Nick again from the Ryman League. 'Ivor, I'm really sorry about what happened at the hotel – but there is another way,' he said.

'What do you mean?'

Please, God.

'There's a league called the Combined Counties League. They will take you.'

I'd never heard of it. 'How do you know they'll take us?'

'First of all, you only need 51 per cent of them to support your entry,' he explained. 'Those clubs will not say no. Even if you only took 200 of your fans to their grounds, it'll be 200 more than they're used to.

'They average crowds of 30 – tops. They will have you, believe me.'

The sense of relief and hope and salvation was overwhelming and I bombarded Nick with questions about the Combined Counties League.

'Is it in the pyramid?' was my first.

'Yes, it's the same tier as the Ryman 3 so it gives you exactly the same route back to the top,' he replied.

I was ecstatic and went running round trying to grab stragglers who hadn't yet left. I then drove home via the Hand in Hand and Crooked Billet pubs, and told any fans sitting outside the news. They listened in disbelief as I yelled: 'It's solved, we've got a fucking league; it's all been a mistake.' I must have sounded deranged and I suspect some didn't even believe me.

When I eventually got home, I hit the phone and urged people we knew to tell the people they knew and spread the word as quickly as possible. Two years earlier we had been a Premier League club, and now we might be in the Combined Counties. Instead of Chelsea, we'd be playing the likes of Chipstead and Cove and Cobham. But, right then, they felt like the big time.

The formal decision on whether to let us in the Combined Counties was to be taken inside a pub near Feltham, close to Heathrow Airport. We revamped our Ryman document but we were still incredibly apprehensive when we turned up. We'd been gifted a second chance, but there wouldn't be any others.

Once again, we had to sit outside, where we met a bloke from North Greenford United. He seemed to be really downcast. They were up for election as well but he had his head bowed over a pint of lager and looked wretchedly unhappy. I introduced myself, trying to be chirpy. 'I'm John from North Greenford United,' he replied in such a despairing tone that I actually wondered if he was suicidal.

'I hope you don't mind me asking, but is something wrong?' I ventured.

'Well . . . it's football, isn't it,' he replied.

'What do you mean, "It's football?"?'

'Players,' he answered. 'It's always fucking players. They drive you fucking mad.

'Fucking players.'

And with that, he took an enormous glug of his beer. *Christ, is this what football does to you?*

I've never forgotten that moment and thought about it time again over the years as I encountered players myself and all the problems and baggage they drag around. And I've decided old John was right. Whenever you have a problem in football, nine times out of 10, it's fucking players.

We eventually got called in, where at least 50 club representatives were sitting in rows inside a typical 'spit and sawdust' pub function room. We were literally in the last-chance saloon. Kris, Trevor and I were invited on to a little raised stage at the front, where we had to answer questions. One in particular kept recurring: 'We are only small clubs. How are we going to cope with all your fans?'

Our reply was quite simple: 'Rest assured, we will provide stewards and we will meticulously plan each game with you in advance.'

That seemed to quell the concerns and the mood in the room was soon upbeat and positive.

They like us.

You could sense they'd all done the sums in their heads and decided we'd be good for business. We'd bring in revenues to their grounds they'd never dared dream about.

Then it came to the vote and we sat in stony silence as the representatives were asked to raise their hands if they were in favour of letting us into their league. I scanned the room: there were all shapes and sizes in there, classic football club types, deadpan faces giving nothing away. Mainly middle-aged, mainly balding, mainly pot-bellied, mainly realising their dreams of running a football club.

Right then these strangers held our future in the palms of their hands. I was willing, praying, urging them to do the right thing. And then it happened, right in front of our eyes. A sea of hands raised high. The relief was monumental. Now there were smiles everywhere: for them, we meant more business, simple as that.

For us, those hands were the difference between life and death. If they'd stayed down, AFC Wimbledon would have died in that room. There would have been no way back, no resurrection, because there was nowhere else to go.

We walked out jubilant and relieved, hugging one another and smiling broadly. Optimism and hope had returned. But, just as I headed down the stairs, I noticed John was still there clutching his pint pot. And I swear I heard him mumble 'fucking players' as we joyously headed into the future.

Chapter 20
COMMON PEOPLE

LET'S recap: we had a home, Kingsmeadow; we had a league, The Combined Counties; we had a fixture, Sutton; and we even had some money in the coffers. Was there anything missing? Oh, yes. We still hadn't got a manager and we still hadn't got any players.

The first was relatively easy to solve. Terry Eames had come into my office immediately after the FA confirmed their decision and he'd never really left after that. It just seemed natural to ease him into the manager's position. He'd already been a Wimbledon player – a gritty left back, signed by Allen Batsford from Crystal

Palace in 1977. He made 47 appearances after that, helping the side get promoted to the old Third Division in 1979.

Perhaps more relevantly, he went on to manage non-league clubs across south London and therefore knew that world. And that was the world we were about to inhabit. He seemed to be the right man, in the right place at the right time.

Naturally, Terry was desperate to start building a squad – but where on earth do you find players when you're starting from scratch? The traditional method is to scout around. But we had no scouts (or coaches). So we did the next best thing: we held a trial. What followed made global headlines.

Just two weeks before we were due to play Sutton, we announced the trial – open to the entire world and absolutely anyone – would be held on Wimbledon Common, on Saturday 29 June. We told the local press, then the national press and within days we had a three-ring circus on our hands. Trevor set up an email address and 250 players messaged within hours.

We literally had players of all standards applying – from hopeless to marginally better than hopeless. They weren't all local, either: one was a Colombian under-21 international while another claimed to be a Finnish under-21. He physically flew in specifically for the trial and I have to say, if he was an under-21, then I'm an England player.

At least 400 turned up on the day, although nobody was counting. Then there were all the television and radio crews and newspaper reporters and around 25 experienced coaches, who were never asked to show but came because they thought we might need help. Others turned up with cones and balls and bibs because they knew we hadn't got any and then two of our ex-managers, Allen Batsford and Terry Burton, also showed.

The heaving mass of players were all standing in one huge block, shoulder to shoulder, arms tightly folded, each in their own kit and boots, desperately waiting for a chance to show what they could do. It was an organisational nightmare, but eventually we split them into smaller, manageable groups and set them some basic drills while Terry Eames ran round frantically writing down the name of anyone who caught his eye.

By the end of that first day, he had whittled it down to about 60 players he wanted to ask back. Some had a tiny bit of pedigree. Later on, we held a closed trial with players Terry had already found – including Joe Sheerin, who became our first captain. Joe was a bit of a celebrity at our level. He'd been on the books at Chelsea and boasted the shortest Premier League career on record – playing for one and a half minutes for the great Gianfranco Zola in 1997 when he came on as sub against, you guessed it, us! Joe then went to Bournemouth, which didn't work out, and then he had a spell with our fellow Kingsmeadow tenants, Kingstonian. I can still hear everyone whispering, 'Fuckin hell, Joe Sheerin's turned up,' when the second trial kicked off. To say he was head and shoulders better than everyone else was no understatement. I remember thinking, 'How on earth did he not become a huge Premier League star?'

Terry also arranged for other non-league players to come along, although we had no idea who they were. None of them were full-time footballers: we had a plasterer, a carpet fitter, a couple of brickies, a plumber, an electrician and two scaffolders. We even had a player who eventually scored our first-ever goal but went on to become the nation's most notorious private detective, jailed for his role in the newspaper hacking scandal. We knew him as 'Trigger' but his real name was Glenn Mulcaire.

By now the Sutton game was looming large. The trial had created an avalanche of interest and we were inundated with calls from fans across the country wanting to know if they could buy tickets in advance. Which they couldn't.

Christ, what have we unleashed?

Chapter 21
HOUGHTON AND CAMPBELL GET SHIRTY

DURING the countdown to the Sutton game I was invited to join broadcaster Nicky Campbell on his *Radio 5 Live* show. The former Liverpool midfielder Ray Houghton was also in the studio and instead of being a love-in, which I'd expected, it felt more like an ambush. I actually came under attack from the pair of them: 'How on earth do you expect a bunch of fans to run a football club properly?'

I vociferously defended myself but they really had a go and seemed to belittle everything we stood for – and everything we were trying to achieve.

'Fans haven't got the expertise, you'll end up squabbling among yourselves, it'll be a shambles, you've got no experience, you need to let proper experts run a club.' That sort of stuff.

I fought back, passionately. 'What you're saying simply isn't true,' I argued. 'We have some incredible skills in our fan base: people with exceptionally smart business brains and acute football knowledge.'

The conversation depressed me, though. Theirs was a narrow-minded, 'you're just a bunch of delusional upstarts' argument. Was this what we'd be up against out there in the real world? For the first time, I wondered whether there was such a thing as bad publicity.

Unbeknown to me, though, somebody called Miles Jacobson had been listening. He was chief executive of Sports Interactive, makers of the iconic video game Championship Manager, as it was called back then. They were literally world leaders in that market and he'd liked what I'd said. He called me the next day. 'Hello there, my name is Miles and I'm the CEO at Sports Interactive,' he explained. I wasn't into video gaming and, truthfully, had never heard of them.

'Hi, great to hear from you. How can I help?' I replied.

'Can we have a meeting?'

'Er, yes, of course, I'd love to meet. But can you tell me why?' I asked, apprehensively.

'I want to sponsor your club.'

Fucking hell. There's no such thing as bad publicity after all.

We agreed a date and then I did some research. This lot were worth millions. We met at his office as arranged. He looked so fresh-faced, like a college grad who'd just been handed a winning lottery ticket – which I guess he had in the gaming world. He had a strong build but wasn't a whole lot taller than me, and was dressed casually in a T-shirt.

We shook hands and he instantly asked: 'How much do you think it'll cost to run your club for the first year?'

'At least £40,000,' I replied instantly – like it was a figure I knew intimately. I literally plucked it out of thin air.

'Okay, let's do a deal.'

And with that, Miles agreed to sponsor us for the first two years – and paid up front.

Wow.

It was huge for us. And Sports Interactive truly saved our faces when the Sutton game came round. We'd been agonising over who was physically going to manufacture the brilliant kit Jonesy had designed (it was based on the one Wimbledon had worn when we played Leeds in the FA Cup).

Nearly all the major kit companies needed at least a year's notice for something like that. We wanted it inside six weeks and couldn't believe our luck when local manufacturers, Tempest Sports, said they could do it. Their director, Alp Orge, lived in Wimbledon's classy Parkside area, his parents were Turkish and they had a huge factory in Istanbul that manufactured clothing for major UK retailers like Marks & Spencer and Next. One of our fans, Alison Perrone, worked for them and brought them to our attention. We met Alp – who was irresistibly enthusiastic and persuasive – and he agreed to manufacture adult shirts for around £9, which was an incredibly good price. We sold them for £35.

To be fair, we all loved Alp. He had one of those faces that always seemed to be happy with life. There was something can-do and upbeat about him. He truly felt like one of us and we decided to let Tempest do everything. Our shirts, shorts, socks, tracksuits, casual shirts – the works. What could possibly go wrong?

Quite a lot actually. Our big plan was to unveil the new kit at a press conference on the day of the Sutton game, when we knew there'd be loads of media present. Joe Sheerin was going to walk out and, for the first time, the world would see AFC Wimbledon's inaugural kit.

Now Joe is a big bloke, roughly 6ft 2ins tall and muscular with it. We all watched in eager anticipation as Jonesy pulled the shirt out of its box for the first time – and then we froze in complete horror. It looked like a long, flowing evening dress that was literally dragging along the floor. We rapidly put it on Joe and it plunged straight down to his toes. Even the logo, which was meant to be on his chest, was down by his waistband.

It was only then that we realised our kit manufacturer had never made one in their lives before. The thing is, they were just as mortified: it honestly meant as much to them as it did to us. They'd got the measurements wrong, simple as that. Everyone fussed around looking for pins as we desperately tried to tuck the shirt up and make it look shorter on Joe. Presenting our new shirt for the world to see was so important to us. It wasn't just a shirt. It was a statement, physical proof that we were progressing. Mercifully, Joe just about got away with it as we nervously paraded him in front of the cameras and told everyone how wonderful Tempest Sports were.

But that wasn't the only problem. First, the rest of the kits had been held up at customs and wouldn't be with us in time for the Sutton game. Worse, the shirts themselves were all made from an extremely course hessian-type material. If you tried wearing them without a T-shirt underneath, you'd need your nipples replacing immediately afterwards.

And when the kits did eventually arrive – the day before the Combined Counties season kicked off – the Sports Interactive logo on the front kept falling off. They never stopped falling off for the rest of the season. We also discovered that when it rained, the material absorbed all the water and the shirts suddenly weighed a ton. Not that the fans cared. Those shirts became iconic and Tempest couldn't make them quick enough. We sold thousands.

The kits weren't our first official merchandise. When we were still getting off the ground, Marc Jones did a brilliant job of designing our first scarves – with AFC Wimbledon on one side and Super Dons on the other. Charles Koppel sent an officious fax to tell us we couldn't use 'Wimbledon' or 'Dons'.

The arrogance.

We told him, in no uncertain terms, we'd be happy to see him in court. That was the last we heard of it.

The sales success of the first kit wasn't the first concern when it was unveiled. The immediate problem was the Sutton game. We had nothing for the players to wear – until our new sponsors, Sports Interactive, came to the rescue. They had their own staff football team and they let us borrow their kit for the game. And we carried on using it right up to the first game of the Combined Counties season when the Tempest kits arrived in the nick of time.

As for Sports Interactive, the relationship has continued to flourish right to this present day and I'm proud to say it's now the longest-running shirt sponsorship deal in English football.

So chew on that, Campbell and Houghton.

Chapter 22
HALF IVOR HELLER

I'VE WITNESSED plenty of pitch invasions over the years, but nothing like this. We'd just been hammered 4-0 and yet our fans were celebrating like it was the greatest result in the history of the game – which, in many ways, it was. We barely knew their names and yet players who were probably better plasterers, plumbers, scaffolders and sparkies than they were footballers, were being mobbed like they were gods of the game.

All around them, tidal wave chants of 'A . . . F . . . C . . . Wim-ble-don' were sweeping ceaselessly across the Gander Green Lane stadium. Suddenly a microphone was thrust into my hand by Bruce Elliott. 'This is your moment, Ivor. You need to speak to your supporters.' I looked out across the pitch. Every blade of grass had disappeared, buried under a vast blanket of ecstatic fans, all singing, dancing, waving, punching the air – celebrating something magical they didn't want to let go of.

The cacophony slowly began to fade as they realised I was about to say something. I mumbled a few 'thank yous' and then let roar: 'AFC Wimbledon is born tonight.' The place erupted and another chant we'd never heard before suddenly filled the space. I stood, dumbstruck, as I began to work out what they were singing: 'Half Ivor Heller . . . there's only half Ivor Heller.' For the first time in my life, I felt six feet tall. The smile on my face stretched the full width of Sutton's main stand: it was hilarious and it was humbling and from then on I'd hear the same chant just about every time I walked into a pub on matchdays. 'Half Ivor Heller' would burst out and there'd be howls of laughter as I headed towards the bar.

The Sutton game was everything I could have ever prayed for. Even the 4-0 defeat felt like a resounding triumph. Nicky Campbell had needled me and put doubts in my mind. This felt like our emphatic response. All the smart-arse questions – all the cynical comments 'can fans really run a football club, can they put a team together, can they do this, can they do that' – had all been comprehensively answered in the space of 90 historic minutes.

Yes, we fucking can.

Everything went right that night. We miraculously survived our 5 p.m. press conference when we told the world that Sports Interactive were our new sponsors. At least 70 national and local newspaper reporters were there, plus TV and radio crews, and none of them suspected a thing as Joe Sheerin paraded our new Tempest shirt. It's amazing what a few safety pins can do.

Once the conference was over, someone pulled me aside and said: 'Ivor, you'd better take a look outside. There's a hell of a lot of people queueing down Gander Green Lane. They're never going to get in in time.'

I'd promised Bruce we'd bring along 2,000 fans but the queue outside Sutton's ground started around 3.30 p.m. By 7.30 p.m. it was still so long that kick-off had to be delayed – twice. We'd planned several things as part of the celebrations. One was a presentation on the pitch when thousands of yellow and blue balloons would be let off. Claire had sorted them all, everything was ready to go, the players were about to walk out when suddenly we were told: 'Stop! There's still thousands stuck outside trying to get in.'

Remember, this was a pre-season friendly against Sutton – hardly Wimbledon v Manchester United in the Premier League. Some fans were climbing trees, others scaling fences. It was pandemonium and they actually gave up counting after 4,650 had somehow got in. The ceremony eventually went ahead once the teams walked out. The two sides exchanged pennants and then Sutton, who were magnificent hosts, presented us with a little cut-glass trophy.

Then we all watched in awe as Claire's yellow and blue balloons were finally released and sent spiralling off into the night. I remember praying they'd all head straight for Soho Square and form a huge pile right outside the FA's front door. 'Welcome back to work – from A . . . F . . . C . . . Wim-ble-don.'

Sutton themselves played a blinder and it feels now like they've become important people in our history. They spectacularly ran out of everything: toilet rolls, crisps, burgers, chips, chocolate, lager – you name it, it vanished. We'd been allowed to design the match programmes, printed thousands and they'd all sold out long before the game kicked off.

Even though we were playing at their stadium, they allowed our master of ceremonies, Chris Philips, to take over the Tannoy announcements. I'll never forget him reading out our starting line-up. We all listened and cheered and then went, 'Who the fuck is that?' as we heard names for the very first time.

There was Mehmet Mehmet (so good, they named him twice). He had an England schoolboy cap and I'm pretty sure his dad owned a kebab shop, while Carlo Castronova's dad owned a popular Italian restaurant by Shannon's Corner in New Malden. Every time I ate there, he begged me to give his son a trial. Then there was Akin Gallimore – and our number nine, 'Trigger'.

There was one name I did recognise: my mate Dave Fry. He was a genuine Wimbledon fan and had always played at a good level of non-league football. He eventually scored our first goal at Kingsmeadow and for someone like him, you couldn't put a price on that.

In fact, that was true for a lot of our players. They were used to playing in front of crowds of 30, never mind 3,000-plus. These games, these occasions, were every bit as memorable for them as they were for us. They were experiencing their own personal cup finals each time they stepped out. We were a magnificent creation.

The game went by in a blur and I spent a lot of it looking up at stray yellow and blue balloons that were still hanging around as though they wanted to see the match for themselves. And I remember thinking: 'Is this the turning point?' Is this our stake in the ground moment? We've kicked a ball, we've played as a team, in front of our fans, in our backyard. We've done exactly what the FA told us not to. 'We've told the whole football world that Wimbledon is back, and that we're not on buses and trains heading for Milton Keynes.'

Was that what our game against Sutton was all about? I think it was.

Chapter 23
GOOD RIDDANCE

EVERYBODY told me not to go. 'We've moved on, Ivor; it'll rebound on the club. Leave the past behind.' But I couldn't. There was still some unfinished business to attend to. I needed closure. The week before our opening Combined Counties League game at Sandhurst, another team called Wimbledon played Gillingham in the old League Division 1 at Selhurst Park. They hadn't yet moved to Milton Keynes, this team called Wimbledon, and this was their first game of the new 2002–03 season.

WISA called for a demo outside Selhurst Park and we held loads of meetings about what to do. During one of them, Erik turned to me and said: 'You must not go to that demonstration.'

'Nothing will stop me, Erik,' I replied. 'I'll be careful, I won't do anything, but there's no way I'm missing it.' Quite a few agreed with Erik, though. They feared it would undo all the good we had been doing with AFC Wimbledon.

But something deep inside convinced me I had to go – and I'm really glad I did. It felt cathartic, like a letting-go process that I had to experience. It was also visible proof that people were on our side. There were way more outside Selhurst Park than there were inside. Thousands of us did a giant conga all the way round the stadium, with banners and posters that read: 'Say no to the franchising of football'.

This was us putting up a final two fingers at the FA. They'd ordered us not to start again – we ignored them; they expected us to travel 70 miles to Milton Keynes – instead we travelled seven miles to Selhurst Park to say, 'Good riddance.'

We were on our own now and would have to shape our own future. Not have it imposed on us by imposters governing the game. It was closure, all right. It was the final kiss goodbye. It was fuck off. I didn't give a shit about that club masquerading as mine any more. Instead, I loved the fact that more people had turned up not to see the game. In fact, we persuaded many to change their minds just as they were going in. 'You've come to watch the wrong Wimbledon,' we told them. Plenty turned round and joined our giant conga instead.

The fact they barely had 2,000 in the ground felt like a victory, especially when we took more the following week to Sandhurst. Even Gillingham's own fans boycotted the game and that felt like victory as well. In fact, that was something else that beleaguered this other team called Wimbledon from then on: visiting fans stayed away to show their support for our Wimbledon team, the real Wimbledon team, at Kingsmeadow. Some even came to watch us rather than be seen at Selhurst Park.

The Wider World of Football had decided whose side it was on. It wasn't the FA's, and it wasn't that other team called Wimbledon, either. The Wider World of Football was on the side of the people who matter the most in the beautiful game. The fans. The Wider World of Football was supporting AFC Wimbledon – even though the adventure hadn't even begun.

But, on 10 August 2002, it got off to a wonderful start. We were all in The Foley when the BBC *Final Score* teleprinter flashed up on an overhead television screen and we all roared euphorically as we saw:

Another Team Called Wimbledon 0 Gillingham 1.

Chapter 24
BOTTOMS UP

I'D BEEN to all the great, truly historic Premier League grounds with Wimbledon: Old Trafford, Anfield, Stamford Bridge, St James' Park, Highbury, White Hart Lane. Arenas that gave you goosebumps. When the crowd roared, the noise would be so deafening you'd still hear it years later. I'd watched some of the game's greatest players in those stadiums: David Beckham, Alan Shearer, Ruud Gullit, Patrick Vieira, Michael Owen, David Ginola, Ian Wright. We had a few of our own, too: Vinnie Jones, John Fashanu, Dennis Wise. The list is endless.

On 17 August 2002, I went to a field in Berkshire where there was a recognisable football pitch but no physical stands anywhere. Scattered here and there were some hay bales for shorter fans like me to clamber on. On this day, I watched players like Tony Readings and Sim Johnston and Dave Towse and Neil Robson. Instead of terracing and executive boxes and rows upon rows of leather-padded seats, we were surrounded by layers of colossal sycamore and oak trees that had stood there for centuries. They were so tall, they made floodlights look like tiny candles.

I remember looking round and thinking about the Stretford End and the Kop. They'd always be rammed and I'd watch, spellbound, as great tidal waves of fans would sway backwards and forwards across the terraces. The only things swaying now, ever so slightly, were the blazing green leaves fidgeting about whenever a rare breeze drifted over. I wouldn't have swapped it for the world.

Just 81 days after the FA told us to lie down and die, we were officially starting all over again in the sleepy backwaters of the football pyramid. Old Trafford and Anfield were a million miles away, but we were still having a party. Around 2,350 of us were encamped at the gloriously named Bottom Meadow to see AFC Wimbledon's first Combined Counties League game against Sandhurst Town. The attendance was 2,449 and, to this day, that remains a record for the home club.

The national press were there in force; one photographer even stood on top of the dugout because there was nowhere else for him to go. Sandhurst did have a clubhouse – midway between a right-hand goalpost and the corner flag. To be honest, it looked more like a groundsman's bungalow. There was also a Portakabin where directors congregated for teas and nibbles. All the old emotions still came flooding back, though: 'We've got to win this; it's important to get a good start; if we can't beat Sandhurst, who can we beat?'

So far, the omens hadn't been great. Pre-season had largely been calamitous. We'd bigged ourselves up and made T-shirts with 'Wombles on Tour' emblazoned across the back, selling them from a converted ambulance which doubled as a mobile club shop. We called it the 'Wombulance'.

We'd established an identity, but were getting consistently stuffed in pre-season friendlies at places like Dulwich, Wealdstone, Leatherhead and Walton. We were losing regularly and we were slowly starting to see a different side to our manager, Terry Eames.

After one defeat, he resigned in fit of pique, screaming and shouting at the players and storming off to his car where he sat, alone, stewing. Our brave new world hadn't even begun and I'd already seen enough. If a manager wants to go, then let him. That was my attitude. The others disagreed, though, and they persuaded Eames to stay. To be fair, we had been playing teams that were much higher than us in the pyramid and even I could see any manager would need time to mould new players into a unit.

We hadn't scored a single goal, though, in something like six games. Then came a midweek fixture against Bromley. They'd taken the lead when, suddenly, Trigger got the ball on the edge of the box, feinted, then hacked it straight into the top corner. Boom.

Everyone went mental, like we'd won the World Cup. We still lost 3-1 – but at least we'd scored.

Our first game at Kingsmeadow followed, against fellow tenants Kingstonian. Over 2,500 fans turned up for a non-league friendly. Khosla was ecstatic because it was a taste of things to come, and although we lost (again), my mate Dave Fry scored a stonking half-volley. I've always marvelled at the ingenuity of fans and how they can spontaneously launch into a brand new chant. Seconds later, they were singing their own adaptation of the R. Kelly classic: *'I believe I'm Dave Fry, I believe I can touch the sky.'*

Brilliant.

We then lost at Windsor and Eton, where I met their president, the legendary TV football commentator Barry Davies. What a lovely man: he was a real gent, behind us all the way and extremely encouraging. Little moments like that meant a huge amount to us.

We didn't actually win until our final game at Enfield, who were much more our level. Then came another nightmare. To my horror, Claire announced that her sister, Stella, was getting married 24 hours before our league opener at Sandhurst. 'But it's our first game the next day,' I protested. 'There'll be loads for me to prepare. I'm not going to a fucking wedding.'

'Oh yes you are, Ivor. Family comes first.'

Mercifully, Claire's brother, Raymond, was a massive football fan and loved the fact I was involved with AFC Wimbledon.

'Any chance you could get us tickets for the game?' he asked. I could have kissed him: it was my get-out-of-jail card. I happily got tickets for him and his son, knowing Claire couldn't possibly argue against that. But it was a close call and possibly an early sign of tensions to come.

On the day of the game, my mobile rang around 11 a.m. It was Steve Elson and there was a barrage of noise in the background. 'Where are you?' I yelled.

'We're in the Batsford Arms.'

'Oh, do fuck off,' I replied. The Batsford Arms had been our beloved pub at Plough Lane and, of course, it had long vanished along with our old ground.

'No, really, I am. You need to get your arse here quick. Sandhurst have recreated the Batsford Arms for us at Bottom Meadow and there's loads of us here already.'

Bottom Meadow looked and felt like an English summer fete when I eventually got there. It was a baking hot day, everyone was in shirt sleeves and shorts, and I half expected to hear a Tannoy announcement saying: 'The children's gymkhana will start in five minutes.'

There were people everywhere, a lot of them pissed way before kick-off. The only thing keeping them off the pitch was a single metal rail that ran round the entire perimeter. Many were leaning against that at dangerously intoxicated angles; others were wobbling about on the hay bales.

And Steve was right – Sandhurst had genuinely built a pop-up bar inside a marquee and called it the Batsford Arms. I was overawed when I saw it. This was a club used to crowds between 30 and 40 and yet they'd gone the extra mile to do something special like that. It was ridiculously wonderful how much they welcomed us. They couldn't have done more and they even let us hang our banners and flags all over their clubhouse roof and on the railing round the pitch. If you go to Sandhurst Town today, they still have memorabilia of that game all over the place. They were a shining example of what true football people are really like. The FA would have learned a lot had they bothered to turn up.

We were undeniably at an unrecognisable level, for sure. Steve and his mates had actually phoned the club and asked if they could sponsor the game. Sandhurst didn't know what to say – or charge – because nobody had ever asked them that before! In the end, he paid £50, which got them inside the directors' Portakabin and access to tea and biscuits. I stood behind one of the goals and was constantly approached by reporters from papers like the *News of the World* and the *People*, all wanting my thoughts on what the game meant and represented.

Fuck, where do I start?

Yes, I thought about the days spent in the Premier League's greatest stadiums. The contrast was acute and you could argue that we'd fallen a hell of a long way. But the FA had done that to us. They'd pushed us this far back – in fact they didn't want us congregating in that field at all. So I told Geoff Sweet from the *News of the World* that this was our resurrection. We were starting again, free from all the evils that had destroyed the club we'd supported before. Our destiny was now in our hands and I wanted this version of the club to go the whole way, right from the bottom and stick two fingers up to the FA at every single stage along the way – starting in a field in Sandhurst. Every time the FA looked in a mirror, I wanted them to see our reflections staring right back at them. That's what I told him.

The game itself passed in a blur of yellow and blue. The players looked like pros in their new Tempest skin-chafing kit and Kevin Cooper got us off to a dream start when he slotted home our first league goal. Keith Ward made it 2-0 with a powerful header; the roar from our fans comfortably raised the non-existent roof off the non-existent stand. Sandhurst were no pushovers, though, and they pulled one back just before the break. We then had to survive at least 12 minutes of added time to hang on 2-1 winners.

After that came pure drunken elation and I squeezed into the Portakabin with Steve and his mates. Steve was battered by then and I'll never forget him trying to sell a caravan – presumably because it felt like we were standing in one – to the totally bemused Mayor of Sandhurst, who was proudly there in his full regalia with a bloody chain and medallion round his neck. Steve had never owned a caravan in his life and still doesn't.

I couldn't have been happier. I didn't rue the fact we weren't at one of the big grounds. At the same time as we were beating Sandhurst, another club called Wimbledon were losing 3-2 at

Watford. Those imposters were still using our old name, and they didn't physically move from Selhurst Park to Milton Keynes for another year.

But it never crossed my mind to pine for the good old days because, deep down, I knew we would get back there. I was in it for the journey, for the getting there – that was as much a part of the package as being back at the top. We'd sold 1,100 season tickets by now, phenomenal for that level. And after Sandhurst came our very first League game at Kingsmeadow.

First, though, we did an extraordinary sponsorship deal with the advertising guru Trevor Beattie. He was chairman of the agency TWBA at the time and helped get Tony Blair elected as Labour Prime Minister in 2001 and 2005. He was also the brains behind the 'fcuk' campaign and 'hello boys' Wonderbra adverts with supermodel Eva Herzigova.

I was introduced to him by his design director, Wimbledon fan Paul Silburn, and Beattie generously agreed to pay £5,000 to sponsor our first home match. It didn't buy him very much: Beattie had to sit on a concrete step throughout the match because fans grabbed his designated seat for themselves. 'I don't give a fuck – this is absolutely brilliant,' he smiled.

He also agreed to shoot an iconic TV advert for us that showed our supporters building a new fans' stadium. Top-flight companies would have paid many thousands of pounds for that.

The other big PR opportunity that came our way was when the actor Alun Armstrong, a mate of mine and a passionate Wimbledon fan, called to say he'd accepted a part in a new show – and had specified his character would be an AFC Wimbledon supporter on screen! He needed a shirt as a prop – but all the replica kit had sold out. So I sneaked into the dressing rooms when everyone had left and grabbed a player's strip for him. The show turned out to be *New Tricks*, the hit comedy police drama with the likes of Dennis Waterman and Tamzin Outhwaite, and it went on to become one of the UK's most exported programmes. The producers even wanted a picture of Alun's character with one of our players, which ended up appearing alongside other strategically placed merchandise in almost every episode.

Despite losing our opening home game, we won nearly all our matches after that. But that was another unexpected lesson as well. We finished the season with a bumper 111 points – and yet that still wasn't enough to get us promoted. Only one team went up from the Combined Counties – Withdean 2000 – and there were no play-offs.

Chapter 25
VIOLENT TIMES

I'VE BEEN knocked unconscious and carried across the pitch on a broken advertising hoarding; I've witnessed *Strictly Come Dancing* star Alesha Dixon knocked to the floor at one of our home games and I've pleaded with thugs – the snarling, deranged types – who've turned up at a Wimbledon away match purely to hurt someone. I've also watched our players punching opponents in an ugly pitch fight after an alleged racist remark. We got fined for that. The racism could never be proved.

None of us had the faintest idea what we were letting ourselves in for when AFC Wimbledon's journey began at the bottom of the football pyramid. We hurtled head-first into the realities of life at a football club and it wasn't always the beautiful game.

It wasn't long after we'd enjoyed the genteel surroundings of Bottom Meadow that we experienced the other side of life at stadiums where there were rarely any police, or even stewards. It was 23 November 2002, absolutely pissing down and we took a couple of thousand fans to Wallingford, who were neck and neck with Withdean 2000 at the top of the league. The rain was so heavy, games at Oxford, Reading and Swindon were all postponed. Unbeknown to us, their most violent thugs headed for Wallingford instead.

These were real hard-core troublemakers and there was next to no security at the ground. We were already losing 2-0 when I got a phone call from a mate who was in the clubhouse bar, immediately behind one of the goals. 'Ivor, you need to get in here – fast. It's all kicking off; there's a fucking riot going on and some of our fans are getting hurt.'

I was with Kris, and by the time we got there everything inside had been smashed, broken or upended. Glasses and bottles lay shattered across the floor, chairs were upside down, their frames splintered or torn apart. All around stood moronic groups of snarling nutters, either gawking at one another or picking something else up to hurl randomly into the mayhem. Some had blood pouring down their faces, which they let run freely as if to say, 'Look how fucking tough we are.'

One thug was on a phone and I heard him yell, derangedly: 'You've got to get in here, it's fucking brilliant.' Then a glass ashtray hurtled past his head, missing by millimetres. I looked at the culprit: he was grinning inanely.

Kris and I desperately pushed our fans back – I was using my umbrella – until we heard sirens getting louder and louder and then a helicopter hovering overhead. 'Thank Christ,' I said and we moved aside as a line of police filed in. One by one the baying mob were slowly dragged out. At least 50 of them were rounded up, but I suspect they all got away with it and had a good old laugh when they got back to their local pubs.

Thank God it hadn't happened at Kingsmeadow, but it could have done and we would have been just as helpless. That was the wake-up call. I suddenly realised that we had a new responsibility now. Matchdays weren't just about going to the football and getting drunk and having a big laugh. They were about ensuring everyone was safe and everyone got home in one piece. It was our jobs to guarantee that.

Sadly, the Wallingford Riot, as we came to call it, was followed by two more sickening incidents – one involving our players, plus the music celebrities Alesha Dixon and MC Harvey. We'd reached the last 16 of the prestigious FA Vase and were handed a home draw against Colne, which is near Burnley. Christ, their players were ugly and huge with it: the shortest was well over six foot and they all had shaved heads. Horrible.

It was a great game to be fair, extremely physical and bruising, but there was a tension like I'd never seen before. Our side included the rapper MC Harvey, who achieved fame with the hip-hop band So Solid Crew. He was also a decent left wing-back. His missus back then was Alesha, already a star herself with the band Mis-Teeq. She used to come to our games regularly and was a right laugh. I really liked her – despite her fame, and despite the fact she radiated beauty and confidence, she had no airs and graces.

There were no sides to Alesha: she would smile and chat with absolutely anyone and I enjoyed keeping a fatherly eye on her. Harvey was all street – she was all class.

Alesha was at the Colne game when it suddenly became clear that Harvey was extremely agitated about something that had been said to him on the pitch. The mood turned very ugly, very quickly; players started pushing and shoving and then punches were thrown.

The whistle finally went, and we'd lost 2-3, but both sets of players continued brawling as they came off the pitch. Alesha ran over to calm Harvey down, then got caught in the melee herself and was sent sprawling into a slimy patch of mud outside the players' tunnel. I ran over to check she was okay and then watched in disbelief as Joe Sheerin – our captain and a real gentle giant – started wrestling with their captain, who wriggled free and headed down the tunnel. But Joe stormed after him, launched himself into a thunderous sliding tackle and hurled a ferocious punch that broke the Colne player's jaw in three places.

Both clubs got fined afterwards, money we couldn't afford to lose. No action was taken over the alleged racism. It was the first time we'd been charged by the FA and another lesson about running a football club. We were all responsible for maintaining discipline, and there'd be a cost if we didn't – no matter what the alleged provocation.

We then reached the semi-final of the Premier Challenge Cup against Coney Hall, who were in a division below us. This was very much Millwall territory and the game was transferred to Bromley to cope with the expected attendance. I already knew Bromley's chairman, Jerry Dolke, and our head steward talked to him in advance about crowd safety because we knew we'd bring around 2,000 fans. 'It'll all be covered,' was the response.

Jonesy and I got there early, walked in and there wasn't a steward in sight. Worse, there were two tables outside the main bar overflowing with cans of lager, selling for just £1 each.

Fucking hell.

Erik and I hunted down Jerry and said: 'What the hell are you doing? We've just seen young kids buying four cans each. This is a recipe for disaster. And where are the stewards?'

'Oh, don't worry about that,' he answered. 'You won't be bringing 2,000 with you.'

'Jerry, this is our first semi-final. We promise you, we will.'

Everywhere I looked, there were 14-, 15- and 16-year-old kids – all in trainee hooligan clobber, clutching cans of lager and trying to slurp it down as quickly as they could. 'Jerry, you have to stop this – we need stewards and we need police.'

'I've been doing this for years; there's nothing to worry about,' he insisted.

The crowd kept building, and suddenly a mob of around 300 proper football factory types started gathering. They headed straight for the £1 lagers. It was unbelievable. Genuinely worried, Erik phoned the police and I heard him say: 'I'm calling from Bromley Football Club, where there's going to be a large crowd tonight for a cup tie between our club, AFC Wimbledon, and the local side, Coney Hall.

'We expect to bring at least 2,000 fans but there are already 300 potential troublemakers here and they're drinking heavily. There doesn't seem to be any security or stewards and we wondered if you could send someone along?'

'No, we can't do that,' came the reply. 'If something happens then we will send people in.'

The atmosphere was getting increasingly feral as our fans started to arrive. Erik and I watched them intensely and felt relieved when there didn't seem to be any obvious troublemakers among them. The first half passed incident-free. There was no crowd separation but the Coney fans seemed to be banked on the terracing behind the dugouts, while ours were behind a goal.

We took the lead after the break but then Coney equalised. Suddenly cans half full of stale beer were getting chucked at our management team from behind the dugouts. Some thugs were openly urinating into cups and hurling them at our staff.

Our fans realised what was happening and both groups started baying at each other. The game went into extra time, the atmosphere became even more incendiary and I saw two groups edging closer and closer.

Memories of the Wallingford Riot came flooding back and I rushed towards our fans, pleading with them to stop. 'Lads – think about what you're doing. They're trying to wind everyone up, you need to back off or someone will get seriously hurt.

'If there's trouble here, it will rebound badly on our club.'

I thought I'd convinced them but then a fight broke out on the upper terracing above the dugouts, and rapidly spiralled down towards us. Bodies suddenly piled into me, I stumbled backwards, fell, and my head crashed heavily on to the concrete steps – knocking me out completely.

I'm told I was unconscious for a few seconds and then slowly opened my eyes. I remember my head was pounding and then I realised fans had formed a circle around me and were bending down to see if I was okay.

The referee abandoned the match and ushered the players off

the pitch, realising there was no police or stewards anywhere to be seen. I got carried across the pitch on a broken advertising hoarding, half-conscious and still very groggy. Jonesy drove me home and I woke up the following morning with a huge bump on my head. I remained concussed for at least three or four days afterwards.

The game still needed to be rearranged and we all sat together in a board meeting trying to work out how to avoid another riot. Although I largely blamed Jerry for ignoring our pleas, I also knew our fans had thrown the first punches.

Erik revealed that he'd been approached as he left Bromley's ground by an off-duty police sergeant, who had said: 'I saw everything. I'd like to be a witness and help because you have a couple of people you need to get out.' Brilliant, we all agreed. Except Erik had lost his name. 'I don't know how to trace him,' he groaned.

And that's when Trigger, who hadn't yet become embroiled in the phone-hacking scandal, came to the rescue. He was running our reserve team by then but had told me he did a bit of private investigation work on the side. So I got him on a speaker phone and said: 'Trigger – we need to find a police sergeant who was at Bromley two weeks ago and witnessed everything.'

We gave Trigger a description, which was hopelessly vague, and a name – which was almost certainly the wrong one because Erik couldn't remember it. 'Yeah, OK, give me a few minutes,' Trigger replied. He phoned back 10 minutes later and gave us the sergeant's full name. 'Just so you know, he's just this second left a post office in Caterham and he'll be home in about 10 minutes. Here's his phone number!'

So we waited and then Erik rang him on the speaker phone. 'Hello there, I don't know if you remember, but we met at the Bromley game and you kindly offered to be a witness for us.'

'Oh, yes, I remember. You're lucky to catch me – I've just come back from the post office!'

None of us had the faintest idea how Trigger had done it. When the hacking scandal did break, I got called in three times by Operation Weeting. The detectives couldn't make any sense of notes he'd made from his days at the football club.

'What is this code for – 'the Weird and Wonderful Rematch?' they asked me.

'That's when we played Liverpool in a charity match,' I explained.

'Do you recognise any of these numbers?' I looked, and they were simply members of staff.

'Who's Nicky Nine Toes (RIP)?'

'He's one of our fans,' I replied. 'He goes in the bar every week.'

I had to laugh when they added: 'There's something about "Salad" all over the place. What's that all about?'

Smiling, I said: 'He's another fan – that's his nickname. He's forty stone, so everyone calls him Salad (RIP)!'

I wasn't shown a single thing that felt wrong. It was all innocent and easily explainable. And the police sergeant that Trigger had helped us find was a huge help as well. Two fans were banned: one for chinning a much younger fan who'd been walking along with drinks in each hand. He served his sentence, returned, and was never a problem again. The other – who tried to justify himself by claiming he was 'defending the club's honour' – also got banned. He never returned.

The rearranged game was held at Sutton with a full-scale security operation in place. The Coney Hall fans were segregated and we won 5-0. We were in the final, where we'd play North Greenford United at Woking. I spent much of that game looking for old John, whom I'd not seen since the Combined Counties meeting when we were accepted into their league. I never did find him, but after we'd won 4-1, I like to think he left the ground mumbling, 'Fucking players.'

Chapter 26
HATED FOR SACKING THE MANAGER

GETTING rid of our first manager Terry Eames – and what happened afterwards – was the closest I ever came to walking away for good. The fans never knew the real reasons why he was sacked and I can only hint at them now. It didn't help that he'd become a hero with our supporters. He'd amassed a staggering 111 points in his first season (not enough to get us promoted but that didn't matter) and he'd even begun a historic unbeaten run of 78 games, which remains a record at any senior level within the English game.

Halfway through his second season, it became obvious we were going to win the Combined Counties League by a mile – and most likely one of the cup competitions as well. The team was riding high under his leadership: we were about to win trophies and we were having a ball.

But the fans didn't know the Terry Eames that we knew. Behind the scenes he seemed to be an entirely different animal. We couldn't tell them that he seemed to have become increasingly distant, refusing to talk to us – or even attend board meetings. Then there were some bonus payments allegedly promised to our players that we knew nothing about.

He didn't talk to us at all during the summer prior to his second season. Then his wife, Ann, started claiming that we were to blame. She claimed that we weren't inclusive, that we treated the club like we owned it, and we were big-time Charlies.

None of this was true but it added to the bad feeling. What on earth are you meant to do when your manager won't talk to you, his wife thinks you're aloof and power-crazed – and yet the team are flying high, top of the table, and halfway through a historic unbeaten run?

Then came our point of no return: we discovered Eames had apparently sacked a load of club staff without telling us first, or explaining why, or seeking approval. We demanded he came in to see us, unsure whether he'd actually show. We were surprised when he did and so we told him, straight to his face, what we thought, saying: 'We're going through a process that could lead to your dismissal.'

He stormed out and then it all kicked off on social media. All sorts of wild lies and accusations started flying around. He was then invited to another meeting, which he didn't attend. We sacked him in his absence and Kris, still our chief executive at the time, announced that – regrettably – Terry Eames was no longer at the club. That sparked uproar and it quickly turned extremely nasty.

We were called every name under the sun: we were diabolical, incapable of running a football club properly, we'd lost sight of our principles, we thought we were gods, we'd forgotten it was a fans' club, we needed to resign, etc. All spiced with a barrage of swear words and personal insults.

It was a real onslaught. His missus, Ann, even stood for election to the Dons Trust and won, only to resign the following week. Her mantra was being swallowed hook, line and sinker – her husband was whiter than white, he'd done nothing wrong, he'd been picked on by the nasty board members. I remember saying to Kris: 'We're getting screwed here. The fans are believing everything they're being told and we can't tell them our side of the story.'

After we dismissed him, our next game was against Chessington at Leatherhead. I've never experienced so much poison at a match. The atmosphere hissed with violence when Kris and I walked into the bar. I was so certain we were going to be hit that I grabbed an empty bottle of beer and kept it in my pocket the entire time.

Kris got jostled and pushed and shoved out on the terraces. Jonesy and I stood with him and we were all subjected to a barrage of disgusting insults and comments all through the game – even though we won 9-0. Yes, that's right: NINE-NIL. We'd put assistant manager Nick English in charge and the transition had clearly not affected the team.

That still didn't lighten the mood, though, and – as I was leaving the ground – I suffered the worst personal abuse I ever encountered at an AFC Wimbledon game. A car drove past me, the window came down and one of our fans – John Venables – leaned out and sang a crude adaptation of the song we used to sing to Charles Koppel: 'Heyyyyyy, heyyyyyy, Ivor – ooh, arrh – we want to know, know, know, why you're such a cunt.'

It caught me at the wrong moment. I can look at it now and know it was just words, sung by an imbecile. But right then it lit a fuse deep within me. Had I gone full circle? Had I turned from hero to villain? Was I just like Koppel? Egotistical, out of touch? Had I put myself on a lofty perch and totally alienated the people I was meant to be representing? Was I no longer one of us – but one of them?

Is this what it had all been about? All the minutes, hours, days, weeks and years devoted to saving my club. I'd spent more time with Wimbledon than I had with my wife. I'd spent more time at work sorting club problems than I'd spent looking after my own business. Had it all been for this? Was it time to walk away?

All of us were feeling low and angry and victimised afterwards so Erik, Kris, Trevor and I called a meeting with the players. Nobody had explained to them why Eames had been sacked and we wanted to know how they felt. Their reaction was a total shock: none of them were bothered. In fact, the only response we got was: 'What about our bonuses when we win the league?'

'What bonuses?' Kris replied, completely bemused – as we all were.

'The manager promised us a big bonus.' When we asked how much, the response blew us away. It added up to a quarter of a million pounds.

The room fell totally silent as those numbers turned over in our heads.

Fucking hell, that's 2-5-0-0-0-0 and I could see the individual digits turning over like they were spinning numbers in a casino slot machine.

Such a number was impossible at our level. To be honest, £10,000 between them all would have been hard enough. We might have thrown a party and given them a few hundred quid each, perhaps. These were part-time players on £50, £150, £200 a week. We weren't in the fucking Premier League.

'We have never, ever discussed a bonus scheme with Terry Eames. He wouldn't even come to a meeting with us, so how could we have done?' I said.

The players didn't look too surprised. Maybe they'd exaggerated the number themselves just to chance their luck – but Kris added: 'If any of you feel that you can't play any more because of this, then we will reluctantly understand.'

There was a big advantage to our conversation with the players. We knew they'd get straight on to social media and start telling everyone. Which is exactly what they did. For the first time, fans started to hear our side of the story.

Sure enough, people began apologising at our next game. 'We were bang out of order last week' – 'We'd no idea what was going on' – 'Why didn't you tell us?'

Eames's departure had no impact on the team's performance from then on. Nicky English continued on the unbeaten run and even led the team to a league and cup double.

But it had been another, very steep, learning curve. This time, we learned that if you don't nip a bad situation in the bud, it will fester and snowball. If you want to run a football club successfully, you have to keep control.

Chapter 27
EL PRESIDENTE

ONE of the greatest things we ever did was ask Dickie Guy to be our club president. I am unashamedly biased when it comes to our legendary goalkeeper. Dickie was my boyhood hero from the moment I first saw him play at the old Plough Lane. He never let us down: he got us, and he got the club. The pinnacle, of course, was the moment he saved Peter Lorimer's penalty in front of 45,000 fans packed into Elland Road.

I still tease him about that penalty today. In my mind, Dickie hurled himself acrobatically through the air to fingertip Lorimer's ferocious drive past the post. It wasn't until I saw *The Big Match* the next day that I realised the Scottish international had mishit his shot and the save was easier than I'd imagined. 'He completely scuffed it,' I tell everyone – even if Dickie's alongside me – and a great, big, cheesy grin spreads over his face. He can take a joke and I like him even more for that. He stayed 11 seasons at Wimbledon, once making 275 consecutive appearances and only missing one game in a run of 449 matches between 1970 and 1977.

I got to know him as a person, and not just a hero, as I started arranging golf days. Turned out that my hero was a warm, friendly, funny human being, with deep family values and immense loyalty. What wasn't there to like? Inevitably, his career waned, but his love for our club never ceased. He stood shoulder to shoulder with us during the protest years and then shared our excitement and determination as AFC Wimbledon rose from the ashes. In fact, Dickie was there for our historic Wimbledon Common trials and helped us sift through all the goalkeepers who turned up.

AFC Wimbledon's first president was Allen Batsford, and

nobody would dispute his credentials, either. But when Allen decided to step down, we needed someone just as legendary to fill his shoes. There was only one contender for me, so I talked it over with Kris. He agreed immediately.

The moment came as we celebrated our 2004 league and cup double, having won the Combined Counties and lifted the Premier Challenge Cup. After a civic reception in Morden town hall, we all decided to head back to the Alexandra pub in town – a favourite watering hole for many Wimbledon fans. Many of us headed upstairs to the pub's open-air roof terrace, including Dickie – who'd been at the civic reception – and his family. I noticed he was leaning over the wall at the front of the pub, looking down on the main street below. I turned to Kris and said: 'Let's do it now. Let's ask Dickie to be our new president.'

Kris nodded approval and we walked over. 'Dickie – can Kris and I have a chat with you?' I asked.

'Yeah, of course,' he replied, a little startled. He'd absolutely no idea what was coming.

'Well, as you know,' I continued, 'Allen has stepped down as president.'

'Yeah, yeah,' he answered.

'Well – Kris and I were wondering if you would like to take over and be our next president?'

He welled up instantly. The look on his face was priceless: he hadn't expected it – that was for sure – but it was the emotion that made it all worthwhile. He was truly honoured and grateful and it clearly meant a hell of a lot.

'I can't believe it. Are you sure?' he stammered, totally shocked and overcome. Make no mistake, this giant of a human being was moved to tears. 'No, really, is this what you want?'

And then the words we wanted to hear came: 'Yes, of course, it would be a total honour. I can't thank you enough.'

We let him wander off to tell his wife, Josie, and smiled at the sheer joy and pride beaming across his face as he started telling everyone. He was so thrilled and he got nicknamed 'El Presidente' straight away.

Just how devoted Dickie is to our club was underlined when he came with us on a pre-season tour to the La Manga complex in Spain. He has suffered horrendous health problems over the years and had just had a voice box fitted after a second bout of throat cancer. It was a huge operation and he'd barely come out of hospital.

We landed and, inevitably, ended up in a bar. Dickie asked for a beer – but also a separate empty glass. 'The valve on my voice box has a leak,' he explained, stoically. 'I'll have to thicken the beer and that should stop it dripping into the valve.' I then watched him pour a full sachet of powder into the empty glass – and then tip the beer on to it. The concoction frothed up immediately like some horrible chemistry experiment gone wrong – and exploded all over the table. We howled with laughter, but deep down I knew we'd just witnessed how brave the man is. There he was, absolutely determined to be with the club he adored. There was more to come, as well.

There's always an initiation ceremony on these trips – people who have never been before have to sing something in front of everyone. We were all in the sprawling La Manga Square one evening, and getting a lot of attention from all the other holidaymakers there, when I realised Dickie hadn't sung anything – for pretty obvious reasons. But I was feeling mischievous: 'Listen, Dickie, you're not getting away without singing just because you've got a voice box.'

'Don't be stupid,' he replied, his voice box unavoidably making him sound robotic.

'No, really – I have the perfect song for you,' I replied. Straight away, I gave him my own rendition of 'I Was Born Under A Wandrin' Star,' in my own, very gravelly, Lee Marvin voice.

Dickie saw the opportunity immediately: 'I can do that,' he smiled.

It was a beautiful, warm evening, everyone was in a party mood so I went for it. 'Right, everyone – Dickie is going to sing.'

The whole square fell silent instantly – and I don't just mean us lot. Dickie stood on a chair in front of everyone and blasted out the entire song. You could hear a pin drop: nobody uttered a word. Only when he finished did the place erupt into a crescendo of applause and cheering. I genuinely think it was the most selfless thing I'd ever seen or heard. He was the bravest man I knew for going on the trip in the first place – but then he found the courage to go and do that. Why? Because he's so fucking proud of our club.

Even today, Dickie's had several more major health problems but he still joined us for the 300-mile round trip to Grimsby on the last day of the 2024–25 season. Sometimes I think we keep him alive – and, in return, he keeps us alive.

God bless you, Dickie.

Chapter 28
LET'S BUY KINGSMEADOW

IT FELT like doomsday. The end of the road after just one season. We'd have to pack our bags and find another home because Kingsmeadow, or rather its owner Rajesh Khosla, was bleeding us dry. Ground sharing should have cost around £20,000 – that was the deal. But that was nowhere near accurate. By the end of our first season, playing at Kingsmeadow cost us closer to £100,000 – and Khosla wanted to increase the rent for season two.

Erik was pulling his hair out. 'I don't want to give him another penny.' Everyone on the board agreed and relations with our landlord hit rock bottom. Kris even started to look seriously at groundshare deals with other clubs. It seemed like we only had two choices: cough up more rent – or get out. But then I came up with a third option: one that would reshape our entire future.

When we first negotiated our ground share with Khosla, we assumed we'd be playing in the Ryman League. That only had 16 teams – so, allowing for a modest cup run – we were happy to pay £20,000, thinking it would be for 20 matches, tops. If we played more, then we would pay more and that was agreed. It soon became obvious that 20 games was nowhere near enough. The Combined Counties League was much bigger (24 teams) and we enjoyed lengthy cup runs.

Khosla also charged us for any extras we requested, including the tiniest ground improvements. Many board members felt these should have been freebies, but Khosla saw them as opportunities to demand more money from us. It didn't help that he was also pocketing every penny we earned from selling food and drinks to our own fans. That was always the agreement from the very beginning – but it definitely jarred.

Despite the rising bills, I always understood Khosla. He was an out-and-out businessman, and he put a value on everything. Nothing was free, and if you accepted that, then he was someone you could do a deal with. But there was little softness in him. When people demanded favours, their requests usually fell on deaf ears. A lot of it was a breakdown in communications. They simply didn't talk each other's language and, as a result, they wound him up – just as much as he needled them.

If I wanted something, for instance, I'd maybe start the conversation like so: 'Hello, Mr Khosla, how are you, how's the family,' and then listen attentively as he told me his latest news. Then, when the moment felt right, I'd drop the bombshell: 'By the way, Raj, I was just wondering, is there any chance that we could use that little bit of space in the fridge for our energy drinks . . .'

Usually, the reply would be: 'Yeah, no problem.'

Put like that, it was a deal. Put the other way – 'we need to use that space in the fridge' – the reply would likely be: 'How much are you going to pay?'

Most of our board members hated him when he wouldn't jump to their requests. And when word spread that he wanted to increase our rent for season two, the relationship plummeted further. By then, I was literally the only person he'd talk to – which actually put a lot of unwelcome pressure on my shoulders. People were constantly saying, 'I need this, I need that – can you sort it, Ivor?' What they actually meant was, 'Can you sort it for free?'

There's no doubt, Khosla would charge the bollocks out of absolutely any tweak we wanted at the ground, especially if he was asked the wrong way. The more it happened, the more people talked about moving to another club. I got very aggravated about this because I knew Kingsmeadow was perfect for us. Others naively thought we could just move and everyone would happily trot along. As far as I was concerned, we had to put down roots and build a proper home, not become wandering nomads.

Our average attendances were over 3,000; geographically, we were in the best place we could realistically hope to be. Many of our fans already lived in that area, plus we had two big bars and a decent smaller one to accommodate them all. In my mind, it made far more sense for us to physically own Kingsmeadow, rather than rent it or leave it. That would secure our future and give us control of our destiny and revenues.

It got to a point where I turned to Erik and said: 'Why don't we just buy Kingsmeadow off Khosla?' I then repeated the suggestion at a subsequent board meeting but it got pooh-poohed by pretty much everyone. 'We haven't got the money,' was the stock reply. To be fair, we hadn't.

But a momentum was building that I couldn't stop, and a showdown meeting was called with Khosla in early March 2003. It's no understatement to say the mood was tense, especially when he confirmed: 'I intend to increase your rent next season.'

I could see Erik and Kris were on the brink of exploding so, without any prompting, I looked at Khosla and said: 'Why don't we cut through all this. Why don't we buy Kingsmeadow off you?'

Silence. It was the first time anyone from AFC Wimbledon had put that thought in his head. It was truly a crunch moment. The room stayed chillingly quiet and I could feel daggers being plunged into me there and then. We hadn't pre-planned this moment or agreed a joint strategy. I'd just gone for it on my own.

I knew exactly what I was doing, though. I didn't want the meeting to end in turmoil with everyone storming out and I knew we were perilously close to that. Someone had to cut through all the sniping and raised eyebrows and get straight to the point. That was the only language Khosla understood.

'How much?' he said, breaking the silence.

Yes.

I'd already played this part of the conversation over in my mind while the room had been paralysed into silence. There was no point giving him an insultingly low number. I knew it had to be realistic to get his attention.

'I have no idea what the real valuation is, Rajesh,' I replied. 'However, if we could get this ground for £2.5 million, then it would be a decent deal as far as I'm concerned.'

I must stress I said all this entirely off my own back. I hadn't checked it with Erik or Kris beforehand. I'd simply gone rogue with no mandate. Silence again. The knives that had been in my back earlier were now sticking out of my neck; I was sure of that. We were in the boardroom at Kingsmeadow and nobody dared say a word until Khosla responded.

As we sat there, my eyes turned to a framed photograph on the wall. It was a big picture of Kingstonian winning the FA Trophy and I wanted it to be us. If we got the keys to Kingsmeadow, we'd start making real money and we'd have many framed photos of our own on that wall in the years ahead.

'I think we can work around that,' Khosla suddenly responded. I could see everyone else shuffling papers and glancing up to the ceiling. I'm pretty certain they were thinking, 'What the fuck has the little cunt done now?'

But I had no regrets at all: I instantly knew I'd done the right thing. However, Khosla then dropped a bombshell of his own. Knowing his relationship with everyone else was on the floor, he continued: 'There's only one thing you guys need to know. I will only deal with Mr Heller.'

Oh, fuck. Please don't say that.

But he did, and everyone in the room nodded and weakly mumbled, 'Okay.'

Kris didn't like what I'd done at all. He didn't like the idea of buying the ground and thought we should explore other alternatives. He even entered into negotiations with Tooting and Mitcham Football Club. Bizarrely, that unexpectedly worked in my favour. Tooting were owned by Steve Adkins. Although he wanted us there, he also knew it would stifle our progress because we wouldn't generate anywhere near enough income. Two years further on, we'd be looking for somewhere else again. It would have killed us and even he saw that.

I couldn't see any advantage in the Tooting option but there were some technical issues that complicated buying Kingsmeadow. There was a second lease on the physical perimeter of the ground, which was owned by Kingston Council. This was the land people had to cross in order to access the turnstiles and stadium itself. By now, though, Erik had got accustomed to the idea and was 100 per cent on board. He and I went to see the council and they, too, were persuaded. If nothing else, it would help secure Kingstonian's future, as well, because we wouldn't kick them out.

There were still two almighty hurdles in front of us, though. Where on earth would we find £2.5 million – and would our fans, now our owners, give their approval? The situation brought the best out of Erik, who hatched an ingenious plan to launch a public limited company (plc). He would explain it far better than me but, in a nutshell, the club became 100 per cent owned by a new company – AFCW plc – which, in turn, was 75 per cent, plus one share, controlled by The Dons Trust. The remaining shares could be sold to our fans.

First, though, we needed to gauge whether they'd be on board, so we invited every Dons Trust member to attend another historic meeting at Wimbledon Theatre. I was there to rally everyone and whip them into a state of excitement. Erik was there to talk some actual sense and make sure everyone fully understood what we were proposing.

It was an Erik Samuelson masterclass and a truly defining moment. Around 600 turned up and he patiently explained why we needed to raise the funds and what the shares would cost. At one point he told them: 'If everyone was to invest £3,000 each, then we would be home and dry.'

We all knew that wouldn't happen and that many would simply invest the minimum permissible amount, which was around £90. We then held an indicative vote in the theatre and the overwhelming majority gave us the green light.

The work and the hours Erik poured into the project after that was breathtaking and the club can never repay him adequately. He attended endless meetings with legal experts and brokers and then attended more meetings with us, patiently explaining all the rules and regulations and steering us through all the potential pitfalls.

Then we had to go to legal chambers in town to get it all signed off. I found that an intolerable slog but it was nothing compared to the hours Erik had put in. Fuck knows how he did it.

In the end, we produced a printed prospectus that was smart and professional. However, it came with a huge warning. For legal reasons, we had to tell fans that this was actually a bum investment! They'd never get a dividend and they'd never get their money back. Our prospectus basically said, 'You'll all be idiots if you buy these shares but you'll be helping the club own a home if you do.' They'd also get a share certificate that would say, 'You own shares in a plc that owns AFC Wimbledon.'

Can you put a price on that?

That was the gamble we were taking. We were appealing to the very core of what every true football fan feels deep within their hearts and souls. The sheer unadulterated and unconditional love of their club was the only reason why they might invest because, financially, it was a big, fat dud.

We were appealing to the very emotion the FA could never – and have never – understood.

It could have spectacularly backfired as well. To be a success, the share issue had to raise over £1 million, otherwise we would have to give everyone their money back – and pay costs. It was a big gamble for a small club but Erik didn't flinch. Nor did I.

We all believed that wouldn't happen and we were full of optimism when we sent out the prospectus – and then waited for the cheques to come in. Which they did – thick and fast. For a while, at least. Everything was through the post. Cheques were coming into Kingsmeadow and Erik was there every day, tearing open envelopes, counting how much – and keeping a running total up to date. Sometimes he'd ring me and, in his sombre voice, mischievously make me think nothing had arrived. Then he'd say: 'We've had one or two, though.'

'How much, Erik?'

'Well, actually, £150 grand. Oh, and did I mention there was another £120,000 the day before?'

As predicted, many fans invested the minimum, but those cheques quickly added up. Some supporters did much bigger sums, even though it didn't buy them any extra privileges. Then, around two weeks later, we hit a brick wall and the envelopes stopped arriving. We were still about £250,000 short. For the first time, Erik seemed concerned. 'I'm getting worried,' he groaned. 'Maybe we've been too ambitious. I'm not sure we'll get there.'

I'm more of a glass half-full bloke and replied: 'No, people who are planning to buy large amounts need time to withdraw their savings. There's more to come, I'm sure of it. They'll get us over the line, Erik.'

Neither of us knew for sure. With a week to go before the deadline, I was pulling my car into Kingsmeadow and the spot where I always parked. The phone suddenly went and it was Erik on the line.

'Are you sitting down?' he said, deadpan.

'Er . . . yes . . . why?'

'We've had £250,000 in today.'

'You're fucking joking me,' I replied.

'No. It's real. We are there, Ivor. We've done it.'

It was a massive moment and I slammed my hand across the steering wheel in sheer joy. I couldn't stop smiling. But I also remember thinking, 'It's going to get complicated now.'

In all, we needed £2.4 million for the ground and another £100,000 for the perimeter second lease from the council. Erik had masterminded that deal as well. The share issue had raised half that amount – but how were we going to raise the rest? We most likely needed another £1.25 million. We'd already talked to the high street banks and mainstream finance lenders and they didn't want to know. We were a fledgling club, with no real financial history, and football for them was an extremely risky business. So I went back to Khosla. 'We've already raised over £1 million from the share issue but it's still not enough. Will you lend us the remainder, Rajesh?'

Kerching.

He agreed. Course he did. He'd be lending us £1.25 million on paper but he'd never have to physically hand over any money at all. Now, though, he could charge an extra 10 per cent in interest on top! Even Erik said: 'I'm reluctant about this but it's the right thing to do.'

If I thought negotiating all our extras with Khosla had been bad, I didn't know half the story. What a nightmare – it nearly sent me over the edge. He drove me mad. Every single thing I talked to him about was met with: 'No, no, that's not included. How much extra will you pay?' Everything. And somehow I had to get him out of the building ASAP. I hit breaking point very quickly.

For instance, there was a pile of rubbish under the stand and he insisted: 'That's staying there.'

'But we don't want that,' I replied. 'It's yours, you have to get rid of it. It's rubbish.'

'Absolutely no – don't push me, Ivor. I don't want to have to call the deal off over this.'

For fuck's sake.

'Okay, okay, we'll clear that shit,' I reluctantly conceded. And that's how it felt all along the line. We even got down to negotiating over crockery.

'It would be nice if you left us the basics so we can trade,' I appealed.

'Well you're not keeping the Wedgwood; I'm taking that.'

'What fucking Wedgwood?' I said, genuinely alarmed.

'It's mine and I'm taking it.'

I didn't even know there was any Wedgwood. 'Where is it? Show me, will you?' I pleaded.

So we went to a room behind the back bar and he opened a cupboard I didn't know was there. Inside was a load of plates, cups and saucers, which I turned over. Stamped underneath were the words 'British Airways'. To be fair, they were full Wedgwood sets.

'OK, Rajesh, you take the Wedgwood, but you've got to leave us the rest.' The rest was a load of utterly worthless crockery.

Then we went into the kitchen, where nearly everything was shit. I was at the end of my tether: 'I don't want any of this, none of it fucking works, none of it has been checked, it's all useless,' I said. He turned round and said: 'Well, that may be – but I'm taking the ham slicer.'

And with that, I snapped.

I'd had enough and slammed my hand down on the sink and roared: 'No!! No! No! You're dumping the biggest load of rubbish on us and you're not having the only thing that might actually work.

'You're not having the fucking ham slicer. The ham slicer stays with us.'

My temples were bursting. Even Khosla was in shock: I could see his eyes nearly exploding from their sockets, he was that alarmed by the ferocity of my outburst. 'Well, if you feel *that* strongly about it, Ivor, then I suppose I can make this one exception.'

Chapter 29
SHAME ON YOU, RON NOADES

RON Noades and Chris Kelly – aka the Leatherhead Lip – nearly screwed us over. You couldn't make it up. They were meant to be football heroes, weren't they? Well, that went straight out of the window. Just when it looked like we were going to be the new Kingsmeadow owners, they both leaned on me – desperate to block the deal. They weren't acting in unison: this was two separate and unpleasant attempts to stop us. They behaved like playground bullies and, if they had succeeded, the AFC Wimbledon story would never have happened.

I never expected it of Noades. He had history with us, after all. He'd bought the club in 1976 and, a year later, he'd helped persuade reluctant club chairmen to let us into the English Football League in an era when there was no automatic promotion.

Why did you try to screw us, Ron?

Chris Kelly had no such affinity with Wimbledon, other than he achieved some minor celebrity as a player at the same time we were beating Burnley – and nearly beating Leeds United – in the FA Cup.

His club, Leatherhead, had beaten Brighton in the third round and Kelly was dubbed the Leatherhead Lip because of his outspoken comments on *Match of the Day*. His brief fame continued into the fourth round when he scored as Leatherhead took a 2-0 lead at Leicester City before losing 3-2. I knew he'd been a Kingstonian director in the past, and had basically run the club alongside former chairman Alan Kingston. But I was surprised when he rang out of the blue.

'We know what you're planning and we'd like a meeting with you,' said Kelly, abruptly. There was very little chit-chat and he wanted everything to be hush-hush. 'We'll tell you where to meet – but only when we know you're actually on your way.' It was real cloak-and-dagger stuff and I informed our board in advance, just to cover my tracks.

I did as they requested and phoned them while I was in my car. They directed me to a pub and, when I got there, they were already sitting there in a very dark and dingy booth. Nobody would have seen or heard us. The conversation started chummy enough, and then suddenly took a darker turn.

'You don't want to do this deal,' said Kelly. His words felt more like a warning than a friendly piece of advice but maybe the surroundings had made me twitchy.

'Really – why's that?' I asked, warily.

The pair of them launched into an anti-Khosla tirade, making all sorts of allegations, while also explaining they were trying to put together a consortium to take control of Kingstonian. I am categorically not accusing them of doing or saying anything wrong. I simply found the entire meeting uncomfortable; it didn't feel like we were going to be new best friends. In fact, I got the distinct impression I was in their way and I actually said: 'You're not trying to pressurise me into pulling out of Kingsmeadow, are you? I won't be intimidated.'

They instantly brushed that notion aside: 'No, no, of course not.' But the meeting remained tense and when we shook hands at the end there was precious little warmth.

'We'll be in touch,' said Kelly, as I rose from the table.

'Feel free but, be assured, you have no chance whatsoever of stopping us,' I replied.

I didn't hear from them again and thought everything was on track until Ron Noades phoned me. He was chairman of Brentford

Football Club at the time and I vaguely knew he had some sort of option with Khosla to rent Kingsmeadow.

It was another 'let's-dispense-with-any pleasantries' call. 'I don't know what you lot are playing at, but it's a terrible idea for you to buy Kingsmeadow. It's not right for you,' he declared. It felt like he was lecturing me and I half expected him to add: 'I'm the Great Ron Noades and you're a minnow who knows nothing about football.'

Instead, he continued: 'Besides, we have a legal lease on Kingsmeadow. If we take up our option you won't be able to buy it.'

I was instantly irritated and snapped back: 'Well, you'd best take up your option then.'

You used to be our chairman, Ron. Why are you doing this now?

'Stop farting about, take it up and we will all know where we stand, won't we,' I added.

Brentford were a struggling League Two side at the time, and certainly not cash rich. They hadn't used Kingsmeadow while we were there and I knew they'd have to cough up £150,000 to exercise their option. I very much doubted Noades would do that – but I had no way of knowing for sure. The fact he was on the phone making vague threats felt a lot more sinister than my strange meeting with Kelly and Kingston.

Noades could have been a real problem, to be honest. We couldn't finalise our paperwork until the Brentford option had expired. It was put up or shut up as far as I was concerned.

'As much as I respect you know what you're talking about, Ron, so do we,' I continued. 'We think this will be the making of our club and not the breaking – which is what you're trying to suggest.'

To my surprise, he snapped back – and again, I sensed menace in the air. 'You lot will never get this right.'

I wasn't having it. I wasn't going to wilt simply because it was Ron Noades.

'The only person that can stop us buying the ground now will be you and I don't think you'll want that on your hands, Ron,' I told him. I found myself thinking back to the mid-seventies when we won two consecutive Southern League titles but were refused entry into the English Football League each time.

It was only when we won a third, and Noades launched his brilliant Dons4Div4 campaign, that we finally got voted in. Okay, he then dumped us for Crystal Palace – but had he really forgotten all that now? Or were we just another job at another club from another era that he had no deep-seated feelings for at all?

'You did a great thing for Wimbledon once but then you went to Palace for whatever reason,' I said. 'Please don't you be the person – of all people – to stand in our way now. Not when we can build ourselves a future. Don't do it, Ron.'

There was a brief silence.

I've touched a nerve.

But then he snapped, petulantly, like someone not getting his way. 'I think you're all mad and it won't work. Fans cannot run a football club.' Those were his exact words.

Noades created an unpleasant situation, quite unnecessarily. He knew damned well what the deal meant for us and yet he couldn't resist potentially jeopardising our entire future.

Was it about control, Ron? Did you want us to crawl to you?

The relief was huge when the final day came and he didn't suddenly appear with 150 grand stuffed in an envelope. He never phoned, though, to say, 'Don't worry, I won't stand in your way.' Instead, we were left to sweat. Noades died in 2013 and I never got to understand why he put us through all that. He had done a wonderful thing for Wimbledon once – but it was clear AFC Wimbledon meant nothing to him at all.

Chapter 30
THE GOOD, THE BAD AND THE EXTREMELY UGLY

ON DAY one, the Kingsmeadow drains backed up with raw sewage. The smell was vile. Whoever built the ground had used pipes that might have been okay for a normal house – but not 3,000 people wanting to go to the bog.

On day two, I had to tell Kingstonian we now owned their ground. They had no idea.

On day three, our main tea bar was condemned by the council.

On day four, the catering ladies walked out.

On day five, I burnt myself so badly trying to cook bacon rolls for fans, it left a permanent scar on my right hand.

On day six, we held our first pre-season friendly and made £3,500 profit behind the bar. We sold *our* food and drink to *our* fans and *we* kept *our* money. The sense of achievement on day six was colossal.

On day seven, I was accused of stealing club funds . . .

Owning our own ground was no bed of roses, that was for sure. Okay, they weren't exactly seven consecutive days, although it certainly felt that way. Each day seemed to bring a new drama and I very quickly experienced just about everything there is to experience when you run a football club. The good, the bad and the extremely ugly.

Once Kingsmeadow was officially ours, and emergency plumbers had sucked away all the sewage, we were each assigned tasks. Mine was to tell Kingstonian (Ks) that we had bought their ground. Ks had debilitating financial problems. Their fans had formed a trust and now the members wanted me to tell them what was going on.

I agreed but, my lord, I was nervous. I knew what I'd say if I was in their position: I'd be spitting and raging and demanding every assurance under the sun. They had been completely left in the dark about the ground sale – and now they were our tenants, instead of the other way round. There was about 120 of them in a back bar. They all seemed to be clutching pints of lager and I could feel their eyes drilling into me as I walked to the front.

Is this the short-arse who has bought our ground?

I really expected it to kick off but, the more I looked, the more I saw something extremely familiar. They were all wearing the same expressions we had worn when we were fighting to protect our club. These supporters weren't gathered to torment me. They weren't there for a war. They were there because their club was one of the most important things in their lives and the thought of losing it was unbearable.

Where was the FA for them? Who, from the corridors of power, gave a damn about Kingstonian?

'We have bought the ground off Mr Khosla but we will do whatever we can to work with you,' I said. I explained they could stay rent free and that we would give them a 20-year lease. That went down well: we didn't want to be their executioners.

'You will be looked after because it strikes to the core of who we are,' I added. One of their old presidents even suggested the two clubs should merge, but that was a step too far. I ruled that out categorically.

I even offered them a chance to buy back up to 50 per cent of Kingsmeadow if they could raise the money. That fell on deaf ears. Instead, one director – Ron Dixon – asked, 'How would our drinks work in the boardroom?' That angered me: we had just taken over their stadium and yet all he was bothered about was the free drinks.

All human life.

We now had three days left before our first pre-season game and so we called in all our volunteers for a massive stadium tidy up.

We'd kept the rubbish crockery and we'd kept the ham slicer – which also turned out to be useless – but the council inspectors came in and condemned our main tea bar. We were not allowed to use it and that was a disaster.

Our only alternative was a dingy little shack to the left of the directors' box. Inside was black and grimy and disgusting, with one tiny griddle and a chip fryer. It would never pass health and safety today, but we had a team of women who didn't give a damn about all that. They rolled their sleeves up and got stuck in.

I was so grateful that I decided to give them a team talk and a vision of our future. 'We're really glad you're here, and we want to improve things and make your conditions much better. You're the experts – we will work with you to get it right,' I said, feeling all responsible and grown up.

'Great,' they replied, amid much nodding of heads and widespread smiles.

Then I added: 'I just need one thing from you – your names and addresses and National Insurance numbers.'

Silence.

'What do you need all that for?'

'Well, this is a new start and we want to do everything properly,' I explained. Suddenly I didn't feel so happy, clappy. 'We'll pay you the same rate – maybe a bit more – and we will also pay your National Insurance contributions on top.

'Everything will be . . . proper.'

I could feel the grimy room getting even grimier. 'I can't do that,' said one of them. 'I claim this and that and I work 16 hours a week and if I go an hour over, then all my benefits and stuff will get taken away.'

Shit.

I could sense everyone suddenly doing the maths in their heads. I completely understood the dilemma but there was no way we were going to start doing things the wrong way.

'I'm really sorry but you'll either have to drop a couple of hours of your other work – or we'll have to part company. We cannot – and we will not – pay cash in hand,' I declared.

The woman who had spoken left immediately – and others followed. I watched in horror as one after the other filed out. Mercifully, two stayed for the remainder of that day. But none of them ever came back after that.

There was a lesson to be learned. This had been about control: there were too many areas within the club where we were dependent on the mood swings and decisions of other people. So, I immediately decided to strike my own deals with a local butcher and baker to guarantee our catering supplies.

I started with Robert Edwards, who had a butcher's shop in Leopold Road, Wimbledon.

'We'll need around 800 burgers for every match – plus another 500 sausages,' I told him. 'I'll pick them up on the Thursday or Friday before a game.' I'd then get up at 6 a.m. on one of those days and drive round doing my collections. As soon as I got to Kingsmeadow, I'd stick the burgers and sausages in the fridges and freezers.

Next, I sorted bread rolls for the hot dogs and baps for the burgers. Plus we had our volunteer rolls – we were making about 150 of them at every match – and regular bread for breakfast sandwiches. Once again, I used a business I knew – The Park Bakery between Merton and Wandsworth – and struck a similar deal with them, arranging to pick up all the bread on matchday mornings.

I also made sure we had all the oil, confectionery, coffee, tea, soft drinks and sugar we'd need for the tea bar, and picked up ham, cheese, eggs, onions and pickles from a Merton cash 'n' carry.

Claire would even make her own rolls for all our volunteers and insisted on boiling all the eggs herself at the ground. We refurbished the little tea bar and got in a new griddle and chip fryer. The main kitchen got deep-cleaned, one of our season ticket holders – Ashley Walter – installed a new hotplate and we brought in a

Polish chef, called Tomaszewski. He was good but hugely unpredictable and he was partially to blame for me getting so badly burnt. I still carry the scar 22 years later.

I'll never forget that morning: it was 22 November 2003, and England were playing Australia in the Rugby World Cup final. We had a home game that afternoon and loads of people said we must do something at the club so fans could watch both matches. Good idea, so we put out an announcement that we would serve egg and bacon rolls from 8 a.m. and we'd open the bar as soon as we legally could.

I estimated at least 150 would turn up, so much depended on Tomaszewski. Then, the night before, I got a phone call. 'Hello – I am a friend of Tomaszewski. I'm afraid he won't be at work tomorrow. He got into a fight and his face has been badly slashed by a bottle. He is very sorry.'

For fuck's sake.

To be fair, he wasn't lying. When Tomaszewski did return, an extremely ugly and very visible scar ran all the way down the front of his face. Someone had literally sliced his face in half. But it left me completely marooned. I couldn't get anyone else in at such short notice – so I had to give it a go myself. I got to the ground for 7.30 a.m. and had barely been there a few minutes when the kitchen doors burst open and someone shouted: 'They're arriving, Ivor, and they want their bacon rolls before kick-off.'

I eventually got 40 or so rolls made up, stuck them on a trolley and proudly pushed it out into the main room, expecting a warm cheer. Instead, I was greeted with 'about bloody time – but where's the rest of them?'

Back I went to the kitchen, swearing and sweating. I wearily poured more oil on to the new hotplate and then somehow – without thinking – placed my right hand flat out on the top of it. There's still a scorched area on the skin to this day. I literally fried the back of my hand and the scorching heat took off the first layer of my skin instantly. I was in agony and ran over to the sink where

I desperately plunged my hand into a bowl of cold water. It was so painful, I wanted to go to accident and emergency – but still had to flip loads more bacon and eggs. Only now, I only had one hand. The other was wrapped in a sodden tea towel, which I constantly kept dousing with cold water.

So I carried on and kept running backwards and forwards with the trolley. The only person who helped me was Dons Trust chair Lou Carton-Kelly, bless her. Meanwhile, the game kicked off and I could only guess what was happening from the roars or groans that kept breaking out. I slaved away throughout, including extra time.

At least I saw the bit that really mattered. At the very moment I came out with my last trolley load of rolls, I glanced up to the screen and saw Jonny Wilkinson launch his historic drop kick and win the World Cup for England.

'What kept you, Ivor? You've missed one hell of a game.'

I had to smile. Despite all the drama and the pain, everything felt overwhelmingly worthwhile. We had put on our first major event and it had, sort of, worked. 'That was fucking brilliant. Great rolls, Ivor, you must do it again.'

The bar takings that day were phenomenal and the atmosphere in the ground remained jubilant. I went back to flipping burgers with one hand for the football crowd and we beat Wootton Blue Cross 3-0 in the FA Vase.

We'd proved we could use Kingsmeadow for more than just a football match – and make a healthy margin by using local suppliers and having control of our bar takings. I was proud and I carried on doing all that for the rest of the season.

I was doing it all voluntarily but that didn't stop one 'supporter' launching a particularly spiteful vendetta against me on social media. Out of nowhere, this lowlife – I won't print his name – suddenly messaged: 'Ivor Heller is stealing money from the tea bar and feathering his own nest.' Then he launched a poisonous stream of accusations that claimed I was taking cash, I was buying extra stuff for my other businesses, I was using the club. The term 'internet troll' hadn't been invented then, but that's what it was – and it hurt, big time. It was bad enough that he wouldn't stop; worse, I sensed his lies were starting to stick among fans who didn't know me.

So, the next time I saw him at the ground, I marched straight up to confront him. 'You might not like me for whatever reason but I have never stolen a penny from this club and I never would. I will do this the nice way only once,' I yelled. He was rattled, as bullies usually are when you challenge them. 'Stop what you're doing right now. If you do it again, the next time I see you will be different.'

'Are you threatening me?' he whimpered.

'Certainly not. Well . . . not this time.'

He didn't learn, though. A couple of days later he did it again. 'Heller is still stealing; the board needs to investigate.' It was unforgiveable and utterly libellous and wrong. Everyone knew it couldn't be true as they could see all the work I was doing – and all the invoices and bills proved I was doing everything legitimately.

I decided I had to do something properly or it would spread beyond control. I wasn't sure what until one night I saw him walking along the pavement as I drove through Wimbledon. I immediately checked my rear and wing mirrors. There was nobody around so I bumped my car over the kerb and swerved right in front of him, completely blocking his way.

I got out quickly and pushed him up against a brick wall. 'For the avoidance of doubt, I am definitely threatening you now,' I raged, pinning his arms back so he couldn't lash out.

'You can report this to whoever you want but if you do, I will take you apart – not on the internet but physically, piece by piece.'

I wasn't proud of myself but I hadn't created the situation, either. If I hadn't done something, then his vicious campaign would have carried on. These days, internet bullies are a real modern-day problem: this scumbag had felt empowered by a little keyboard to spread whatever lies he fancied about me because he felt he'd never face any consequences.

I must admit I felt let down by the club and totally isolated. Time and again, I'd plead with board members to take a stance but, time and again, I was told, 'Just ignore it, Ivor; he will go away.' In hindsight, I realise none of them had ever experienced a situation like that before. It was an entirely new phenomenon for us all. There wasn't even a label for it back then.

Chapter 31

OUR STAR AND THE MENACING CALLS

OUR third AFC Wimbledon manager, Dave Anderson, had barely been appointed when the menacing phone calls began. A disgruntled player, hugely popular with the fans, was demanding more money – but Anderson wasn't having it. That's when it all got rather dark and sinister.

Kris, Jonesy and I started getting abusive calls from strangers. They never revealed their identities but we had a damned good idea who they were. The player had let everyone know how unhappy he was, how unfairly he'd been treated – and that spurred some nutters to start phoning us, incessantly. Worse, this player even started making the calls himself, stupidly thinking he could disguise his voice. We knew it was him, though. Many of the calls would be late at night. They'd be deeply personal, aimed at me, Jonesy and Kris in particular. It was a really dark time and there was more vile stuff on social media as well.

There were times when it got so sinister, I wondered about calling in the police, although none of us wanted that sort of attention at the club. But the player clearly thought he was untouchable. I suspect he craved the adulation of our fans and loved winding them up. It left us with a stark choice: back our new manager, or pander to the disgruntled 'star'. It was a bit of a no-brainer, really, and Anderson brought in Richard Butler and several others. Butler didn't look promising at first: the stocky, little blond striker was dire in pre-season and fans had him hanged, drawn and quartered before he'd kicked a ball in the league.

As soon as the season started, though, he was banging in goals for fun. In next to no time, everyone had forgotten about their hero and all the chants were about Butler.

Fans can be fickle like that.

The player in question eventually apologised publicly, but I still struggle to forgive him because the incident really upset good people at the time. Many years later, during an evening event at Kingsmeadow, he got hold of the mic and said: 'When I left I was bang out of order with the way I behaved. I owe everyone who was affected an apology – and, in particular, Ivor.' He only apologised to me, specifically, because he knew that I knew what he and his mates had been up to. He'd behaved appallingly. If it had happened today, he'd have been in front of a judge and jury.

We were right to stand by Anderson. However, I never liked the way we'd dismissed our previous manager, Nicky English, who had stepped up when Terry Eames went in February 2004. English inherited a side that was already on its way to winning the Combined Counties League and the Premier Challenge Cup. In fact, it went the entire season unbeaten and was heading towards our record run of 78 games undefeated. But none of us knew that then.

Everyone expected Nicky's appointment to be temporary. None of us thought about him as our long-term manager. But his results were outstanding and, for that reason alone, he didn't deserve the ending he got. It's just we'd already decided whom we wanted in the Ryman League First Division: Anderson. While Nicky was masterminding our 4-1 victory over North Greenfield United in the cup final, Dave was quietly watching in the stands. He had enjoyed considerable success with Hendon and the way he talked was so much more professional than we'd ever heard before.

From Northern Ireland, he oozed experience, instinctively understood what sort of players we needed, who was gettable, and how he would lead them through all the leagues that lay ahead.

We gave him three years to get us up to the Conference South and his first season couldn't have gone any better. Not only did we win the league by a landslide, he also turned us into a proper football club by bringing in a brilliant physiotherapist, imposing much-needed discipline and overwhelmingly making us feel far more professional.

Along the way, he oversaw our unbeaten run. Terry Eames had started it, Nicky English had kept it going and Anderson took us to the finishing line, setting a new record with a final 2-1 win at Bashley on 27 November 2004. The run had started on 26 February 2003 – when we won 3-1 at Chessington. Strangely, it didn't get huge press coverage, even when it came to a halt on 4 December 2004 with a 2-0 defeat at Cray Wanderers.

Now we'd be in the Ryman Premier League. Anderson had two more seasons to clinch one more promotion and get us into the Conference South. By March, though, we really needed to win at leaders Braintree to stay in contention. Their manager was George Borg, who had a terrible disciplinary reputation – and, boy, did it show.

Midway through the first half, Dwayne Plummer broke clear and looked odds-on to put us in the lead. The Braintree 'bench' at the time wasn't an actual bench at all but a line of school chairs and Borg, seeing our man heading for goal, grabbed one of them and lobbed it on to the pitch. It was so outrageous I actually smirked, especially when one of their backroom staff raced on the pitch to pick the chair up. Our volunteer press liaison officer, Laurence Lowne, yelled out, 'Referee, you can't allow that.' At that point, George Borg turned to the crowd and hollered back: 'Fuck off, you cunt.' I have to admit we all fell about laughing.

Needless to say, Dwayne missed his chance and the game ended goalless. We had to settle for the play-offs, only to lose our semi-final clash against Fisher Athletic 2-1. Dave had one more season left to get us up . . .

Chapter 32
THE DARLINGTON DEBACLE

DAVE Anderson's third season got off to a strong start, with only one defeat in our opening 12 league games. Then, in November 2006, we pulled off a master stroke – or so we thought – by bringing one of our former First Division players, Jermaine Darlington, out of retirement. Jermaine was well known to us: he'd made 105 appearances for Wimbledon between 2001 and 2004.

He'd subsequently moved to Cardiff City, where a knee injury effectively ended his career in the top flight. The Welsh club still held his registration, though. His debut, against Tonbridge Angels on 18 November, made him the first ex-Wimbledon FC player to play for AFC Wimbledon. Results were steady and we even knocked out Aldershot, managed by Terry Brown, in the FA Trophy. We followed that with a 1-0 win at Gravesend and Northfleet (now Ebbsfleet) in the next round. Then I got a call.

'We've got a problem,' said Kris, sounding distraught.

'What?'

'Jermaine Darlington's registration is screwed.' The Ryman League had apparently unearthed a technicality: we'd never got international clearance for Darlington to play.

'So what's the big deal?' I asked, non-plussed.

'The "big deal", Ivor, is this,' replied Kris, sounding increasingly agitated. 'The Ryman are going to hit us with an automatic 18 points deduction. Oh – we'll also be chucked out of the FA Trophy

Ivor aged 8 and already obsessed with playing football

Ivor is already a crowd pleaser by his early teens. The outfit was made by his dad, a professional tailor

Ivor aged 13 with mum Estelle and dad Barry

Ivor, one of the naughty elves in *Santa Claus: The Movie*

Ivor on the day of the 1988 FA Cup Final in his Wembley clobber

Ivor's infamous two-finger salute after Wimbledon win the 2016 playoff final. Was it aimed at the FA?!

(Image reproduced by courtesy of English Football League)

Fans hold up posters to show what they think about Dons chairman Charles Koppel

Outside The Fox and Grapes, when Ivor delivers the devastating news that AFC Wimbledon will not be allowed into the Ryman League

Ivor – assisted by Steve Elson – auctions his prized photo of Lawrie Sanchez scoring the winning FA Cup Final goal at the Dons Trust launch in Wimbledon Theatre (Photo: Paul Willatts)

The historic trials on Wimbledon Common to find new players. Manager Terry Eames is on the left (Photo: Paul Willatts)

Celebrating our opening game win at Sandhurst in the Combined Counties League (Photo: Paul Willatts)

Manager Terry Brown and keeper Seb Brown celebrate his penalty saves in the Manchester play-off final

Ivor holds aloft the Ryman clock before smashing it to the ground as AFC Wimbledon are promoted to the Conference South after beating Staines

Gavin Bolger, Luke McKenzie, Charlie Talbot and Kris Stewart help Ivor celebrate winning the Combined Counties League at Walton Casuals

Dons celebrate the club's return to the Football League in Manchester. Among them is kitman Robin 'Rocket' Bedford (third from left) — one of the club's unsung heroes (Photo: Paul Willatts)

Above left.
The steels go in as a new ground starts to take shape back at Plough Lane

Above right.
Ivor with John Scales (left) and Wally Downes on the centre spot as it is now

Right.
The new ground as seen from the new players' tunnel

Right.
Ivor laps up the view of AFC Wimbledon's new home (Photo: Mike Dunn)

AFC Wimbledon's four founders. From left to right: Trevor Williams, Kris Stewart, Marc Jones and Ivor at the front
(Photo: Mike Dunn)

League action returns to Plough Lane with the very first kick-off against Doncaster

Players and staff at Wembley before the 2016 play-off final against Plymouth

The West Stand is full at last as fans are allowed in following the Covid pandemic

Vinnie Jones presents Ivor with his 1988 FA Cup winner's medal which went on display at Kingsmeadow and is now in the club museum

Club president and legendary keeper Dickie Guy — already a freeman of Merton borough — with Ivor as he receives the same honour

Ivor and Haydon the Womble, the greatest mascot in British football

Every time AFC Wimbledon have played at Morecambe, Ivor has taken a picture alongside the statue of Britain's beloved comedian, Eric Morecambe

and forced to hand back the £12,000 prize money we've earned so far.'

Shit.

I tried to absorb what Kris had just said. 'But what the fuck has international clearance got to do with it?' I asked. 'Cardiff play in the English league, so how can that be international? It's not like we've signed him from fucking Brazil or somewhere.'

I then listened in stunned disbelief as Kris explained the bureaucracy of it all. Yes, Cardiff played in the English league, but it was still a Welsh club and therefore independent. Jermaine was registered with the Welsh FA and to play in England he needed international clearance.

Fucking hell.

Getting chucked out of the FA Trophy probably hurt the most. We'd beaten two of the competition's favourites, we'd reached the quarter-finals and we were all starting to dream about a day out at the new Wembley. It was potentially massive. Even though we knew the odds were against us, we protested furiously – and it went all the way to the House of Commons. Erik persuaded our local Labour MP, Siobhain McDonagh, to complain during Prime Minister's Questions that the 18 points reduction was too high. Incredibly, then Prime Minister Tony Blair replied: 'I agree – it's a daft rule and someone should change it.'

That inspired us to put up a serious legal challenge. Our former chief executive, David Barnard – at Stamford Bridge by then but, for ever, a loyal Wimbledon fan – spoke to one of the country's top criminal barristers, Jim Sturman QC, who also advised Chelsea. We also chatted with the sports minister, Richard Caborn, who went to the FA on our behalf, arguing the punishment was disproportionate to the crime. Yes, we had blundered but this was an administrative oversight by a semi-professional football team and its staff. In fact, the Ryman League themselves hadn't even noticed it until we won through to the FA Trophy quarter-finals. Darlington had played around 15 games by then, so they were just as culpable.

In the end, we did the whole of football a favour. Although we weren't reinstated in the FA Trophy, we got the points deduction reduced from 18 to three. Since then, points deductions have never been so vicious. A bad taste remained between us and the Ryman League, although the reinstated points helped us secure a place in the play-offs, where we'd be away at Bromley in the semi-final. But rumblings had already begun by then. Anderson was getting increasingly criticised on social media channels: it was pretty clear that many fans thought he should have stormed the league and secured automatic promotion – despite the Darlington debacle.

Chapter 33
CONDEMNED MAN

HE CUT a solitary figure out on the pitch, like an actor entirely alone on a stage. The floodlights were still blazing down, cruelly illuminating the torment on his face. He didn't deserve to be exposed like that. We watched from the comfort of the directors' box as he stood, hands plunged deep into his pockets, lost in thought. Suddenly, he moved and walked round in an illogical little circle before coming to a standstill. He looked like a condemned man.

I turned to Erik and said: 'He knows what's coming. Let's do it now. Let's do it like men.'

Erik protested a bit: 'Shouldn't we wait, let him have the night to think things over?'

'No, Erik, we can't,' I replied. 'He's kicking his heels out there right now, hurting like hell. We mustn't prolong that; he's carrying too much anguish already. If we leave it overnight, he'll wake up tomorrow morning and think to himself: "Maybe they won't."

'We owe it to him to do this now because it'll hurt even more if we give him a reason to have hope. I know this is wretched but we agreed a deal, and he's fallen at the last. We now have to stand up and do this like gentlemen.'

'I just don't know,' said Erik.

Thousands had turned up for the semi-final against Bromley and we absolutely battered them straight from the start. But then disaster struck: Wes Daly got sent off for pulling back one of their players. He was bereft and we lost 1-0. Bromley should never have beaten us and our fans were in no mood to forgive. As far as they were concerned, Anderson had run out of luck – and time. The club had a choice to make: either ignore the fans and keep him, or end it there and then as he walked alone on the pitch in ever-decreasing circles.

So out we went. He obviously saw us approaching: his face lifted and I felt his eyes drilling into us both, probing for the slightest hint of what was to come.

'Great effort, Dave,' said Erik, and I smiled and nodded.

'But?' he replied, in his broad Northern Ireland accent.

'But . . .,' replied Erik. 'But we explained three years ago, at the very start, that you had three seasons to get us into the Conference South. You know what's got to happen now.'

I had so much respect for Erik in that moment. I knew, deep down, that he still wanted to give Anderson the night to recover. But he also knew it was beholden on him – as our chief executive – to do the deed. Erik was never a man to shirk responsibilities.

'Dave, unfortunately, we have to let you go.'

It was no surprise to either of us how he took it. Like the honourable man we knew him to be.

'Look, I've loved every minute of it,' he said. 'I can't believe it's come to an end but you're right. This is the right time to do it and it's exactly the right thing to do and there's no hard feelings.'

I watched him intensely as he said that. It genuinely looked like a huge weight was lifting away there and then. Suddenly, he looked much better than the anguished human being we had watched pacing the pitch on his own.

It ended with a warm shake of hands, and a very heartfelt embrace from me. 'What do you want to do now?' I asked.

'I'd just like to stay out here for a few more minutes.'

So Erik and I walked off. Dave Anderson was class, a real honest broker and a really lovely man. I still speak to him regularly and, as I do with all our former managers, I still call him 'gaffer'.

Chapter 34

I'D RATHER BE LUCKY THAN GOOD

WE HAD absolutely nobody lined up to replace Anderson but, as we walked away from Bromley's ground that night, I said to Erik: 'There's only one man for this job now.'

'We've got to do this properly, Ivor,' Erik fired back, emphatically.

'You can do it as properly as you like but I'm telling you right now there's only one man for the job. I know who we should get in.'

'Who?' asked Erik, apprehensively, as though he'd be breaking his own protocol by hearing my answer.

'Terry Brown.'

Terry had taken Aldershot out of the Ryman and all the way up to the Conference. He'd given up the job, though, when his wife Susan was diagnosed with leukaemia but now she was in remission. He might be available.

Erik remained adamant, though, that there had to be a proper procedure. Other candidates had to be interviewed. One of them was the former Southampton player Glen Cockerill, who had managed Woking and was well thought of at National League level. I swear his hair walked into the room before he did: he had this big, blond bouffant arrangement in the Rod Stewart style.

My mind was already made up, though, and I found myself staring at Cockerill's hair throughout the interview, barely listening. He was too self-confident for my liking; there wasn't enough humility there. It was like we were lucky to have him in the room. I didn't really hear him explain how he'd physically go about getting us out of the Ryman.

'Erik, you can go through this process as much as you want but our man is out there; we'd best fucking get him,' I said afterwards.

'Okay. Get it set up.'

By an unbelievable stroke of luck, one of my mates actually lived next door to Brown. Between us, we set up the interview and I chatted to him a few times over the phone to give him background info. I probably wasn't meant to – and I'm pretty sure Erik would have hit the roof if he had ever known. Which he categorically didn't. Terry wasn't under contract with anyone at the time, which made him a free agent. He was also a proper football man and already knew loads about our history. There was very little extra I could tell him, although I definitely told him what our ambitions were.

'We are desperate to get into the Conference – and then, after that, we want to get back into the Football League and stick two giant fingers up to the FA.'

Okay, I maybe added: 'You'll piss this, Terry.'

Terry came along with his assistant, Stuart Cash, and they blew us away. Everything he said, and the way he said it, resonated. He talked about training, how they would do it and what style of football they would play. Then he added six magical words none of us expected to hear: 'Listen, nearly all the teams in the Conference are full-time, so you really need to work towards doing that. You need to go full-time.'

Oh my God. Yes, Yes, Yes!!!! Fucking hell . . . yes!

I wanted to hug him. I gave up trying to contain the massive smile that had invaded my face. It was the first time someone had ever said that to us and I actually shivered as the thought rampaged through my mind. Here was someone who knew what he was talking about. Someone we simply couldn't ignore. And he'd just opened a door on our future. It was exactly what we needed to hear. I remember thinking, 'This man is going to lead us to the promised land. We have to have him.'

I glanced over to see Erik's reaction and I'm pretty sure he was struggling to keep his impartiality in check. Once Terry had left, Erik looked at me and said: 'Yes – he's the one, isn't he?'

Too fucking right.

Terry's appointment triggered one of the greatest periods in our club's history. He was fucking wonderful, simple as that. Hilariously, he couldn't pronounce anyone's name and he couldn't spell a thing – but he had the most wonderful manner about him. He'd happily mix with fans and board members and treat them all as equals.

His personality really radiated: warm, kind, considerate. Underneath those layers, though, was a razor-sharp manager and he started recruiting immediately. Bringing in and getting rid of players in the Ryman was easy because most didn't have contracts.

We also benefitted from a freedom that still exists in non-league football today – the seven-day approach. A club can write to a rival one and say, 'We will be taking your centre forward (for example) within the next seven days.' If the player agrees, then it's a done deal. Terry got a lot of players that way during his first season. But there were also loads who left us, often devastated. Terry always told them face to face and never tried to palm that off on any of us.

He was determined to improve everything, and not just on the pitch. He pushed for a gym and better equipment at the training ground, and brought in proper food for the players. Until then, we'd never thought about feeding them after training sessions.

He also had a great saying, one we quickly got used to hearing – and it always made me smile. Maybe we'd managed to hang on for a win after the opposition had absolutely battered us. Terry would walk past, and even if we were up in the stands and couldn't physically hear his voice, we knew exactly what he was saying as he glanced towards us: 'I'd rather be lucky than good.'

Me too, Terry.

HALF-TIME READ

Chapter 35
STEVE DAVIS, JIMMY WHITE AND SOME BLACK ARTS

I GOT hooked on snooker when I was 13 years old. I was bunking off school regularly and disappearing to Zans snooker hall in Morden. I learned more about life in there than I ever did at Garth school – but it was a road that nearly led me to prison. I'd be in Zans four days a week, sometimes from 11 in the morning to 11 at night. It was full of villains and wrong 'uns and I loved the sense of danger that hung over the tables.

Johnny Cash (no, not THE Johnny Cash) had been jailed – cross him and you'd get a clip round the earhole that you could still feel a week later. Tom the Bomb was another – so called because of his explosive temper.

There was no bar, just a grotty kitchen area where they made teas and toasties, and 12 tables split into two rows. I became a competent player and eventually became a Surrey doubles champion, but my height was a big disadvantage. I had natural timing and could see the angles, but I could barely reach the table and had to stand on a box at the start, which I hated. It wasn't cool.

I made some lasting friendships there, including Keith Grossmith, who became a lifelong mate. We were both kids, young teenagers, but it wasn't long before we were playing for money – 20 pence a point.

People did deals in Zans and some of them were dodgy. I was there one day when lads came in with bundles of men's clothing – shirts, suits, sheepskin overcoats – quality stuff. 'What's all this then?' asked Johnny Cash. The club was above an old Burtons menswear store and these two had just cleared it out totally, then run to Zans with armfuls of the stolen clothing. I watched in awe as labels were ripped off in the blink of an eye, clothing was rapidly shoved into black bags and people legged it – quick. By the time the Old Bill came in (which they did) everything looked normal.

And that was the first time I slipped into the twilight zone. I bought a couple of items – a blazer and some cords – and sold them for a nice profit to a couple of mates. Then, in the mid-eighties when I was a bit older, a new snooker hall opened in Morden: the Royal Surrey. I got involved right from the start and helped the owner, Henry West, run the place. Above the Abbot pub on Abbotsbury Road, it was everything Zans wasn't – plush, upmarket and modern.

I met Steve Davis there and, to my immense surprise, discovered he was a thoroughly decent bloke. My heroes were Jimmy White and Tony Meo, whom I became very friendly with, but Davis actually taught me one of the secrets behind his huge success.

'Whenever I make a mistake I memorise it and then do something you should try as well,' he said. 'I practise that shot for two hours solid. It might be the silliest mistake ever but I will go over and over it for two hours without stopping. Give it a go, Ivor.'

So I did. I missed an easy blue cut into the middle pocket not long after and decided to practise that the next day. I swear, I will never, ever, miss that shot again.

Jimmy, however, was never so single-minded. This was typical Jimmy: he'd been in the Royal Surrey one December night and then vanished – leaving his cue in the office. The Mercantile Credit tournament was starting on New Year's Day and Jimmy was playing Dean Reynolds in the first round. On New Year's Eve, the club phone rang and I answered. It was Jimmy: 'Has anyone seen my cue? I'm in Blackpool and I need it tomorrow.' I offered to drive the 260 miles to get it to him. Thankfully, someone had a mate working on the railways and he took it on a train the next morning instead.

The game was on TV that evening and, as soon as we saw Jimmy, we could tell he'd been on the piss for two weeks. It was a first-to-five match, Jimmy went three down, scraped the next frame – and then whizzed through the rest. He went on to win the tournament.

Wimbledon were flying high in the old First Division back then. Alan Cork, one of our legendary players, came in to watch a Davis exhibition and I said to him: 'Why don't you bring the others here; they'll love it. It's a safe place, discreet. They won't get seen and nobody will know what they get up to.'

So Corky turned up with Andy Thorn the following week and before I knew it, the Royal Surrey became a little Wimbledon FC drinking club. Then, one Thursday, Corky turned to me and said: 'Ivor, all the boys are coming in later. You'll have the entire team in here.'

'Brilliant,' I replied, genuinely excited to be so close to my heroes. Dennis Wise was the first to creep in, followed by Nigel Winterburn. Before I knew it, the whole bloody team were there.

Jimmy White and Tony Meo were also in the club that afternoon. They saw the players and suddenly the beers started flowing around 4.30 p.m. An epic drinking session followed and it went on all night. Everyone got battered, except Winterburn, who sat at a table with half a pint of Guinness that he barely touched.

We all ended up in some club, somewhere, and I eventually got home at 4 a.m. on Friday morning. I woke up later with a terrible head, slowly reliving the night. Wow: I'd been on the lash with my heroes. What a night. Then an awful truth began to dawn: they were all meant to be playing Liverpool at Plough Lane the next day.

Oh my God! I've just completely screwed the team.

I went to the game, fearing the worst, then watched in shock and awe as we matched Liverpool man for man to earn a very respectable 1-1 draw. I was in the sponsors' bar afterwards when one of their midfielders, Ronnie Whelan, came in. He turned round and said to nobody in particular: 'Thank God that's over.'

'Why's that?' I asked, intrigued.

'Well, between you and me, me and the lads went a bit too far on Thursday night.'

'Really,' I smirked. I never told him what our lot had been up to at the same time. Football was a different game back then.

Playing snooker wasn't my only activity at the Royal Surrey, though. I also got involved in a bit of buying and selling. I didn't realise what I was getting into – until it was almost too late. One day, John the Rascal walked in, a stranger to me at that point, wanting to sell a couple of beautiful Pakistani silk rugs to the club's owner, Henry. They were real quality and I asked: 'How many of these can you get?' We got talking and I agreed to pay £150 per rug, confident they'd easily sell for double that. I didn't ask where he was getting them from.

They sold like wildfire, word spread, and then some blokes in Eltham ordered 20. They were even willing to pay £250 each for them. John the Rascal smelt a rat, though. 'I don't like the sound of this, Ivor. Do you know these people? Don't use your own name with them – be very careful. In fact, I'll come with you.'

So we went over in two vans – three blokes in one, two more in ours. They stayed hidden while I knocked on the door of a mock Tudor house. Two savage-looking thugs answered and I straight away said: 'My name is Harry. I've been told to deliver 20 rugs to this address.

'Have you got the money?'

'No,' they answered, deadpan.

'Well, there's five men inside those vans so you'd better go and find it.' I couldn't believe I had the front.

It was clearly a trap but they never thought I'd arrive mob-handed. They made some calls and two dishevelled blokes eventually turned up – clearly junkies – with the cash. I signalled to John the Rascal in the van and his men brought the rugs out.

About a month later, I was watching *Crimewatch* on TV and nearly choked when I heard: 'Three weeks ago, police raided a drugs den in Eltham and discovered 20 stolen rugs with a street value of £20,000. They are now seeking information about a man known locally as "Harry from Tooting".'

Up until that *Crimewatch* moment I thought I was a clever dick, bucking the system, having a laugh. Now I wasn't so sure, although I still hadn't learned my lesson. One of the Royal Surrey regulars was a gambling addict. He came in one day and needed cash to play the fruit machines. 'Give us £50 and I'll get you a brand new mink coat in return,' he said.

I agreed and, to my surprise, the coat was immaculate. Turned out he was a warehouseman at a big Knightsbridge store and he offered to supply me with as many as I wanted – for £100 each. They were selling for five grand on the high street.

'OK, it's a deal,' I replied. 'I'll give you £300 for three.'

In other words, I was about to buy £15,000 worth of stolen goods. He delivered the coats, plus a short leather jacket I wanted for myself with mink liners. It was all so easy and I started taking orders.

Then came my next wake-up call. I'd nipped into the Royal Surrey and left a load of the clobber in my car. On the back seat was a black bag and one of the coat arms was visibly hanging out. It was a freezing cold day and, when I went back to my car, I had to scrape thick layers of frost off the windows. As I was doing that, I suddenly noticed a police car with two coppers still inside. They were almost parallel to me.

Shit.

I got into my car, trying to look calm, pulled out the choke, turned the ignition – and flooded the engine. I kept turning the key frantically but the engine didn't want to know. Then I saw one of the policemen get out of his car. I was completely panic-stricken.

He's going to see the mink coats. I'll be in prison by the end of the week.

I closed my eyes and turned the key one more time, praying. The copper was halfway across the road when suddenly the engine spluttered and then sprang into life.

'It's started,' I shouted over to him, trying to look cheerful and law-abiding.

I looked in my rear-view mirror to drive off, saw my reflection and did a double take. It wasn't me staring back. It was someone else, someone who'd been found out. Someone who thought he was a prince of thieves, Robin Hood, doing a bit of buying and selling.

The person staring right back at me in the rear-view mirror was a shambles. I looked long and hard at his face and was ashamed. I didn't want to be that loser. Where was Ivor Heller?

Chapter 36

WE'VE LOST YOUR FRIEND ON THE OPERATING TABLE

IT WAS a devastating motorbike accident, one that ruined everything. First, a policeman told me I had escaped certain death by inches. Then, as I lay in agony on a hospital bed, I was told my best friend had been 'lost on the operating table'. I passed out when I heard that.

I'd got it all worked out until then, as well. I was going to be a master baker and run my own top-drawer patisserie business across the UK. It even looked achievable and I wasn't even 18 years old.

After I started out at Tesco, I worked for the in-store bakery at the old Caters supermarket in Morden. It was the middle of the 1977 national bread strike and we were one of the few places where people could still buy a loaf. I loved it. Starting something with a bag of flour, then turning it into something that smelt divine, and tasted even better, really appealed to me.

I had to start right at the bottom: preparing the trays, putting them in the oven, getting them out – getting burned but learning to crack on. It was tough, physical work and I had to get used to hauling 100-pound bags of flour on my shoulders. I was a strong little fucker, though, and slung them up there – no problem.

I learned so much from John Harvel, a real craftsman. For instance, how to make a cottage loaf – straight to the oven floor and never on a tray. He taught me all the fine art stuff and then encouraged me to move to other bakeries to learn about patisserie work.

So that's what I did, moving from bakery to bakery, learning all the time. I left home when I was 17 and got a job at Goodies in Kenton, living in the flat upstairs. There, I worked with an old baker called Sam, who was at least 75 years old. He had the biggest hands I'd ever seen – and recipes most people would never share. But he trusted me with them.

I adored the sense of creating something with patisserie and became really good at pastries, quality gateaux packed with fresh fruit, flans, specialist breads, continental bakes – stuff you couldn't easily find in those days. I became a really good pastry chef and eventually moved on to Selfridges and the Sheraton Patisseries, and even did stuff for The Ritz and The Savoy. Some of my products were exceptional, especially the gateaux and speciality cakes.

By then, I was starting to dream about running my own business. Places like GAIL's simply didn't exist. I'd seen a genuine gap in the market and found a bakery for sale in Crown Lane, opposite the civic centre in Morden. I was going to call it 'Harry's' – after my middle name. I would bring continental baking to south London.

Then came disaster. My knee remains permanently fucked to this day. I was living near Heathrow Airport at the time and I was going to meet a couple of girls with my best pal, Alan Tucker. It was a frosty night, he arrived on his Honda 125 motorbike, and off we went. I didn't realise he'd forgotten to bring his glasses and couldn't see a thing as we zoomed away. I remember leaning over as we turned a corner in Honeypot Lane, Stanmore – and careered straight into the front of a parked Ford Granada.

I went flying, literally spinning head over heels and narrowly missed a lamp post before crashing down heavily into the gutter. I knew I was badly hurt but I couldn't work out what or where. I sensed my left leg was in trouble and I started shaking violently – either from the shock, or the freezing night air, or a combination of both.

At least I was conscious and I became increasingly aware of Alan, who was screaming incessantly. I looked up and could just about see his left leg had smashed straight through the Ford's front grille and was buried deep into the engine. His other leg was somehow sticking up into the air at a totally unnatural angle.

'My leg, my leg, I can't feel my fucking leg, I've lost my leg, get someone, Ivor, please, anyone – call an ambulance.'

People came out of houses, trying to calm us and wrap us in blankets against the biting cold. We were both completely disorientated, and I vaguely remember a policeman standing over me, shaking his head, and saying: 'You don't know how lucky you are, son. If you'd hit that lamp post, you'd be dead, end of story.'

Alan had smashed his left tibia and fibula – both bones had crossed over and two lumps were sticking out of his leg. We were both taken to the same ward, and he was taken for an operation the next day.

I was lying there, worrying and becoming increasingly concerned that Alan hadn't returned after a couple of hours. Suddenly a nurse came running into our ward and shouted: 'Ivor, what's Alan's home phone number?'

'Why?' Now I was really worried.

'Something's not right; we need to get his parents here,' she replied, anxiously.

'8687977,' I answered. I still remember that number today.

'What's happened then?' I asked.

'We've lost him on the operating table.'

I passed out there and then. I'd just been told my best mate had been 'lost on the operating table' and the hospital needed to contact his parents urgently. That was enough for me. I eventually came round but each time I saw a doctor or a nurse in the ward I'd cry out: 'Have you heard anything?' Every time the reply was: 'No . . . sorry . . . no . . . nothing yet.'

It was fucking terrible, to be honest. I was convinced he was dead. Then, about three hours later, I began to hear an almighty commotion, getting louder and louder. Alan and I had developed a bit of a comedy routine – we were only kids, remember – and if we saw someone sitting on a pavement, we'd say 'afternoooon' and crease up with laughter.

Suddenly, all I could hear coming steadily towards the ward, was someone shouting: 'Afternoooon, afternoooon, afternoooon . . .'

I could feel an enormous smile spread across my face. He was alive and he was taking the piss out of everyone. They hadn't 'lost him on the table' at all, although I later learned he had suffered a massive asthma attack under the anaesthetic and had momentarily stopped breathing. He was drugged to the eyeballs as they pushed him into the ward and had no idea what he was doing or saying.

The relief was off the scale: Alan was my first proper pal, and we have remained unconditional friends ever since.

Chapter 37
YOU MUST MARRY ONE OF MY DAUGHTERS

I TOOK a huge gamble in January 1983. The season was going really well: Dave Bassett was our manager and we looked certainties for promotion into the old Third Division. Something inside me yearned to do a bit of travelling, so I packed my bags and left the UK, knowing I'd be back in time for the following season.

The adventure didn't go quite as I expected, though. Wimbledon went up while I was away. That was good, but an Israeli army major tried forcing me to marry one of his under-age daughters. That wasn't good.

I'd decided to visit Netanya, a holiday resort on the Mediterranean coast, where I knew an old mate, Andy, lived. I instantly fell in love with the town centre; I could actually believe its huge open market hadn't changed much for centuries. I tracked Andy down to the top floor of a small block of flats, knocked on the door and, sure enough, he answered – looking much hippier than I'd remembered. 'What are you doing here?' he grinned.

Back in the UK, Andy had been an electrical engineer. Now, as I quickly discovered, he was dabbling in drugs. His rooftop flat was party central, with lots of dodgy dealing. I wanted nothing to do with it. So, after a few days, I started looking for work around the main market square. I literally followed my nose and wandered down a narrow street where the familiar smell of a bakery came wafting towards me.

Two Israelis were working inside. They spoke very little English but I offered to do some European bakes for them and they nodded. 'You come tomorrow morning, 5 o'clock. You start then.' So I did and that's when I met the owner, Simon. I liked him straight away. He'd been a major in the Israeli army, really high up, but I assumed he was finished with all that. We clicked straight away: he wanted to learn English, I wanted to learn Hebrew and we became great friends. I even learned what my Hebrew name was: Itzik. I liked it. I still do.

It was a proper bakery and I was able to show Simon how to make plaited breads correctly. When we took them out of the oven, he was dancing with joy. Now he could sell to Europeans in the town. Within six weeks business was booming. And before I knew it, Simon was saying to me: 'New shop. New bakery. You and me – partners.'

'No, no, no – I'm happy just working for you, Simon.' I didn't want anything more than that. I was loving the routine, the work. I felt healthy, strong. Life was good.

But we moved all the same, to a bigger bakery and a bigger shop front. It was an instant hit. Then war broke out in Lebanon. I went to the bakery the next morning but Simon wasn't there. Then I noticed a note on the table. It read: 'Dear Itzik – gone to war. Others are with me. I need you to run everything until we come back.'

And that was it. I had no other explanation. A young Arabic boy who helped out in the bakery wandered in, and it was down to us to run the entire operation. So we rolled our sleeves up and worked harder than ever before. Simon reappeared two weeks later. He was in full military uniform and said: 'War is terrible, Itzik, but I know you've been doing an incredible job for me. I'm so sorry you were on your own but I'm back tonight.'

'Tonight?' I gasped.

'Yes, tonight. I'll be off again tomorrow.' Then he added: 'When I come back from the war we need to talk.'

The conflict ended a couple of weeks later, and Simon returned and arranged a huge party to belatedly celebrate moving into the new bakery. Or so I thought. All the family came along, and friends and neighbours were outside in the street laughing and joking and drinking and eating. Then, totally out of the blue, Simon grabbed my arm and said: 'You and me. We talk – now.'

So off we went into a side room where he said: 'You and me, partners. You are family now.'

And that's when his wife came in with their three daughters. The oldest was 15 years old, the other two were 13 and 12 respectively. Their mother and father stood beside them, pride bursting from their hearts and souls. Then I realised the party outside had stopped and everyone was listening. Simon took a step forward, looked me straight in the eyes and said: 'Itzik, you will offend me if you don't take your pick. I want you to marry one of my daughters. You must now name which one.'

Oh fuck.

If it's possible for your jaw to hit the ground, mine hurtled straight into it there and then. In his mind, Simon had just bestowed on me the greatest honour any father possibly could, offering me the pick of one of his daughters. The fact they were all significantly under age was not in his thinking. I'm pretty certain my entire future flashed before me – but this wasn't in the script. Instead, I became fixated on one all-consuming thought.

I've got to get out of here.

'Er, Simon, I am flattered of course, but in my culture this simply doesn't happen,' I mumbled.

'But you're family now. You will have 50 per cent of the business and you will marry one of my daughters. You must name which one,' he insisted, eyes blazing like he was issuing a battlefield command.

Mercifully, everyone who had been quietly waiting outside couldn't wait any longer. They were desperate to know the outcome: the door was pushed open and in poured loads of excited aunts and uncles and nephews and nieces. It broke the tension and I got swept away as all the guests tried to establish what had happened. I'd promised Simon I'd 'think about it' and that was the last we spoke that night as the party got back on track. A party that was really to celebrate my impending marriage.

I went back the next day and everything was normal. Fraught – but no funniness. Simon kept persevering and even offered me 50 per cent of the business *without* having to marry one of his daughters.

'My life is in London, Simon. I was never coming here to stay for ever. My life is back there,' I insisted. 'I love you, your family, your kindness and warmth and generosity but please don't make this more difficult. It's a terribly hard decision to make.'

In the end, he reluctantly accepted my reasoning. We had a warm, friendly farewell party – albeit tinged with sadness – and we simply stayed friends in our hearts. All I could think about on the plane back was the West Bank – and not the one on the Gaza Strip. I realised the rest of my life, one way or another, would have to be based round football. Almost six months in Israel had taught me that I couldn't live without it.

Chapter 38
THE DON OF DONS

JOEY Pyle was a man to be feared. Google him and see for yourself. He mixed with notorious gangland villains like the Krays in the London underworld. It's said the New York mafia called him the 'London Don of Dons', which – given my obsession with Wimbledon – struck a chord. Intimidating and, quite frankly, pretty fucking scary, he looked like a retired champion boxer: heavyset with a broad build and powerful arms and shoulders.

Whenever I met him, he wore a black open shirt unbuttoned sufficiently to reveal a heavy gold chain that clung tightly to his six-lane-motorway chest. Attached to the chain was a tiny pair of boxing gloves. You wouldn't choose to say 'no' to Joey Pyle but that's exactly what I did – twice.

At the time, I was friendly with a club promoter and we thought we could earn some decent money by organising pub functions. I was 19 years old and had not long returned from Israel. The Crown in Morden's London Road seemed an ideal venue. There was a room upstairs with a big stage, so we talked the landlord into letting us run a 'gentlemen's evening'. We booked three strippers, a comedian and a saxophonist. Classy. Tickets were £15 each, we prepared a cold buffet ourselves and about 150 people turned up.

It was all going beautifully when, about two thirds through the evening, in walked Joey Pyle. Unbeknown to us, he owned the fucking pub. In fact, it was his palace. I watched as faces turned towards him – and then looked away just as quickly. They all knew who he was. Then he headed straight for me: 'Very good do you've put on here; good crowd you've got,' he said as he towered over. 'In fact, I've got a few dos that need arranging myself. We'll have to have a chat about them some time.'

'Yes, absolutely, of course, Mr Pyle,' I stuttered. He then walked off, satisfied.

I thought no more of it – until I met him again, this time in a local William Hill betting shop at the Beverley roundabout. I was into horse racing and used to do the Tote dual forecast. Back then there was a loophole in the system which, theoretically, meant you could win way more than a straight forecast.

It was pissing down with rain on this particular day and there was live racing at Ascot. I did the dual forecast and needed my picks to finish first and second. It came in, but I didn't expect a huge payout. The ground had been soft and I suspected a lot of other punters would have chosen the same horses. We'd all have to share the same prize pot.

All of a sudden, Joey Pyle was by my side. 'I hear you've had a decent winner,' he said.

'Oh, hello, Mr Pyle, good to see you,' I gulped. 'Er, I'm not really sure, we're still waiting. I think there'll be quite a few others who got it as well.'

'But you just got the forecast.'

'Yes, that's true,' I answered.

'How much are you going to get?' he enquired.

'Honestly, I'm not sure Mr Pyle. I'm waiting to find out.'

Then came the bombshell: 'Tell you what. I'll give you £50 for your winning ticket.'

Shit.

'Ooh, that's very generous, thanks Mr Pyle, but I'd rather wait to see what I've won.' I actually thought he was teasing. But no.

'Come on, it might not even pay that much,' he continued.

'Yes, yes, that's true, Mr Pyle. But it might pay a lot more and I'd rather wait to see. Thank you, though. Thank you.'

But he wasn't letting go. 'I'm guaranteeing you fifty quid. That's a lot of money.'

Fuck.

'I'll let it go all the same, Mr Pyle. But thank you very much.'

To my surprise he turned and walked off. *Thank Christ.* I watched as he headed towards the door but then he stopped, turned and came straight back.

'Right, get your ticket out, lad. I'll give you £100 for it.'

My mind was racing and I calculated how quickly I could leg it to the entrance door. But what was the point of running? Nobody could run from Joey Pyle. So I stood my ground – as politely as I could.

'I'm sorry, Mr Pyle, it's not for sale. I've actually had one that's paid £2,500 before. This won't be anything like that but I still think it could be a lot more than £100.'

But he wasn't giving up. 'Come on, come on – take it,' he boomed. Then he placed his huge boxer-like hands down on a table and hung his face down low. I feared he was about to pick up the table and hurl it out of the betting shop – or go 10 rounds with me.

Fuck, fuck, fuck.

There were about 20 punters in the betting shop but suddenly you could hear a pin drop. The tense silence was only broken as he kept repeating, over and over: 'I'll give you a hundred quid, I'll give you a hundred quid. You should take it. Take it!'

So I did the unthinkable. I snapped. A volcano went off somewhere deep inside and I erupted: 'Why don't you leave me alone.'

The words just gushed out, almost involuntarily, like someone else was saying them and I was just the vessel. Worse, I said them straight to his face. The face of the man who had once been best man at Reggie Kray's wedding.

I watched his chest expand and his jacket strain at the seams as he took in a massive gulp of air. Then he turned and said: 'I came to one of your dos in The Crown, didn't I?'

'Yes, that's right, Mr Pyle, you did,' I replied.

'I thought so – you're Ivor, aren't you? You know what, Ivor, I knew that night you had a bit of bottle. You're going to fucking work for me one day. I love what you did just then. For a little man you've got some fucking huge balls. Good luck to you.'

At that very moment the betting shop loudspeaker crackled and a distant voice announced: 'Dividends from Ascot: Tote win £24, Tote place £6, £4, £3 and Tote dual forecast . . . £103.'

One hundred and three pounds.

The place erupted and a huge grin spread over Joey Pyle's face for the first time.

'All that for £3, Ivor! Tell me honest – was it worth it?' and, still smiling, he gave me an almighty slap on the back.

Chapter 39
WEST BANK EMERGENCY

I CAME within millimetres of being crippled for life on the West Bank at Plough Lane. It was the May Bank Holiday Monday in 1984 and Wimbledon were already promoted from the old Third Division. We were all pissed up on the West Bank terraces, celebrating our last home game of the season against Gillingham.

I was 20 years old but one of the favourite antics was to pick me up and hoist me above everyone's heads because I was so much smaller than anyone else. I didn't mind, it was a bit like crowd surfing, only this time I got dropped – and crashed heavily on to the concrete steps below.

The pain was excruciating and, worse, I realised I couldn't move or feel my legs. I was screaming and panicking: something was badly wrong and I went into shock. The police came over and decided to drag me away, but not out of sympathy. They assumed I was just another pissed-up football lout and so they pulled me along – two of them, with their arms under my shoulders and my feet flopping up and down over the terracing.

I was in total agony, screaming and yelling, acute spasms shooting all over my lower back. We got to their police hut, where they eventually laid me on the floor until an ambulance took me to St George's Hospital. I was X-rayed but it was a Bank Holiday and there were only junior doctors available. They insisted nothing was broken and I was told to go home.

My parents were horrified when they came to collect me and laid me on the floor, realising I couldn't possibly climb any stairs to a bedroom. I was really rough for several days and then, just before my 21st birthday, we got a phone call from the hospital. 'We need to see Ivor – urgently.'

Mum and Dad drove me in, where a consultant told us that I'd fractured my fifth lumbar vertebra, but the break hadn't been spotted when I had my X-rays. 'An eighth of an inch over and it would have snapped your spinal cord,' he said. I would have been a paraplegic for the rest of my life.

He wanted me to stay in hospital but I wasn't having that. I preferred to recover at home although I carried on lying on a wooden board in our living room for seven weeks. I couldn't face food and my weight dropped to about six stone. I'd no energy, could barely move and zero idea what I was going to do with my life.

My bakery plans were out of the window, especially when the consultant warned me against carrying heavy weights. 'Put it this way, Ivor,' he said. 'If you carry on physically demanding work – such as humping great, big heavy bags of flour – then you will end up crippled for life.'

Then an unexpected letter arrived in the post.

Chapter 40
MY BIG ROLE IN *SANTA CLAUS: THE MOVIE*

I OPENED the envelope. Inside was a newspaper cutting and a note from my pals, no doubt trying to have a laugh at my expense. A film company was looking for extras to appear in something called *Santa Claus: The Movie*. The only requirement: you had to be under five foot two inches tall.

Ha, bloody ha.

Then I thought a bit more about it. My plan to run my own bakery was dead in the water, and I had no idea what to do with my life.

Why the fuck not? I'll show those clowns.

I submitted some photos and a covering letter but I'd pretty much forgotten all about it when the phone rang one day: 'Mr Heller, we would like you to audition for *Santa Claus: The Movie*.'

'Great, where's that?' I replied, barely able to suppress my laughter.

'Pinewood Studios near Slough.'

It was one of the funniest days of my life. As I pulled into the car park, all I could see was loads of little people – everywhere. There must have been at least a thousand of the buggers.

I've no fucking chance.

But being under five foot two was the most important thing and the more I looked, the more I could see people who didn't look quite right. Some were clearly taller but trying to disguise it by walking with bended knees. We were all split into groups and then told: 'Let's see if you can move to music.' With that, some diddly-diddly-type tune blasted out and we had to walk in time to it – but not actually dance.

As it progressed, people were tapped on a shoulder – but not me. *Shit.* Then I realised they were the ones being asked to leave. So I kept on bobbing along, up and down, until there were only 10 of us left in my group. 'Right, stop. Everyone left can get some food and we will regroup in an hour. Thank you very much.'

I was starting to make friends by now, all people like me – working class with no acting experience, none of us taking it too seriously. One of them was nicknamed Stumpy and we were soon branded 'the naughty elves'.

Everyone remaining was called over, one by one, to a desk where there were five supervisors sitting in a line. 'Name – check; age – check; height – check.' When I went up, someone shouted 'height' and I replied, loud and proud: 'Five foot and an eighth of an inch.'

I watched one of the supervisors write down 'five foot'. I immediately protested: 'No, no . . . you've got that wrong. I'm five foot AND an eighth of an inch.'

'Who cares about an eighth of an inch,' he replied.

'Well – I fucking do,' I answered and the entire room erupted into laughter. Unbeknown to me, the directors and producers of the film were quietly watching and I'd just been noticed. Now I was moved into a different group, including Stumpy, and we were told to keep two dates free for costume fitting. We were in.

We still didn't know much about the film, although we knew the star was Dudley Moore. He was five foot three and at the peak of his career after appearing in the Hollywood blockbusters *10* and *Arthur*. All the elves had to be shorter than him.

While I waited for the costume fitting, I got another call to be told our rates of pay. We'd get £160 for an eight-hour day – plus an extra £30 for every hour if it went over. We'd also get free meals. If we did anything extra, like stunts, we'd be paid extra for those. I eventually got singled out to do Dudley's stand-in work and was paid extra for that as well.

We had two costume fittings and I ended up with a red-and-blue polka dot top, with an orange waistcoat, a green and orange floppy hat, orangey-red curled-up boots and hessian trousers with stockings underneath and huge stick-on sideburns!

Then we got called to the set. There were about 150 of us, and we arrived for 7.30 a.m., got into costume, then hung around for ages, sitting and talking and having a laugh. We quickly realised that the more we fucked up scenes, the longer we'd have to stay – and the more overtime we'd earn.

Our set featured the Toy Tunnel, which cost over £1 million to build and was truly magical. It was a work of art really, with wooden toys hanging metres high from huge wooden walls, and three walkways covered in salt to look like snow.

We got introduced to the cast on the first day proper. They included two stars from the television comedy *It Ain't Half Hot Mum* – Don Estelle and Melvyn Hayes – who were really chatty. Judy Cornwell was Santa's wife Anya, Peter O'Farrell was another big name and we were also introduced to Dudley, who was the main elf and Santa's right-hand man, Patch.

I was chosen to do his stand-in work mainly because they'd seen me move in time to music – and also because, back then, I looked a little bit like him. Dudley himself was great. Very down to earth, very friendly, chatting with everybody and laughing endlessly. He never minded wasting time just to have a giggle. There was a piano in one of the rooms we used and he'd sometimes play us tunes.

We tried to find the Pinewood bar on the first day of filming but got totally lost on the vast complex. Suddenly, I saw a very tall bloke in a black karate outfit walking towards us. 'Excuse me, mate, do you know where the bar is?' I asked. Instead of replying, he just looked at me with complete contempt and stayed silent.

'Do you understand English?' I snapped. 'Listen, you might be a lot bigger than me but you can still be polite. I'll ask you one more time: Where is the bar?'

He looked at me contemptuously but before it got ugly, nine elves rushed on top of me and pulled me away. Then Stumpy said: 'You can't have a fight with him, for fuck's sake.'

'Why the hell not?' I asked.

'That's Christopher Walken, that's why not.' The James Bond film *A View to a Kill* was being filmed at Pinewood at the same time – and he was the villain.

The best bit for me, though, was meeting one of my film heroes, the Hollywood legend Burgess Meredith. He'd played the Penguin in *Batman* and also the grumpy old coach in the *Rocky* movies. Now he was the Ancient Elf and his big role was to walk up the Toy Tunnel, where he got presented to Santa Claus.

Burgess had Parkinson's disease by then and I was asked to look after him for a couple of days. I'd be his cloak carrier in his big scene and also spend time with him off set, making sure he was okay and had someone to chat to. 'Fucking hell, yes, I'd love to,' I replied. I spent ages talking to him about all the films he'd been in and then came the moment for his big scene. Burgess had to walk along the Toy Tunnel, with the entire cast lined up either side, while I stood behind, holding on to his cloak.

Although I wasn't in view of the camera in that moment, it still felt like absolutely everyone was staring at me. Don Estelle and Judy Cornwell were on one side, all the elves were lined up, and Santa started coming down as Burgess began his lines. About half-way through, though, he got tongue-tied and the words 'cut, cut' rang out. By now, the entire set had to be re-raked and tidied and all the continuity worked out so the next shoot would be identical to the first.

That alone took an hour and a half. I went back with Burgess to his changing room and kept calling him 'sir' because I didn't know how else to address him. 'Hey, Ivor, call me Buzz, everyone calls me Buzz,' he insisted. But I couldn't. I had too much respect. He was wonderfully nice but the telltale signs of Parkinson's were clear to see.

In the end, the scene had to be reshot four more times that day because he kept messing it up. Then the director said: 'Look, we just about have enough time in the day for one more attempt, otherwise we will all have to come back tomorrow.' By now, all us elves were thinking exactly the same thing.

Please fuck it up, Buzz, one more time – so we can get paid extra.

There was a real sense of pressure: Burgess started and was word perfect. However, there were live reindeer on the set, we were all on the snow, and suddenly we could hear a loud crackling sound, like Rice Krispies at full volume. The reindeer had started pissing all over the salt that was laid down to look like snow, and then I heard the first explosion of laughter – Don Estelle and Dudley Moore were creased up and that got me, and everyone else, going.

Oh joy – another day's pay!

It took two more goes the next day. And I do appear in the scene – after Burgess finishes his speech he goes back up the Toy Tunnel. As he turns, my face is clearly visible for a full second!

The entire experience definitely left me thinking about acting as a career. By complete coincidence, I knew the daughter of one of the world's top film editors, Archie Ludski, and he invited me to a drinks party in the Pinewood bar a couple of days later.

I was introduced to all the right people – including Sir David Lean CBE, who directed a host of classic films including *A Passage to India*. It was all going extremely well until I suddenly saw Christopher Walken enter the room and heard Archie shout: 'Christopher – over here.

'Christopher, Christopher, I'd like to introduce you to this up-and-coming actor I know.'

I turned round, praying he wouldn't recognise me but, mercifully, he was already laughing. 'Hey, pal, we've already met, haven't we?'

We shook hands and that was it, no hard feelings. I was liking this life: the treatment, the pay, the bar – and getting fed all the time. I walked round the party and I asked every page-three girl there for a date. Even Grace Jones – who played Walken's bodyguard May Day in the Bond film – bounced me up and down on her knees. She definitely took a shine to me but, my God, what a scary woman.

Then I made one of the worst decisions I'd ever made in my life.

Someone who had taken all my details at the party phoned me a few days later and said: 'We have an opportunity for you but it'll mean going up to the Scottish Highlands. Six weeks, you'll be well paid and you'll have a small speaking part in a film called *Highlander*.'

At that point, Santa Claus wasn't completely finished, although I wasn't needed for any more filming. But I still considered myself one of the naughty elves, I was one of the guys, and I wanted to go to the after-party with them all.

'Can they wait a week?' I asked.

'No, you need to go next week; that's non-negotiable, Ivor.'

'But I need to finish the job I'm on; it's the decent thing to do,' I naively replied.

'Well, that's very admirable but also very stupid. Chances like this won't come around twice in this industry.' And they didn't.

SECOND HALF

Chapter 41
I WANT TO BUY YOUR CLUB

WHEN I first met Darragh MacAnthony, he was surrounded by bodyguards. 'I've probably pissed off both the Spanish and Turkish mafias,' he laughed. 'You can't be too careful.' Days later, this young, cocky and super-confident Irishman made a serious offer to buy AFC Wimbledon when we were still in the Ryman League. It triggered panic and horror in our boardroom like I'd never seen before. To be honest, I don't think any of us emerged with any great credit.

Jonesy and I were running our print design agency in 2006 when one of our clients and a hugely important Dons supporter, Xavier Wiggins, said: 'There's a bloke I know called Darragh. He wants to meet you – there might be stuff he can do with the club.' We did some homework. Darragh was only 30 years old, yet ran his own company – MRI – and was seriously wealthy, having earned a fortune from the overseas property business. By chance, a print exhibition was being staged at Olympia the following Saturday, so I arranged to meet him there.

I was waiting outside when he suddenly appeared, surrounded by an entourage of bodyguards and advisors. He was a big, imposing bloke and said: 'Hi, I'm Darragh. Hope you don't mind but I'd like to go to Kingsmeadow and have a look round. Maybe we could have some lunch on the way and get to know one another.'

Two huge BMWs then emerged. 'Where shall we go? I don't know Wimbledon,' he added.

'Might as well go to the Dog and Fox,' I replied. 'We can drive past the old Plough Lane along the way.'

As we approached our old ground, Darragh suddenly spotted the greyhound stadium, which was still in use. 'What's that?' he asked. 'That's the dog track, been there for years,' I answered.

'That looks brilliant; let's take a look,' he said, calling his chauffeur to pull over. He then blagged his way into the stadium and the pair of us ended up walking along the track.

'This would make a football stadium, wouldn't it?' he said. 'Yeah, I guess it would,' I replied. 'But I think you'd have to knock it down and start again.'

We then headed to the Dog and Fox. As we entered, I noticed one of the bodyguards was already sitting by the main entrance, while another was positioned by another set of doors. The rest of the entourage had settled round tables further inside the pub. Darragh and I sat at our own table and he asked: 'What are we talking about here then?'

'Basically, we need money and we need sponsorship,' I answered. 'Ideally, I'd like your company to become our main club sponsors.'

'How much?'

'£100,000 a year,' I replied, without blinking. I could see little reason why Kingsmeadow couldn't become the MRI Stadium.

'I like the sound of this,' he responded and then called over one of his entourage. 'Ivor – tell my colleague what the deal is.'

'Well,' I said, 'there's definitely an opportunity to become our main club sponsor for £100,000 a year.'

'That sounds great,' said the advisor, 'but . . .'

Fuck. He just said 'but'.

'But – Darragh – you don't want to be a sponsor. You want to own a club.'

That ain't happening.

I didn't want to give up, so interjected: 'Let's talk some more and see what we can do.'

But MacAnthony was clearly having second thoughts. 'He's right, Ivor. I'd find it very frustrating to just be a sponsor.'

'Well, there are other things we could let you do,' I volunteered.

'Like what?'

'You could stand for the board, for example.'

'Nah, I wouldn't want to do that,' he admitted. 'I'm not standing for election – I'd rather buy the club. In fact. Tell you what: I'll buy the club.'

Fuck.

'The club isn't for sale,' I replied.

'Everything is for sale,' he snapped back.

He still wanted to look at Kingsmeadow, so off we went. I made sure the club shop was open and he headed straight there, spending big on shirts and scarves, even though the season was over.

We talked some more and then he said: 'Right, I've seen enough – we'll talk again . . . soon.' I watched him leave: he was showy and big – just like the Beamers he drove off in. Early the following week he rang and said: 'I'm ready to buy the club.'

My first duty was to tell our board execs – and their instant reaction was horror. A meeting was set up but when Darragh arrived there was no attempt at small talk. Straight away they asked: 'What kind of owner do you want to be?'

His reply hardly helped: 'Dictator.'

But Darragh was never rude or offensive. If anything, the antagonism was aimed at him. 'We don't want a dictator. Don't you understand what this club is about?' was the response.

Looking back, it was a conversation and an offer that nobody knew how to handle. I would never have sold the club to Darragh MacAnthony – but I was intrigued at the way he'd identified the greyhound track as a means of getting us back to Plough Lane. If anyone could pull that off, it was probably him.

I'd hoped we could focus on that; instead, he was unfairly portrayed as the Devil. Soon after, he took control at Peterborough United and he's done a pretty decent job there. They've been in the Championship a couple of times and their ground has been remodelled. A lot of staff who were at the club when he took over are still there. Darragh MacAnthony wasn't the enemy – he was just offering us an alternative. We could have turned him down with a little more grace.

Chapter 42
READY TO RESIGN

I WAS ready to resign and walk away from AFC Wimbledon for good. We were about to make a ruinous decision and it needed to be stopped. From day one, Jonesy and I always believed our club couldn't be considered a proper continuation of Wimbledon FC unless it was physically based somewhere in the borough of Merton. Kingsmeadow was a blessing but, at the end of the day, it was in Kingston.

Darragh MacAnthony had got me thinking overtime when he saw the greyhound stadium. He was the wrong man at the wrong time but the idea was still good. We wanted to go home. Even if it was a dream, it's what we wanted. Instead, we came perilously close to staying in Kingston for ever.

Not long after we bought Kingsmeadow, a stadium working group was formed to consider any ideas that might take us back to Merton. The greyhound stadium had been considered but the idea was always shot down. 'We could never afford to make it happen,' was the common response. I had no answer to that.

That didn't rule out somewhere else in the borough, though. The stadium working group considered everything and anything. Roger Hobkinson, in particular, wasn't afraid to think big: there were sites around Merton that needed regeneration and we could, potentially, become part of a grand development project on any one of those.

That wasn't a view shared by everyone, however. Many felt we should instead devote all our attention on improving and developing Kingsmeadow. They wanted us to work within our means. In particular, David Cox – then chair of the Dons Trust board – and Tom Adam, chair of the stadium group, were focused on staying put.

Without me realising, they quietly produced legislation for the trust to adopt. It was only when I read the paperwork closely that I realised we were about to take a vote to drop Merton altogether – and concentrate solely on staying in Kingston. For ever. I immediately raised an alarm with another trust board member, Aideen Rochford, and said: 'Someone needs to object to this. We need to reverse the situation or it will get bloody.'

'What do you mean "bloody"?' she replied.

'Someone will end up resigning over this – and it could be me,' I answered. 'I will walk away from the club for good if this goes through.'

The trust board met a few days later and Aideen made sure everyone understood what was at stake when she announced: 'I'm not happy with this proposal. I want us all to vote on it.'

I pitched in and a mini-revolution broke out. Like me, other board members hadn't realised the road we were hurtling down. The proposal was rejected but, as I feared, there was a casualty: David Cox resigned as trust chairman.

After that, the idea of finding a long-term home back in Merton really gained momentum. Loads of groundbreaking schemes were considered: one involved building a stadium that would be suspended over the railway sidings at Morden. The overground would become underground and we'd be above it, in a huge complex at the end of the Northern line.

Another was at Merton Abbey Mills, on land owned by the insurance and pension giants, Aviva. That was a £600 million proposal that would have triggered widespread redevelopment of the entire site, with new housing, shopping precinct and a stadium for us. It was prohibitively expensive.

At least the principle had been established that we belonged in Wimbledon. But how on earth could we afford it – and where could we go? At the time, Jonesy and I employed a big Dons fan, Ben Adams, at our print design agency. Each day he'd ask me what the chances were of us getting back to Wimbledon. At this stage my answer was always the same: 'About 5 per cent.'

Then came the breakthrough . . .

Chapter 43
WIN THE POLITICS, WIN THE WAR

AS FAR as I was concerned, Wimbledon and Plough Lane came hand in hand; one was never complete without the other. But going back there was just a fantasy. It couldn't happen. Then, in 2008, I met a miracle man called Stephen Alambritis and everything changed.

Stephen was leader of the opposition on Merton Council. I'd met him briefly when he led the Federation of Small Businesses, and I'd assumed he was therefore a Tory. I'm not big into politics but I was gobsmacked when I discovered he was actually a Labour man. Not that I minded – he seemed the sort of Labour politician I could identify with.

We met at his office and I noticed straight away the wall was covered in historic scenes from around the Merton borough, all of which I recognised. He looked dapper – in a 'Man from Del Monte' kind of way – and he welcomed me with a big smile and a very firm handshake. He wasn't a whole lot taller than me but his presence seemed to fill the room. It was easy to imagine him dominating a council chamber.

He got down to business straight away and asked me what our plans were for the club. I told him our ultimate goal was to get back into Wimbledon – and then I spelt out why that would benefit the entire community and not just us. I must have rambled on for a good 20 minutes. 'We'll create a hub, a venue where local societies, clubs and charities can meet,' I told him. 'We could open a surgery for GPs and dentists; we could house a library or a school. People could hold events at the ground – weddings and birthdays – and we could stage business functions and cater for hundreds. We'll bring people together. On matchdays, our fans will go into local shops and use local cafes and pubs and all those businesses will flourish as a result.'

I meant every word and got the impression Stephen was hooked. He listened intently but then said something nobody else had dared utter: 'Ivor, I've seen all the schemes you've been looking at and I've got to tell you the council will block every single one. None of them stand a hope . . .'

Silence.

'You sure?' I muttered as I let his words sink in. 'I mean, that's pretty devastating . . .'

'Except for one,' he continued, and I watched a smile slowly creep across his face.

'What's that?' I enquired.

'The greyhound stadium.'

'But I've been told by our people that's a non-starter. We'd never get it,' I argued.

'Well, I think they're wrong. I think the greyhound stadium is the one and only idea that stands the slightest chance.'

But we can't afford it.

I think Stephen could second-guess what I was thinking because he then proposed two strategies that would put us on the right road – and cost us nothing.

'First of all, we need to secure all-party support for the principle of AFC Wimbledon coming back to the borough,' he explained. 'Nobody in their right mind is going to stick their arm up and say, "I object," but we need to get it established so it's irreversible. Secondly, we need to get the club's return written into the long-term development framework. That would make it the council's official business to get you back. And we must make sure that bit refers specifically to the greyhound stadium.'

Fucking brilliant.

For the first time, I was listening to someone who knew how the system worked, inside out. Stephen was opening a door I never knew existed. He was laying the critical groundwork: without these foundations, we'd never get started. I'd never given a shit about politicians before, but he'd just guaranteed my vote, for sure.

Then he said something that I haven't forgotten to this day: 'Ivor, if you can win the politics, you can win the war.' That resonated with me, big time. All the lights went on inside the Heller brain and I left his offices elated, truly believing we were on to something massive.

Then Erik shot me down in flames. 'Look, I think there's a guy you should meet – Stephen Alambritis, he's the leader of the opposition,' I gushed.

'Why on earth should I meet him?' replied Erik. 'He might be great but he'll never get elected here.'

Shit. I hadn't thought about that.

Erik was being pragmatic. The Labour Party had about as much chance of winning control of Merton Council as we did of buying the bloody dog track. I didn't let go, though. 'But he's really supportive about Plough Lane and he can see a route through. Just come and meet him, please; we've nothing to lose,' I implored.

The pair of us met Stephen a week later and he revealed a motion was already being drawn up to cement cross-party support. We kept talking but I could see Erik was itching to escape. 'It's all cuckoo land,' he said as we walked away. 'He won't win the next election, simple as that. Labour are getting panned everywhere across the entire country.'

I knew Erik had a valid point. 'But what if we tell everyone what Stephen is doing?' I argued. 'What if we tell them Labour might hold the key to us coming home? What if we persuade our fans to vote Labour? That's quite a lot of votes, Erik.

'After all, this is a council election and that might be easier to sway on such a huge local issue.'

A few days later, Ben in the office asked me once again about returning to Plough Lane: 'What's the chances now, Ivor?'

'It's doubled – about 10 per cent.'

'That's good, isn't it?' he replied. 'How come it's gone up?'

'Well, if someone called Stephen Alambritis wins our local election, he could actually make it happen.'

Voting day was still over a year away. In the meantime, Stephen successfully engineered the wording on the borough's 2008 long-term development plan, so it read something like: 'Any future development of the greyhound track should be for sport intensification and, specifically, a home ground for AFC Wimbledon.'

Genius.

Okay, I took Erik's point that it was just words. But they were words that were now set in concrete, irrespective of who won an election. They were words that would stop anyone objecting to planning approval in the future.

I started spreading the word about Stephen and told everyone who he was. 'Trust me, if he wins the election, he will get us back to Plough Lane. You mark my words.'

Win the politics, win the war.

Chapter 44
BROWN'S BOYS

EVERY manager we had did something significant. Terry Eames got us started, Nicky English kept the momentum going and Dave Anderson brought in another level of professionalism. Then came Terry Brown. Terry Brown got us back to the promised land. Terry Brown let us stick two fingers up to the FA.

But it so nearly ended in disaster. With 10 minutes left of the 2007–08 season, Terry Brown was failing to get us out of the bloody Ryman Premier. We'd finished third in the league, and then beat Hornchurch 3-1 in the play-off semi-final. The game will forever be remembered for Jon Main's unbelievable solo goal – the greatest I ever witnessed at Kingsmeadow. He literally took the ball from the edge of our box and raced the entire length of the pitch, weaving past stunned defenders before firing home like he was the non-league George Best.

Next, we faced Staines in the final at their compact Wheatsheaf Lane ground. With 10 minutes left, we were trailing 1-0 and Erik leaned towards me to say: 'This is slipping away, isn't it?'

'No, no – we still have hope,' I insisted, not entirely sure. Moments later, Luis Cumbers headed home an equaliser and then substitute Mark DeBolla, whom Brown had only just brought back to the club, deftly curled a free kick round the wall and into the net. Cue hysteria.

This was a milestone in the club's history, progression, a huge step towards the seemingly impossible – a return to the Football League. Now we'd be in the Conference South – and that felt a long way from Bottom Meadow.

Brown started to assemble a new line-up after that. In came the likes of Mickey Haswell and Elliott Godfrey plus we still had Jon Main up front. Danny Kedwell joined us later on and that was another huge signing. 'I like our chances. I think we have a good team here,' cooed Brown.

Just how good was put to the test in our first match, away at Newport County, who were considered hot favourites to go up. We'd last faced them in 1984 in the Third Division. It felt like our biggest league game ever as AFC Wimbledon, and we took 1,200 fans there – in torrential rain. The weather was so bad we thought the match would be cancelled, but it went ahead and we won 4-1, largely thanks to a Jon Main hat-trick.

It was a breathtaking display and we'd played really good

football. As we clambered back into the car – looking like drowned rats – I remember saying: 'We're going to win the league.'

'Don't be so bloody stupid, Ivor,' came the reply. 'It's the first fucking game; we've got a whole season to get through.'

Surprisingly, our nearest rivals turned out to be our near neighbours – Hampton and Richmond. And that was a worry: they were indisputably our bogey team. Whatever we did, we never seemed to beat them. Perhaps we'd get a player sent off, or another badly injured. Nothing ever went our way.

It was nip and tuck between us and them for automatic promotion until there were only two games left – and the first was at The Beveree. The former West Ham United hero Alan Devonshire was their manager. What a top bloke. We had over 3,000 fans at their compact ground, and this was a highly pressurised game for both sides, and yet Devonshire showed real class to help me out minutes before kick-off. I'd got an unexpected phone call from our main sponsors, Sports Interactive. 'Ivor, we're outside but there are no tickets in the ticket office for us. We can't get in.' I knew Devonshire's wife, Christina, ran the boardroom. She was lovely and I headed straight for her. 'I've got a massive problem – our main sponsors can't get in, even though their names are definitely on the list,' I explained.

She immediately called her husband. 'Tell Ivor to get down to the changing rooms right now and see me,' he told her.

This really wasn't his problem but I ran down and he was by the door waiting. 'How many do you need?' he asked.

'Six,' I replied, apprehensively. With that, he plunged a hand into his tracksuit pocket and pulled out a clump of tickets. 'There you go, Ivor – bang, bang, bang . . . six tickets, all yours. Good luck.'

The relief was unreal but can you imagine any other manager helping an opponent out just minutes before a game that will decide the destiny of either team?

The ground was rammed and looked wholly inadequate for the number of fans packed in. Nevertheless, the game kicked off and it quickly became a familiar story: we couldn't score – but they did. Absolute depression kicked in, and we kept pressing but couldn't hit the net. Then we got a break. The ball went out to the left, Chris Hussey prepared to receive it, but two Hampton players rushed in, trying to intercept. Instead, they ran straight into one another, their heads clearly colliding. They both fell, poleaxed, to the ground. Today, the ref would stop the game instantly, but that wasn't a thing back then. Play continued, and the ball ran through to Hussey. He raced down the wing, crossed – and Main scored a sublime equaliser as the two Hampton players remained floored.

Our fans went berserk, jumping up and down, and suddenly part of the terraced structure where they were standing collapsed. At least 50 fell to the ground below, but fortunately no one was badly injured. The ground just wasn't equipped for that size of crowd; it could have been a far more sinister outcome.

The game ended in a 1-1 draw and our fans ran on to the pitch towards the Hampton supporters and scuffling broke out on the terraces near me. I could hear their chairman groan: 'Bunch of animals.' I'm not condoning the fighting, but what did he really expect? We had effectively won the league and completed the formality by beating St Albans 3-0 in our last game.

We would now be in the Conference – the highest level of non-league football. We'd be up against teams with big histories, like Luton, Oxford and Wrexham, only now we were rewriting history ourselves and rapidly becoming English football's most outrageous success story in our own right.

Chapter 45
GOING FULL-TIME

THE night before the 2009–10 season started, I was listening to talkSPORT radio. Our former manager, Bobby Gould – who'd led us to our FA Cup final triumph in 1988 – used to do a late-night show and I loved listening to him. Everyone was talking about the new Championship season kicking off, and which big games they liked the look of, when Bobby said: 'Listen, the biggest game of the lot, the most remarkable of them all, is none of the ones you lot are talking about. Forget West Brom v Newcastle or Reading v Forest. The big one tomorrow is Wimbledon v Luton Town.'

I wanted to reach into the radio and hug him for so many reasons but, most of all, because he'd just called us Wimbledon. Then he added: 'It's unbelievable that in 1988 we played Luton in the FA Cup semi-final and now we're playing them again, only this time in the Conference. That's the biggest game in the country for me.'

I fucking love you, Bobby Gould.

I was excited. We had a decent team, we still had Kedwell and Main, but we also had a big decision to make. We had done all we could to prepare for a new life in the Conference – except for one thing. Our players were still part-time. They'd train on Tuesday and Thursday evenings and squeeze in their other jobs in between. One worked for London Underground and would sometimes come in for training and then rush off for a night shift. Madness.

Most of the players had coaching jobs, some worked for other clubs, while some were winding down from full-time careers. It was a right hotch-potch and not how most clubs in the Conference operated. We were one of only four part-time clubs at that level and Terry Brown was desperate for us to step up.

The issue was debated constantly. I agreed with Terry 100 per cent, but the overwhelming concern was cost. There was a real fear that we could never afford it so Terry and the players struggled on and, against huge odds, finished an extremely creditable eighth in our first season.

But Brown never stopped chipping away. He had a very good relationship with Erik and suddenly, towards the end of the season, a proposal appeared before the board for us to go full-time. 'We'll get better players if we do – and it won't cost us significantly more money,' Brown argued passionately. 'If we never do anything else, we must go full-time.'

It was a no-brainer in my book. Playing games all over the country on a Tuesday night and then watching players trudge off to work the following morning was no way to run a football club in what had become, to all intents and purposes, the country's fifth division. There was no argument really and the decision was approved.

I got a real insight into how Brown handled his budget shortly afterwards. I'd gone along to the training ground when he said: 'Look at this, Ivor. We have three fantastic players here – but I only have enough money left to pay one of them.' He then pointed out the three and added: 'Just watch them and tell me what you think.' So I did, and they were all good. 'But I've only got £650 a week left in the budget,' said Brown as we carried on talking.

It seemed a dead end – until Brown brought the three together and said: 'Listen, lads. I'm really sorry but I've barely got the money for one of you, never mind all three. What can we do?'

It was a master stroke. The three of them went off for a chat and came back to say: 'We'll split it.' They'd agreed to become our full-time players on a third of £650 each because being a full-time player was what meant the most to them.

Fraser Franks played for Luton, Stevenage and Newport after that; Ed Harris continued playing for Dover and Dorking, while Sammy Moore carried on scoring goals for us before joining Leyton Orient.

Our playing budget didn't go up much – I think it rose from £450,000 a year to around £550,000. That was still one of the smallest in the Conference, but at least we would start the 2010–11 season knowing our players only had one job to perform.

Chapter 46
THE SPEECH

TERRY Brown really bought into the Wimbledon story and used it constantly to motivate his players. At the start of the 2010 season, when we went full-time, he asked me to say a few words to his squad about our history: who we were, where we'd come from, what we'd suffered and how we'd fought back. He passionately believed our story had the power to lift his players just that little bit more. I believed it as well, and every year I'd meet and greet new players and tell them everything I could. I never tired of the task.

I wanted the players to know about our exemplars. What did I mean by that? Well, Alan Cork and Mick Smith were exemplars: they both played in all four divisions for us. I believe that's an impossibility these days.

Dickie and Cookey – they're definitely exemplars – and Simon Bassey was another. He joined Wimbledon when he was eight years old, played for us and had two spells as our caretaker manager. Our current goalkeeping coach Ashley 'Bayzo' Bayes is an exemplar. He joined in 2013, and different managers have come and gone, but he's masterminded unbelievable success with our keepers throughout.

Our former youth team manager Geoff Taylor was another. Geoff sadly died in March 2025, but what a legacy he left behind. He took kids and turned them into Premier League stars in the 1980s: players like Andy Thorn, Neil Sullivan, Paul Miller, Glyn Hodges, Kevin Gage and Mark Morris. All his players were sold on for fortunes.

Not everyone shares my view on this. Some believe I'm stuck in a time warp, reminiscing about a bygone era. Their view is that modern players aren't interested in our history, that it's got nothing to do with them and they're only here for the pay cheque.

However, two or three years ago, me, Kris, Jonesy and Trevor – the four founders – were asked to do a pre-season induction. I was to speak first: so, I stood in front of the players and the following is what I said. Is it still relevant today? You decide:

'You guys are too young to remember what this club is really all about. You probably know we don't like the team in Milton Keynes – we call them 'the franchise' – because they took away our League place in 2002. But you need to go back a bit further than that to realise our club was built on great, great things.

'We had the best FA Cup run for a non-league club when we beat Burnley and then drew with Leeds United. The captain that day is still with us – and the goalkeeper is now our club president. I want you to think about that. Their success happened in 1974–75 and here we are, 50 years later, still honouring the players who did those great things for our club.

'Ninety-nine per cent of the people who come here believe you are the players who inherited the mantle of Wimbledon Football Club. Not the franchise. That means YOU are the same team that won the FA Cup, YOU are the team that didn't lose a league game at Arsenal for 11 seasons, YOU are the team that helped start the Premier League and stayed in it for eight seasons. The club YOU now represent produced legends like Vinnie Jones and Dennis Wise – and now it's down to YOU to be the next legends.

'So, the question I want to know now is: Which one of you is going to be our future club president? Who's going to write their name in our history and become part of this set-up in the same way Dickie Guy and Ian Cooke are now for what they did all those years ago? In 50 years' time, I want to think that you are going to be our exemplars in 2075.'

Chapter 47
GOING TO THE DOGS

SOMETIMES, things are written in the stars, aren't they? They're meant to happen. It's fate. On 6 May 2010, something incredible happened that was to reshape and redefine AFC Wimbledon's future: Stephen Alambritis took control of Merton Council. Labour didn't win the election outright but they had more councillors than anyone else. They could call the shots. Only two boroughs across the entire country had changed hands to Labour – and we were one of them.

Thank you, God.

Nobody had seen such a result coming and I'm certain we were a massive reason for it. Stephen unashamedly made our return to the borough a huge part of his manifesto. There were still many hurdles ahead, though. Not least the Prime Minister, Gordon Brown, who had decreed super casinos could operate in the UK.

That prospect had persuaded Risk Capital Partners, a private equity company run by former Channel 4 chairman Luke Johnson, to buy the old Greyhound Racing Association. It owned six dog tracks, including Wimbledon, where there was plenty of adjoining land to build a giant casino and hotel. They weren't looking to provide AFC Wimbledon with a home – they were counting all the jackpots that might be coming their way.

Then, unbelievably for us, Gordon Brown completely ditched his super casinos project. Luke Johnson's company was now stuck with decaying greyhound stadiums, all losing money. Oxford rapidly got sold off for housing development and it seemed a safe bet that something similar would happen to Wimbledon. I then got a call from a neighbour, Alan Johnson (no relation to Luke), who worked with housing associations.

'Ivor, this is completely hush-hush, but a deal's been reached for the Wimbledon dog track,' he confided. 'You need to talk to a company called Galliard Homes. They'll be redeveloping the entire site.'

I told Erik but he remained sceptical about Plough Lane. He still feared it was something we couldn't realistically afford or make happen. Besides, Alambritis had already introduced us by then to an Irish property developer called Stephen Sexton. He'd done some rough drawings of how the site could be redeveloped and what our stadium might look like. 'I can make this happen and you'll get a free football ground out of it,' he kept telling us.

We liked Sexton and agreed to give him a six-month exclusivity period to see what he could do. Erik and I started talking to him regularly and, after each phone call or meeting, Ben in the office would ask: 'What do you think?'

'Fifteen per cent now,' I replied.

'Really?'

'Yeah, really.'

But it was all about who owned the land. We were two months into Sexton's exclusivity period when my phone went and someone called Michael Watson introduced himself. 'I'm one of the directors of Galliard Homes.'

Oh my God. I nearly dropped the phone there and then.

This is it: first contact. Earth to aliens.

He instantly sounded like a no-nonsense businessman and before I could even respond, he carried on: 'I'm not going to beat around the bush. It's very unlikely, but there is a possibility, we could do some business.'

'Er, right, yes, er – what exactly do you mean?'

'We have control of the land down at Plough Lane in Wimbledon and we need planning approval to build dwellings there. However, some bits and pieces have somehow got into the long-term development plan. Apparently, part of the land is earmarked for you lot.'

Once again I tried to respond, but he wasn't stopping.

'The easiest way round it is probably to do a deal. We will build you a stadium and then it'll be happy days all round.'

Has he finished?

'Well it's not quite as easy as that,' I ventured, hesitatingly.

'No. Indeed, it's very far from being as easy as that,' he replied. 'But, in principle, that's what we are talking about. I realise you're not on your own in this – who else do you need to talk to?'

'Quite a few actually but I have to tell you we are already in agreement with someone else at the moment – and that's slightly awkward.'

'Well, if you lot want to do anything, you'll have to get a fucking move on.' And just as I was saying, 'Okay, I'll get back to you,' he hung up.

My head was spinning and I rang Erik immediately. 'I need to see you right now. It's urgent,' I blurted. There was no way I could tell him over the phone. Technically, I had now broken our exclusivity agreement with Sexton just by taking the phone call. I knew Erik would be horrified by that in itself – never mind what we had talked about.

I was right. He hit the roof when I walked in and explained what had happened: 'You can't do that; you should have put the phone down straight away,' he protested.

'Erik, come on. If nothing else, we have smoked out the reality.'

That much was true but we also had a situation. At the next Dons Trust board meeting, Erik told everyone the problem: we had received contact from the people who actually controlled the site but we also had an exclusivity agreement that technically stopped us talking to them.

Behind the scenes, I was frantic and constantly in Erik's ear: 'We fucking need to talk to Galliard. If we let this go, it'll be treasonous as far as the club is concerned.'

I actually used that word: treasonous. We risked blowing our only chance to ever get back to Plough Lane. Where we truly belonged. Then Erik did what I admired most about him. He thought the problem through carefully, then came up with a quite brilliant solution.

'Let's bring in a consultant,' he said. 'We probably need one in any case but if we engage a consultant now, and he talks to Sexton, then we're not technically breaking the agreement.'

We quickly appointed Andrew Williams, who lived in Wimbledon and knew all the right people. I then spoke to Watson and explained that our man would be the point of contact from then on. Soon after, Andrew contacted Watson and started reporting back to us regularly at our football club board meetings. I returned to my office, where Ben once again asked: 'What do you think?'

'Thirty-five per cent.'

'Fucking hell – why?'

'Because now we are talking to the people who actually have control of the land and they are showing a willingness for us to have a stadium.'

Sexton's exclusivity period eventually ran out and, not long after, we had our first face-to-face meeting with Michael Watson. That's when I knew we were coming home.

Galliard were willing to work on a Section 106 for us. Put simply, that meant a sum of money would be paid by them to the council – and then forwarded to us to help pay for a new stadium. In return, Galliard would get the green light to build surrounding flats and homes.

I walked back to my office immediately after that meeting. This time, Ben simply said: 'Well?'

'Seventy-five per cent.'

'You're joking! 'Bloody hell, Ivor.'

Chapter 48
OUR TIME

THE microphone was thrust into my hand and a voice said: 'Tell us, Ivor. You've been at the club from day one – what are your thoughts right now?' Everywhere I looked was pandemonium: a yellow and blue eruption, players jumping around manically, trying to get into the crowd, trying to be mobbed, celebrating like they'd never celebrated before.

I looked at the mic. Every sinew in my body wanted me to scream: 'This is for those fools at the FA. This is for those tossers who told us we shouldn't exist. Well, just look at us now – the club you tried to wipe out, the people you told to go away. You can all fuck off, the lot of you.'

I swear the words were queuing up on the edge of my tongue, trying desperately to cascade out. All the anger, all the resentment, the injustice, the sheer fucking cruelty and absurdity, all the hatred and heartache that had been boiling away for nine years. I'd never stopped believing this day would come. It was our atonement, our revenge, our vindication. The club the FA had tried to wipe off the map was back from the dead.

I opened my mouth, ready to say all of this – and more – when, suddenly, I heard feedback crackling through the stadium's PA system. Only then did the penny drop: I was being interviewed live by Premier Sports, and every word I was about to say would be going out completely uncensored. I checked. Instead of saying 'fuck them all', I drew back and yelled: 'We've shown them all.'

But I really wish I'd been brave enough to say what I wanted to say. Right from the heart: 'fuck them all'. I wish I'd mentioned the pariahs in Milton Keynes who happily received a new football club on their doorstep without ever questioning where on earth it had come from. How come the entire football world understood the injustice of what had happened – and yet so-called football supporters in Milton Keynes never blinked an eyelid. Where were their principles?

It was something that needed saying. It was something the FA – and the football world – needed to hear. It was something I should have said, and I should have said it right then, raw and unashamed, instead of being diplomatic. Fuck diplomacy. Where was diplomacy in 2002? I didn't, though. Maybe I was overwhelmed by the occasion – it was, after all, an incredibly dramatic ending to the greatest season of them all. Maybe I can be excused for not finding the right words given the millions of emotions that were stampeding chaotically through my mind.

Our second season in the Conference had quickly turned into a prolonged battle with neighbouring Crawley Town for the top spot. Brown's insistence that we went full-time had paid dividends: there were some big teams in the league – Grimsby, Darlington, York and Luton among them – and we were competing with, and beating, the best of them.

Except Crawley. On 18 March 2011, we lost 3-1 at their place. A demoralising defeat – but one that brought the very best out of Terry Brown. From that point onwards, we were all privileged to witness an inspirational example of how to manage a football team. Instead of clinging to a forlorn hope that we might still overtake them and seize top spot, he focused everything on making sure we finished second, and therefore guaranteed the easiest possible route into the play-off final. Everything he did, said, organised and analysed was geared towards getting us to the City of Manchester Stadium, where the final would be played two months later. It was unbelievable. Textbook. Everything was meticulously planned from start to finish and he got the entire club – not just the players – focused 100 per cent on that one single mission.

As a result of his single-minded focus, the team went unbeaten for the rest of the season and the spirit within the club was at its peak when we needed it most. We finished second by miles and had to play Fleetwood over two legs in the play-off semi-final. Their playing budget was miles more than ours – yet I reckon our performance up there was the best AFC Wimbledon performance I'd ever seen. We absolutely took them to the cleaners and won 2-0. The return leg at Kingsmeadow was a rout: we beat them 6-1 – Kaid Mohamed bagging a hat-trick – to secure the biggest winning margin ever in a play-off match. Suddenly, we were one game away from the Football League.

If anything would prove that we'd been right to relaunch our club, right to defy the FA, right to fight for something that had been stolen from us, then getting back into the League would do it. The excitement was off the scale, but Brown kept us focused and we were determined to do everything right. The tiniest detail might make a difference – as we soon found out.

Me, Claire and my commercial executive Keith McGuiness were anxious to look after our loyal sponsors, so we asked City if we could visit their stadium to work out seating plans.

The team also arranged a training session on the pitch, but when Luton asked to do the same, City said, 'You're too late.' They even switched dressing rooms to give us theirs – and asked how we would like the grass cut! Why? Because they never forgot former Hatters manager David Pleat dancing on their old Maine Road pitch in 1983 when his side avoided relegation with a last-minute winner against City.

It's all going our way.

I couldn't sleep that night. I kept thinking about all the things and all the people who had lifted us to this point and I kept returning to one moment, right at the start, that set us on our way: David Fowkes filling in the London FA form and writing down our name for the first time on official paperwork – AFC Wimbledon – and then writing down the year we were formed: 1889.

I was so thrilled we'd reached the play-off final, and I was sensible enough to know it could all go pear-shaped. But I desperately didn't want it to end like that. I couldn't shake off the thought that we'd be carrying 112 years of history with us into the City of Manchester Stadium and my mind started churning over all our club's historic achievements. Winning the FA Cup was right up there, of course, but also winning the FA Amateur Trophy at Wembley, when that competition really mattered, and beating Burnley and nearly beating Leeds when we were still non-league.

All this was whirling around in my restless mind. Then I started thinking about Dickie, and Allen Batsford and Dave Beasant and Bobby Gould and Vinnie and Wally and Lawrie and Corky and all those Crazy Gang heroes. They'd all been part of what made my club so special. Jonesy and Kris and Trevor drifted into my fitful slumber and I saw how devastated we all looked when the Ryman League refused to let us in.

Then Erik appeared and Stephen Alambritis and more and more faces until I was standing in front of a packed terrace. It was the old West Bank at Plough Lane: my mum and dad were there and David, and the football coach who took me to Plough Lane for the first time and my mates – the Batsford Boys – the people, the friends and family, whom I loved and cherished most. As I looked up and down the concrete steps, I recognised more and more familiar faces: Tim Hillier, who ran our merchandise operation for free at Kingsmeadow, was standing next to the entire 1974–75 squad! Just above them stood the ever-loyal David Barnard, Peter Miller and Aideen Rochford.

Then I found myself waving at the Ashington Wombles, a supporters' group who'd regularly come all the way down from the North East to cheer us on. My best mates, Alan Tucker and Keith Grossman, were at the front, leaning against the advertising boards – and so, too, was my mum's sister, Aunty Myra. She's 95 years old now and still says 'good result on Saturday' every time I see her.

Then I saw all the volunteers and sponsors and local businesses and everyone who, at some point, had drifted in and out of our club. Some were still with us, some weren't, but they'd all made a contribution somewhere along the line.

If we won this last game, if we got back into the Football League, then the victory would be for all of them – and for everyone else who had ever been involved in our history since 1889. The achievement would be right up there with all our club's previous triumphs. We'd have earned our rightful place alongside our ancestors.

No wonder I couldn't sleep.

Fucking hell. We've got to win.

Inevitably, we got to the stadium way too early. But our nerves calmed down as our guests started to arrive and we began escorting them to hospitality and their seats. Marcus Mumford had driven all the way to Manchester on his motorbike, Dave Barnard was sitting next to me in the directors' box and Miles Jacobson was there as well.

My heart was racing when the teams emerged. On paper, man for man, Luton looked the better team – but then that's the Wimbledon story in a nutshell. Liverpool in the cup final had the better team; Burnley in 1975, Man United home and away, Chelsea away, Arsenal at their ground, Tottenham away, Man City away – they were all better teams and yet we'd beaten the lot of them.

But this meant so much more. This was our day in court. This was when we could prove to the world that we deserved to exist. Lose, and I could imagine the FA sneering with delight. In fact, I bet they were praying we'd fuck it up.

The game went by in a blur. We matched Luton completely but they had a real chance towards the end. It looked like the ball was going in; instead, it hit the post and rebounded straight back into our keeper's arms. I turned to Claire and David Barnard and said: 'We're winning this.'

The score remained deadlocked, though, at the whistle. We were unlucky not to edge it in extra time, when Luton looked really knackered and were there for the taking. But it stayed goalless – and that meant a dreaded penalty shoot-out. Our keeper was Seb Brown. Unbelievably, he'd supported Wimbledon as a boy: aged 10, he was at The Dell in 2000 when we got relegated from the Premier League. He'd even joined the Selhurst Park protests. Now everyone was praying that boy would be the man to take us back to the promised land. And, boy, did he do just that. The advantage swung our way immediately when Seb dived low to his right to save Luton's opening penalty.

Our fans were right behind the goal making as much noise as they could each time a Luton player stepped forward. Then, on their fourth spot kick, Seb did it again. Once again, he dived to his right but looked beaten when Alex Lawless chipped his kick straight down the middle. Somehow, Seb recovered mid-dive, stretched out his left arm and palmed the ball away to safety.

Our nerves shattered, though, when Mohamed – who'd been suffering badly with cramp and could barely run – saw his effort saved. We still had the advantage and the stage was set for our skipper, Danny Kedwell, to take us into the Football League with the final penalty. I've thought long and hard about what happened next. Kedwell turned to his team-mates before taking his spot kick, and said: 'This is our time.'

Why did he say that? Was it because he had absorbed those little speeches I'd given the players at the start of the season, reminding them about our history? Had it actually sunk in – or was I deluded? So I asked him: 'What did you mean when you said, "This is our time," Danny?' I'll never forget his reply: 'I meant it was the moment for the whole club, but specifically for us players, to put right what had happened.'

They fucking understand all right.

Kedwell didn't simply place his spot-kick into the net. Instead, he hit it with thunderous ferocity and now I understood why. When he struck that ball into the net, he knew it was carrying 112 years of history. Everything after that was ecstasy. Kedwell ran over to the left-hand corner to be mobbed by our fans.

Everyone was hugging and going berserk, smoke bombs were exploding, bedlam everywhere – and that's when I got the microphone shoved in my face: 'It has taken us nine years to do this. Nine years to prove the FA were wrong.' At least I said that much. Our victory was indisputable proof we had a right to exist. We'd proved the concept, we'd proved the FA were hideously wrong and we'd proved that fans are the real power behind the throne.

Don't fuck with us.

AFC Wimbledon had achieved what I was thinking back in 2002 when I said: 'Right. Fuck the lot of you. Let's go again. Let's keep our club alive.'

This was a victory for the little guys against the big guys; we'd achieved what countless numbers of people thought we couldn't – and had even told us not to try. And we'd done it with nothing but sheer willpower and determination. We'd done it because we were victims of the biggest injustice in the history of the game.

There were quite a few people at the game who had nothing to do with our club, yet they were moved by the raw emotions afterwards. They were football people – City legends Mike Summerbee and Dennis Tueart among them – and they shook our hands because they understood the crime committed against us. Like us, they were rejoicing that justice had finally been done.

I'd never experienced solidarity like that among football's nobility before. It meant a lot.

In fact, some years later we were walking through Manchester's Piccadilly railway station to get a connection when I bumped into Summerbee. We shook hands and he said: 'I remember you very well. That was an unbelievable day.'

'Incredible – and I'm really glad you were there to witness it,' I replied, sincerely.

His response amazed me. As a player, he'd known unbelievable highs in the game with City and England, and yet he still said: 'That's the most emotional day I have ever experienced in the game.'

Football people got what had happened. They still do. It's just the FA who haven't a fucking clue.

Everyone was staying in The Village Hotel in Bury and, naturally, everyone headed for the bar as soon as we got there. We were celebrating everything: not least the amount of time it had taken us to get back into the Football League.

Nine fucking years. Unreal. Nine years since we'd turned up at Bottom Meadow, having miraculously put together a team from absolutely nothing. Nine years since we'd been told we weren't in the wider interests of football. Where were the snivelling cowards who had made that repulsive declaration? Where were they hiding now, their vicious words well and truly rammed down their throats by the very people they wanted to exclude from their cosy ranks. It only took us nine years to prove every one of them wrong. Wrong to take a club away from its heartland. Wrong to shovel away its supporters. Wrong, wrong, wrong.

AFC Wimbledon v Luton Town, City of Manchester Stadium, 21 May 2011: my favourite game . . . ever.

Chapter 49
YELLOW, BLUE AND GREEN

I HONESTLY thought it was a wind-up. 'Ivor, there's some bloke on the phone. Says he's been trying to get through to you.'

'What's his name?' I shouted back and our new commercial director, Sam Grayson, replied: 'John Green. Sounds American.'

Now, I had a pal called John Green and he liked a practical joke. 'Nah – John Green's not a bloody Yank,' I replied. 'He's pulling your plonker.'

I'd known John since childhood but hadn't heard from him for ages. *What the fuck does he want?*

Sam put the call through and I picked up. 'Hey, Ivor, it's John

Green,' came the voice, in what I thought was a rather fake American accent.

'Yeah, yeah,' I replied.

'I want to sponsor the club.'

'This is a fucking wind-up. I know who you are, Greeny.'

But something didn't quite add up. If it was my mate, why the American accent? Worried I might have got this all wrong, I quickly added: 'What do you want to do then?'

'I want to do something major with the club,' came the response. He sounded suspiciously serious.

'But what?'

'I don't know – sponsor something,' he insisted. It really didn't sound like my mate.

'Okay, do you want to sponsor a stand, maybe, or some advertising hoardings? What exactly are you thinking?' I asked, cautiously. I hate being mugged.

'I'm not sure,' he replied and by now I was back to thinking, 'This is definitely a fucking wind-up.'

'Okay, John, look – before we go any further, who are you and what do you do? Tell me a little bit about yourself so I know what we are talking about here.'

'I'm an author,' said the voice instantly, and this time I paid a bit more attention. There was no way my mate John Green would have ever said 'I'm an author'.

I had my laptop open so I frantically typed in the words 'John' 'Green' 'author' and straight away there was an explosion of images and words on my screen. *Fucking hell.* My eyes started bulging as I absorbed sentences like 'Film being made by John Green'; 'John Green's best-selling book'; 'Hollywood blockbuster'; *The Fault in Our Stars. The Fault in Our Bloody Stars.* Even I'd heard of that.

I was so gobsmacked I just let the words tumble out of me: 'Fucking hell, you're THAT John Green.'

'Yeah – I'm THAT John Green,' he replied.

'Right, okay apologies, I thought you were my mate who is also called John Green. Would you believe it – what a coincidence, eh? So, John, what are we going to do?' Without even realising it, I was now sitting bolt upright in my chair.

Then he came out with the line: 'I'm going to be playing the FIFA soccer game soon on YouTube. I want to donate the money I earn from that to your club. What d'ya say, Ivor?'

It sounded great but, truth be told, I hadn't a clue what he was talking about. Who on earth was going to watch John Green the Author playing FIFA? It might as well be John Green my prankster mate.

'Er . . . wow . . . but tell me, John, how exactly does that work?' I asked. *He thinks I'm an imbecile.*

'Just so you know,' he continued, 'hundreds of thousands of people around the world will be watching.'

Incredulous, I quickly opened YouTube and then saw how many people had watched his videos.

'So, let me get this right, John. You'll play the game as us – AFC Wimbledon?' I asked, nervously.

'Yeah, that's right. But I'll probably call the team something like "The Wimbly Womblys". They'll play in blue and yellow and I'll use real player names – as well as some made-up quirky ones.'

The YouTube game was a huge success, and brought in at least £20,000. I actually think we became the first UK football club to earn money like that from Esports. More importantly, it marked the start of a treasured relationship with John Green the Author, who remains a loyal supporter and friend to this day.

He really was nowhere near finished either, and completely bamboozled me when he announced: 'There must be a way I can use the Nerdfighters to help the club. What d'ya think, Ivor?'

Nerdwhatdidhesay?

Again, I hit Google. John and his brother, Hank, had established a colossal online community and its mission was to fight just about anything and everything that 'sucks' in the world. The Nerdfighters were people who maybe didn't quite fit in, often extremely intelligent and caring and massively into Harry Potter and stuff like that. And there were millions of them.

John wanted the Nerdfighters to sponsor our players' shorts, so proposed a competition for them to design a logo. It's the same one that's on the back of AFC Wimbledon's shorts right now – the letters: D F T B A. In case you don't know, that stands for: Don't Forget To Be Awesome.

John also took four hoardings – one simply said 'Nerdfighteria' – and they ran along the perimeter of the Kingsmeadow pitch. Some years later, we hosted the European Nerdfighter Conference at the ground and it was totally awesome. At least 120 turned up and I'm still friends with many of them today. AFC Wimbledon got some lifelong fans out of the Nerdfighters.

I spoke at their conference and told them all about our story. They all looked like they'd just walked straight out of the latest *Harry Potter* movie, with their little round glasses and scarves. In fact, the finale of the day was a game of quidditch on the car park outside. It was hilarious: they had all the gear, broomsticks and pointy hats, and two teams ran at each other throwing God knows what through the air. They may have looked like misfits, but the amount of charity work and fundraising they did was a lesson to us all.

John started coming over to watch matches and I really got to know and love him. There's no side, or airs and graces, with John Green, the Author. He's a genuine, 100 per cent decent bloke, who always finds time for anyone and everyone.

He wasn't finished there, either. We unexpectedly needed one of our end stands sponsoring when Nongshim, who made Korean pot noodles, pulled out because of their own internal issues. It was a big blow – just before the new season – but John called and said: 'I really like the idea of having a stand named after me.'

'Great,' I replied – a bit apprehensively. He wasn't a company after all. 'John, won't that be a bit weird?'

'No – not at all. I'll be advertising my books,' he explained and suddenly it all made sense. John Green the Author was very much a business – the business of books.

We agreed a deal for £20,000 – on top of the other twenty he'd already handed over. Now he'd become a very significant sponsor. And I have to say the way he maximised his stand sponsorship was inspirational. Not only were the words 'The John Green Stand' permanently emblazoned on the stand itself, images of his books then ran underneath along the perimeter boards.

One day he phoned me to say: 'I'm in London next Friday. Do you fancy meeting up?'

'Great,' I replied.

His PA phoned two days later and told me to meet John at the Leicester Square Hotel at 4 p.m. the following Friday. When I got there, Leicester Square was heaving with teenagers, all milling round the main cinema entrance. I headed straight for the hotel, walked into the main foyer, and immediately noticed posters on the walls: John Green, *Paper Towns.*

Then I spotted a reception desk, introduced myself and was handed a VIP pass. 'What's this for?' I asked.

'John is doing a preview for his new movie, *Paper Towns*. He thought you'd like to see it and then catch up afterwards.' *Brilliant.*

I headed back to the cinema, waved my pass at the security guards and stood in the entrance hall, staring at all the people pouring in. The entire film cast were there – including Cara Delevingne and Nat Wolff, plus loads of influencers. Suddenly everyone started cheering and applauding. I looked up and there was John, standing dramatically at the top of the main stairs. John smiled and waved and then held out his arms to quieten the crowd down, before saying: 'Ladies and gentlemen, I love you people, but there's a very special guest among you right now. Will you all please put your hands together for Ivor – Ivor from AFC Wimbledon.'

What the fuck.

Everyone started turning towards me and carried on cheering like I was the person they'd really come to see. I then got escorted to the VIP seating area and watched a tsunami of 16–20-year-olds – mainly girls – come rushing in.

Then the lights went down, and two YouTube influencers did a warm-up before a voice filled the arena: 'Now, ladies and gentlemen, the man you've all been waiting for – Mr John Green.'

The audience went mental and John strolled out like a superstar: 'Hi, London, it's great to be here.' He then let the cheering drop a few decibels before adding: 'But you all know why I really love London.

'There's one reason above everything else. And I'm delighted to tell you, we've got the guy who started it all right here in the audience – right now.'

All of a sudden a huge spotlight flashed on and, somehow, singled me out. He obviously knew where I'd be sitting. 'Stand up, Ivor!'

'I am standing up,' I joked. I actually thought that was quite a good line but nobody could hear me against the roar. I was like a rabbit in the headlights. This was as far away from a football crowd as you could get, so I waved meekly and smiled embarrassedly and sat down as quickly as I could.

Afterwards, there was a reception and the cast were all there, along with the director. John and I talked to them for hours – and the only thing they wanted to know about was AFC Wimbledon.

Chapter 50
HONOURABLE TO THE END

I NEVER witnessed an ending like it. Our most successful AFC Wimbledon manager knew his time was up – without anyone needing to tell him. We were languishing near the bottom of

League Two. There was unrest among the fans and we were playing Torquay United at home in a game Terry Brown simply had to win. Only we didn't. We lost 1-0 to a farcical goal that somehow summed up everything: keeper Seb Brown kicked the ball away, only to see it hit a Torquay striker on the arse and trickle back into the net.

Time was up for Browny, and everyone present knew it. At the final whistle, and without any announcement, the crowd rose to give him and his assistant Stuart Cash a standing ovation as they walked together round the pitch. It was one of the most emotional moments I ever witnessed at the club because nobody had said a word about their futures. He hadn't been dismissed, there'd been no statements. He just knew – and so did everyone present.

What a man.

Browny then walked back into his little office with this huge rapturous applause still echoing round the ground. For a few minutes it was just the two of us, and I looked into his eyes and immediately phoned the bar. 'Send the beers in – and keep them coming.'

People started gradually coming in until it felt like 30 of us were packed into this tiny, shoebox space – and we didn't leave until something like 3 a.m. the following morning. We were singing Wimbledon songs endlessly and I can still hear us belting out 'Terry Brown's Yellow and Blue Army'.

We talked about the wonderful memories and the camaraderie and I found myself thinking, 'This is typical Browny. He's gone out on his shield; he's not ducked anything.' It just showed the measure of this unique man. Like I said, at no stage did anyone formally say, 'It's over.' It was just understood. Then we started the hunt for a new manager.

Erik was determined to make it a formal process. He even insisted we would ask questions that weren't solely about football but reflected the changes in modern society. Like: 'What would you do if a player racially abused a team-mate?'; and 'How would you respond if a player told you he was gay?'

We received about 150 applications and used Dave 'Harry' Bassett to help us whittle them down to a shortlist. There was me, Erik, Nigel Higgs, David Charles and we all sat in awe as Harry started zooming through the names in front of him. 'No – no – no – no – maybe, then a two-second spiel on why we should rule that one out, then back to: no – no – no. Then came a moment that had me in stitches. Harry suddenly stopped in his tracks as he studied the next name on the list, then looked up and declared: 'Absolutely no. You can't have a fat cunt as your manager!'

I fell about laughing. So much for moving with the times. It was the funniest line I've ever heard in any kind of recruitment debate, ever. You wouldn't see that in an HR pamphlet. Harry was Crazy Gang, bless him.

We finished with a shortlist of about six and held the interviews at the swanky Grosvenor House Hotel in London's Park Lane. We started with the football stuff and Bassett would say: 'Right, there's a whiteboard over there. I want you to show me your best set piece.' The candidates would then stand up and scribble away, explaining the theory behind the lines and squiggles they were drawing. It was fascinating to listen to and watch.

Simon Bassey, who'd been standing in after Terry left, was one of the first to be interviewed. He did well but within a minute of him leaving I checked the betting odds and, to my utter amazement, saw the bookies had made him odds-on favourite. I was genuinely shocked, so when the next candidate came and left, I checked again. Lo and behold, that person was suddenly the new favourite. And it went on and on like that for the whole day. Someone at the hotel was clearly phoning the bookies the second they saw each of our candidates walking away.

And yes – we asked them all our revolutionary questions. What would you do with a bully, how would you protect a gay player, that sort of stuff. Nobody said anything stupid, in fact the answers were surprisingly sensible and uniform: 'We'd look after them, make sure they were safe.'

'There is no place for racism or any form of prejudice in my dressing room.'

It was obvious stuff really, but I'd never seen or heard any of our previous potential managers deal with those sorts of issues before.

Neal Ardley was one of the six we interviewed. He'd been a massive star for us as a player and was now head of the Cardiff City academy. We were pals, we'd played golf occasionally and I really liked him as a person. He interviewed brilliantly and, to me, he was the obvious appointment. He took over in October 2012.

His first priority was to keep us up and I remember him saying to me on New Year's Eve: 'We'll need to hit promotion form between now and the end of the season to stay up.'

My God, it was close. Everything boiled down to the last game, which we dubbed Survival Saturday. None of us will ever forget that day. We had to beat Fleetwood Town or we'd be relegated back into the Conference. Who knows how disastrous that might have been. We piled on the pressure right from the start and, after an hour of near misses and hitting the woodwork, took the lead when Gary Alexander headed home.

The celebrations were silenced two minutes later, though, when Fleetwood equalised and we were all suddenly staring into the abyss. Anxiety swept across Kingsmeadow: I remember looking up to the skies and all I could see were dark clouds bearing down.

The minutes were slipping away, and the trapdoor was absolutely wide open when Curtis Osano was dragged down in the box and everyone in Kingsmeadow roared 'penalty'. It was clear-cut but you could have heard a pin drop as Jack Midson placed the ball on the spot and then calmly slotted home the spot kick.

Waves of relief engulfed the stadium and when the final whistle went it felt like every single fan clambered over the perimeter walls to invade the pitch. It was an enormously important moment: I'm not sure whether we could have handled relegation after just one season back in the Football League.

Ards had kept us up – but his best was yet to come . . .

Chapter 51
GOOD v EVIL

IT FELT like I was walking into hell. I was going to a place that shouldn't exist. We were about to face the franchise for the first time in our history and I couldn't have felt any worse if I'd been going to my own funeral. The match felt, to me, like good versus evil. When I stepped off the coach, and looked up at their ground, I instantly burst into tears. I literally stood still and sobbed on the spot. My tears were coming from a deep, anguished, guttural place.

It was horrible to see the stadium, it was horrible to walk towards it and it was horrible to actually go inside. I despised everything it represented. To me, their ground was a drab arena plonked in the middle of roundabouts with lots of concrete to enable a shopping centre. Which was pretty much what we'd always said. Our club was sacrificed to enable a property deal in Milton fucking Keynes.

The architect of it all, Peter Winkelman, wanted a league club to play with – so decided to nick ours. If he'd done it the proper way, if he'd started like we did – from rock bottom – and then worked his club all the way up through the leagues, then he would have been a hero and the franchise's story would have been widely applauded.

But no. He wanted one that was oven-ready and we were in the baking tray waiting to get roasted. We call them the franchise because they were manufactured: they had no history, no heritage, no heroes, no stories. They had nothing to be proud of, nothing their fans could reminisce about, because what they did have actually belonged to someone else. Us. The franchise never earned their place in the Football League. They stole it.

Do you understand why I was sobbing?

People often ask me, 'Ivor, do you hate the franchise?' Hate is a deeply offensive word but quite frankly it doesn't come close to the revulsion I feel, even now – 24 years after they stole our club. They masqueraded as us and I can never forgive them.

I despised the town just as much. Jonesy and I went for two business meetings there – one with Kodak, the other with a digital printing company. We walked out of both when the people we were talking to admitted they'd been to see the franchise play.

Now we'd been drawn against them in the FA Cup second round, to be played on 2 December 2012. They were League One, we were League Two, so they were firm favourites with home advantage.

There was a huge amount of debate about the game beforehand. Many said: 'You shouldn't go; don't do it, Ivor.' Others said: 'Go – you must.' It was a pretty big split, but on the day we took about 3,500 fans and a fleet of 20 coaches – including one that I filled entirely on my own with friends, family and people I'd known a long time. My brother and nephew were there, along with Jonesy, Ben Adams and some of the Batsford Boys.

By then, AFC Wimbledon fans naturally fell into one of three categories. There were those who absolutely refused to accept the franchise existed. Others reluctantly admitted they existed, looked to see how they were doing – and felt great if they were struggling. Finally, there were those whose blood flowed with pure vitriol. They accepted the franchise existed in the hope it led to violence.

Me? I identify with all three camps. When the franchise are doing well, I don't look; when they're doing badly I can't stop looking because it gives me so much joy. And then there's my third, more animalistic reality. When I'm anywhere near them, I'm consumed by a deep anger that I don't feel with any other club. Why?

Apart from stealing our club, it all comes down to the name.

They insulted us from day one when they carried on calling themselves Wimbledon – even when they were physically playing in Milton Keynes. Then they rebranded and decided to call themselves MK. That was fair enough: if they'd made it MK City or Town or Rovers or – I don't know, MK Fucking Academicals for all I cared – then that might have been okay.

But no. They had to add the one word that Wimbledon were historically associated with. Our cherished, abridged name – Dons. They added that to the letters MK, and that's what they're still calling themselves today. They might as well have carried on calling themselves Wimbledon in my book. What the hell has Milton Keynes got to do with the Dons? Absolutely nothing. Other than it was our name when they took the club from us. I believe they did it to wind us up. That's the only plausible reason I can think off. It's their fuck-off gesture to us. It still makes me feel sick and it was absolutely one of the reasons why I sobbed as I stepped off the coach. There, emblazoned on their stadium entrance, was OUR name.

All the injustice and all the anguish produced those tears. All the fighting and worrying and campaigning and struggling that had been raging inside me since 2002 came flooding out. There'd been a lot of noise in the build-up to the match. It was decided that Erik would be our only spokesman because he'd be more measured and grown up than the likes of me.

That just wound me up even more, to be honest. I was bursting to say my piece and remind the world what the franchise represented. In my opinion, we should have gone over the battlements and let them have it. We shouldn't have been afraid to turn round and say, 'We fucking hate them.' It's what we all felt – so why not say it? Instead, we got consumed by diplomacy. 'Oh, we mustn't say this, we mustn't say that.' Why did we have to be so ashamed of telling the truth? This was good v evil after all. We hadn't started this.

I didn't feel any better once I got inside the ground. Seeing thousands of our fans in such a wretched place made me completely nauseous. There was a huge police presence, stewards everywhere, and everyone got searched. It just seemed wrong: there was no happiness, no pre-match excitement or joking. Just raw, acrid tension and hostility. It felt dystopian.

There were clearly people there who'd got tickets purely to cause trouble. Some of them were fans I'd see week in, week out, only they looked totally different. They looked possessed. Even the usually placid, normal supporters were swearing and cursing and trying to be intimidating. It was like someone had flicked on a switch. Everyone had 'We Are Wimbledon' posters then, after 30 minutes, we all looked up to the heavens as a plane flew over trailing a banner that carried the same message. It was probably the best bit of the entire game, which was being televised live on ITV.

Naturally we all prayed for a miracle. Winning would have been divine, but the odds were stacked heavily against us, especially when the franchise took the lead. However, Jack Midson levelled – triggering an ugly pitch invasion by some of our fans. Just when it looked like we were going to bring them back to Kingsmeadow for a replay, the franchise grabbed a last-gasp winner in the dying minutes.

Coming away from the stadium was just as bad as going in had been. It was clear there was going to be trouble outside and, sure enough, I heard what sounded like a fight breaking out. I instinctively turned towards that direction when, thankfully, Claire grabbed me forcibly round the arm and yelled: 'No. No you don't.'

Chapter 52
MY DIVORCE

PRINCESS Diana very famously said: 'There were three of us in this marriage.' I knew what she meant. In my case, it was me, Claire and AFC Wimbledon – and not necessarily in that order. Truth be told, I spent more time saving the football club than I did saving my marriage. Football wasn't the only reason we got divorced – but it certainly played a part.

During our very first date, I turned to Claire and said: 'Don't ever ask me to miss a football match. If you do, I will leave you. You can ask me anything else – but never ask me that.' We'd barely known each other a week and I wasn't kidding. To be fair, she only did it once and she never did it again. I'd upset her and then coldly announced: 'Right, I'm off to the game now.'

'Ivor, how can you walk out and leave me like this?' she sobbed.

But I was immune. 'Bollocks, I'm going,' I replied unashamedly as I marched out of the door. It was November 1995 and we were playing Middlesbrough at home. The weather was terrible, the game was terrible and it ended in a terrible 0-0 draw. Served me right.

Claire wasn't anti-football by any means and she definitely helped us get AFC Wimbledon off the ground. She'd listen patiently as I told her about the bastard Koppel, and moving to Milton Keynes, and the protests and the plans to start all over again – and she supported all of it, passionately. Way more than I suspect many wives would have done.

But I could never get the balance right between spending time at the club and spending time at home. I was enjoying a bachelor life inside a marriage, too wrapped up in myself, my football and being with the lads, to notice. For example, what partner would have put up with the following – which was a typical week in the life of Ivor Heller:

Monday – play poker. It'd be rare if I was back by four in the morning. Sometimes I'd leave our flat saying, 'I'll be home later,' then return the following Tuesday night. Actually, that used to happen a lot.

Tuesday – usually off to an evening match. If it was an away game, I'd get back well after midnight – or not at all.

Wednesday – my day of rest. So what did I do? Watched football on the telly, that's what.

Thursday – take work clients out for a slap-up meal or piss-up.

Friday – I used to get excited about Friday on a Tuesday. That's when I'd let loose and do whatever I fancied. There'd always be horse racing somewhere in the afternoon, or I'd go to the snooker club, or maybe a poker game in Wembley. Usually without Claire.

Saturday – matchday. If there wasn't any football, I'd go to the snooker club. I might agree to go for an evening meal with Claire and some friends – but I'd always cut it fine getting back. I'd walk in and she'd be sitting there, all dolled up and ready to go, whereas I'd be dishevelled and half pissed. 'We won't be late, so what's the problem, dear?'

I must have been a fucking nightmare. My entire regime was about me and doing my stuff – whether Claire was there or not.

We met when I was running my printing business and about to get a new contract with Liberty's store in London. I went in one day, and one of their researchers, Jane Docherty, teasingly said in front of a room full of young women: 'Ivor, how's your love life? I don't know why you don't take Claire out.'

Before I could respond, Claire Stead added: 'I can't go out with him: he's not a six-foot high, three-foot wide rugby player.'

I took the bait. 'Just for your knowledge,' I replied, 'I don't need to be six-foot high and three-foot wide to take you out, luv. You'll never go out with anyone like me.'

'Oh . . . really?' she giggled.

'Yeah – Sunday.'

That got a few shrieks from all the other girls listening intently in the office – and that was the start of our romance.

Scottish and feisty as fuck, with big, blonde hair and a trim figure, Claire was 23 then – so three years younger than me. Her family worshipped Celtic and she confessed to 'quite liking football'. That's when I warned her to never ask me to miss a game.

'That's not going to be a problem, Ivor,' she replied. 'I'll even go with you from time to time. I'd love to.'

We definitely had chemistry, we made each other laugh and I quickly started to think, 'This is the one.' We started dating regularly at the start of the 1990–91 season – our last one at Plough Lane. The first game I took her to was against Liverpool – it ended in a 2-1 defeat and with me about to thump their defender Barry Venison, the England international, after he barged Claire out of the way on his way to the bar in the tiny sponsors' lounge. He hadn't been playing, but had been drinking. It took Ronnie Whelan, another of the Liverpool party, to step in to keep the peace. Liverpool staff appeared from nowhere, all fussing around Claire and me, apologising profusely. Venison was sent to sit on the team bus.

Despite the bust-up with Venison, Claire had loved being at Plough Lane. Here was someone I could share my love of football with and that was a big deal for me. I also believe she felt a warmth for the club itself. She wasn't just coming along to please me. Having someone who properly got football – and my devotion to it – felt like the full package and so I took the plunge and proposed. At home, while we were watching *EastEnders* on the telly.

'I think we should get married,' I suddenly announced, then lifted myself out of my chair and bent down on one knee. 'Do you want to marry me?'

'Yes.'

We didn't go on honeymoon until Christmas Day 1997 when we flew to Sri Lanka. But Claire became perilously ill the moment we landed and was rushed to hospital with crippling sores that were attacking both the outside and inside of her body. She could barely breathe. Her condition was so bad that a specialist advised me to phone home and warn her family that she might die. I'll never forget that moment, phoning Claire's sister, Stella.

Mercifully, Claire started to revive slowly. By New Year's Eve we were able to hold hands as we sat on the roof of Nawaloka Hospital, watching and listening to firecrackers zigzagging and exploding across the Colombo night sky. It's fair to say we both appreciated being alive in that moment. We returned home 10 days later and our own doctor diagnosed internal chickenpox. He told us many people end up in wheelchairs after that, and it was rare for Claire to still be walking.

Even though the ordeal was over, I still had no intention of becoming a stay-at-home hubby. Don't get me wrong, we weren't living separate lives all the time. Claire really got into the fight against franchising and the move to Milton Keynes. When we smuggled posters into the directors' box at Selhurst Park, she was right there, sticking her poster straight in front of Koppel and his acolytes.

She understood the cause and supported it completely. We'd talk about it at home, and she loved the idea of fan ownership. 'It'll be better when that happens,' she said repeatedly. But relaunching the club took me away from home even more, especially in the early days. A lot of stuff went on at night: there'd be Dons Trust meetings, special general meetings, stadium group meetings, working group meetings. The bloody meetings were endless.

Then there was the work that went into staging all the matches – sorting the food and catering at the ground, picking up supplies at six in the morning, keeping the bars stocked. There were so many needs. It was a pretty demanding environment – for me and for Claire. She volunteered for the first 21 years of the club's life and she carried on long after we eventually divorced in 2015 – sorting buffets in the boardroom, helping in hospitality. But she got the balance right.

Me? I kept blundering on, oblivious to the selfishness of my lifestyle. As far as I was concerned, we were still happily married – until we came under huge financial stress. And that was probably because I was more bothered about the football club than my own business. There's no doubt I was spending more time on AFC

Wimbledon work than I was with my own business clients. I was losing my love for the print industry – running a football club was far more fun.

In the end, my company went tits up in 2006 when a major client, who owed us a load of money, went into liquidation and we were left penniless. I then went into business with Jonesy, still print stuff, but Claire and I were forced to sell our flat. That was a massive strain on both of us. Her own company also started to struggle at the same time – she had launched the country's first bespoke gift-wrapping business, based in the Brent Cross shopping centre. She turned over £20,000 from a standing start in the first six days.

By the 2010 World Cup, though, we were squabbling over the tiniest things. Tension was always bubbling away under the surface – and then it came to the boil on quarter-final night when she said: 'I want us to have a trial separation.'

She was clearly down. Everything had been going wrong: we'd remortgaged, she'd taken a business loan that was weighing heavy, I'd paid off bills – but there was no money left. I let it all sink in. 'Okay, right, I'm going then.' That wasn't what Claire had meant – she expected me to sleep on the sofa, not leave our home altogether. But I wasn't willing to live in a state of separation under the same roof. For me, it was over.

We tried counselling, we limped on – me sometimes staying in hotels, sometimes sleeping on the sofa, sometimes meeting other women – but it was all downhill. Football on its own didn't break our marriage. But the sheer volume of what needed to be done to launch a club, and the time that consumed, definitely contributed. I can still hear Claire, in the heat of a row, saying: 'You love that club more than me.'

'No I don't,' I'd reply, lamely. I don't think I ever genuinely did but I certainly devoted far more time to it than her.

My instinct was to always prioritise Wimbledon. For instance, I would never abandon a football club meeting just because I had to take Claire out for dinner. Ironically, I get on better with her now. She is still very active, she still loves the club and she got really upset when the current board tried to impose a different ownership structure, one that would have left fans with a smaller stake. She genuinely fears people will take the club away from us one day.

Inevitably, the players had the next word on my private life. They'd twigged that Claire and I had parted and set me up with a Tinder profile while we were on a trip back from an away game in Exeter! I did meet someone online thanks to that intervention from the team. We got on well, but I knew – deep down – it was a frivolity. A rebound that couldn't possibly last. Besides, someone else was on my radar by then. Lisa. There was something about Lisa that I knew was right for me and we've been together ever since.

Chapter 53
ERIK STANDS AND DELIVERS

ON 10 DECEMBER 2015, we got the planning permission to build our stadium at Plough Lane. We were all packed into Merton town hall, including fans squeezed into the public gallery. Many of them were wearing our yellow and blue shirts and, by the amount of noise they were making, I suspect they thought they were at one of our games. There was a real buzz in the room. I was feeling really punchy: this was a major moment in our history.

Win the politics, win the war.

Stephen was leading the proceedings and kicked off with 'other business' first. Then came our big moment. By then, Erik had insisted the stadium design must future-proof the club. He didn't want to see us get into the Premier League, for example, and then be told the stadium was inadequate. He was determined our new home would be fit for the long haul.

The pair of us had visited other newly built grounds, looking for ideas and inspiration. Sandy Park had been one, built in 2006 and home to the Exeter Chiefs rugby union club. I was impressed – it was cheap, cheerful and functional, but Erik surprised me. I was looking to cut corners and costs but Sandy Park was a bit too close to the bone for him. 'It's not good enough for us,' was his withering verdict.

When Wimbledon next played at Shrewsbury we took a microscopic look at their stadium, New Meadow, which had been built in 2007. Again, there seemed little wrong with it to me: four stand-alone identikit stands, perfectly neat and tidy. I turned to Erik and said: 'This would do.'

'No,' came the emphatic response. 'I can't stand stadiums that don't have the corners filled in. The stands should be connected to one another.' I respected what he was saying. He wanted our home to be fit for generations and competitions and leagues to come. He was absolutely right.

Loads of meetings were held to debate what our stadium needed to have. For me, in my role as the club's commercial director, state-of-the-art hospitality facilities with proper catering, executive boxes and a banqueting suite were essentials. We had to earn new money.

Erik listened to and absorbed everyone's ideas and opinions and then literally went into a bunker with our consultant Andrew Williams and architect Derek Wilson to come up with a design that would guarantee planning approval and give us a stadium that would serve our needs whatever happened in the future.

Erik really seized control at this point and his single-minded pursuit unquestionably got us over the line. He effectively pushed for two stadiums: one with a majestic main stand and three smaller, temporary stands that would serve us well in League One and League Two.

But his vision went way beyond that. Erik also wanted planning approval in place so the three smaller stands could one day be increased in size, should we need more capacity. When we return to the Premier League, for example.

In the end, as we all held our breath inside Merton town hall, the council couldn't say no. I don't remember anyone raising any serious objections. Then came the vote and a sea of hands flooded the room as the motion sailed through. AFC Wimbledon could come home. I doubt anyone cheered so loudly over a planning decision in Merton ever before; we were all hugging and waving and taking photos and savouring the moment.

I got so battered that night I couldn't find my car for 36 hours afterwards. I knew I'd parked it somewhere near the town hall but couldn't remember where. I literally wandered the streets of Merton trying to find it.

Back at work, I answered Ben's question before he even asked it: 'One hundred per cent. One hundred bloody per cent.'

There was only one problem left. I genuinely didn't know how on earth we would pay for it. At the time, the perceived wisdom was that a new arena would cost roughly £1,500 per seat. In other words, a 15,000-seater would total £22.5 million. The section 106 would give us roughly £14 million, so the next priority was to sell Kingsmeadow. But what would we get for that – and who would want it?

Once again, fate seemed to be on our side. Women's football was starting to take off like never before. Chelsea needed a new home for their team and slap bang in the middle was David Barnard, who used to be our chief executive but was now a much-revered director at Stamford Bridge. They were the right people, in the right place, at the right time. This really was Erik's baby but I took great satisfaction from knowing that I had negotiated the original deal to buy Kingsmeadow off Khosla for £2.4 million. Thanks to Erik, we were able to sell it to Chelsea women for £7.2 million. Not bad.

Everything was looking rosy, until Boris bloody Johnson stuck his big, fat oar in. He hadn't yet ballsed up the country like he did during the Covid pandemic, but he certainly ballsed us up by inexplicably 'calling in' the entire project. He was Mayor of London at the time and hadn't called in a single planning application – until then. Why? Nobody knows for sure but I believe the Wandsworth Tories, who I suspected didn't want another football ground close to their borders, promised to support him for prime minister if he stalled our move. It was a horrible decision, one that would cost us dearly. It meant the project would be on hold for at least another year – during which time building costs rocketed, as they always do. In the end, we reckon Boris cost us at least £2 million.

We all felt devastated, and immensely worried, until – once again – a local election came to our rescue. Thankfully, Sadiq Khan replaced Boris in the Mayor's office in 2016. Once that happened, I knew we were home and dry. Sadiq kicked the project straight back to the local authority, they'd already passed it, so we were back in business.

Thanks, Sadiq.

Chapter 54
TWO FINGERS

THERE'S a photograph of me in the Royal Box at Wembley. I've got a big cheesy grin on my face and I'm merrily sticking a V-sign into the air. Everybody assumed I was telling the FA to fuck off. We'd just beaten Plymouth Argyle 2-0 to win the 2016 League Two play-off final in front of 60,000 fans. Our journey through the divisions was getting better and better, we'd now be in League One and I had every reason to be ecstatic.

I wasn't telling the FA to fuck off, though. I wish I was – but I wasn't. Alan Tucker was in the seats below and had shouted up 'Ivor!' I leant over, saw him making a mocking gesture at me – so

I was simply giving him two fingers back in return. Everyone was laughing – except for Lisa. She gave me a hefty kick on the shin and, pointing to the other end of the stadium, mouthed: 'Ivor, you're on the big screen.' Sure enough, there I was, only it wasn't just the big screen, either. I was being broadcast live by Sky TV into every living room that had tuned into the final. They'd zoomed on to the Royal Box, knowing they'd see a reaction from us at the final whistle. The entire country saw me giving the V-sign. And the entire country thought it was aimed at the FA!

In the summer of 2014, Ards had signed the mountainous striker Adebayo Akinfenwa, nicknamed The Beast and, according to FIFA video stats, the strongest footballer in the world. He was to give us one of our greatest moments. We'd beaten Wycombe away in the FA Cup second round and were praying we'd get a Premier League giant in the next round. Maybe what followed was fate. Of all the teams, of all the tournaments, AFC Wimbledon were drawn against . . . Liverpool. At Kingsmeadow.

It was the only event I ever worked on that absolutely, 100 per cent, took over my entire life. The excitement and the anticipation went off the Richter scale. There simply weren't enough hours in the day to do everything that needed doing. Erik came up with a brilliant idea: peg ticket prices. We could have justifiably increased them, and we might have made a few extra quid, but if we told the world that AFC Wimbledon were keeping their ticket prices the same when they played Liverpool in the cup, how good would that make us look? He was totally right – but we still charged a fortune for our hospitality.

Everyone wanted to go and I was inundated with ticket requests. The national press were phoning constantly and the draw for the next round would be held live in our President's Lounge. There were so many moving parts to handle.

I managed to get the golf superstar Darren Clarke along as a special guest thanks to one of our loyal sponsors, My Golf Travel. I knew he supported Liverpool so our other guest of honour was our 1988 goalkeeping hero Dave Beasant. They both agreed to do a live chat for our hospitality guests but, as I stood between them, I realised people were giggling at the size difference between me and them. Beasant twigged as well and started playfully elbowing me in the right ear – while Darren started doing the same to my left. So, I grabbed a chair, stood on it to be level with them, and then smacked them both in their own earholes. 'Right, now we're even, let's start this bloody interview,' I joked. The entire room was in stitches.

By then, Kingsmeadow was bursting with excitement and expectation and rammed full. We even had Vinnie's FA Cup medal, which he'd donated to the club in 2010, on display in our main entrance. At the time, we were sitting 12th in League Two, while Liverpool were eighth in the Premier. They had some big superstars in their team, not least Jordan Henderson and Philippe Coutinho. Oh, and someone else: their inspirational skipper and England international Steven Gerrard. Could we really stun that lot, like we had in 1988?

Well, we certainly came close, although any hope of an upset looked doomed when Gerrard gave them the lead after just 12 minutes. Then we did what we always do. George Francomb slung over a 35th-minute corner, the ball crashed against the crossbar, players lunged in for the rebound and suddenly Kingsmeadow exploded. The Beast had scored. To this day, he still regards it as the highlight of his career. Liverpool were rattled but Gerrard wasn't having it. First he cleared Adam Barrett's effort off the line just after the break, then, in the 62nd minute, he curled an unstoppable free kick into the roof of our net. Make no mistake, we were brilliant that day. If it hadn't been for Gerrard, we would have won.

We reached the League Two play-off final the next season and faced Plymouth Argyle. The last time I'd been to Wembley with the Dons was in 1988. I was totally pissed getting there and in an even worse state coming back. This time, I drove. I decided to take

Mum and Dad and I'm so glad I did. It was to be the last time they'd both come to a game with me. I never had a single drink that day. Dad was pretty immobile by then and I'd started to reflect on how much I'd neglected them both as I devoted my life to AFC Wimbledon. Wembley let me use a disabled car parking space so we were able to get Dad into the Royal Box alongside me, Mum and Lisa. It was special, and long overdue. Having them there really was the icing on the cake for me. I was fulfilling an ambition to be a club director, to sit in the Royal Box at Wembley – and to have my mum and dad alongside me. What more could I have wished for? Just a win, I guess.

After a goalless first half, Lyle Taylor fired us into the lead after 78 minutes in front of 23,000 ecstatic Dons fans. John Green was among them, although God knows how he made it. The day before he'd been at the Indianapolis 500 motor race, then had flown over to London immediately afterwards! We had to endure 11 minutes of injury time and the tension was unbearable – until Ade Azeez was dragged down in the box and we were awarded a penalty. We then all watched, gobsmacked, as Azeez, Callum Kennedy and Akinfenwa clearly argued over who should take the spot kick. There could only be one winner and The Beast thumped the ball low into the left-hand corner. A week earlier, he'd been told his contract wouldn't be renewed – so the penalty was his last kick for our club.

Once again, we'd smashed a glass ceiling by getting into League One. But there was an even bigger prize waiting for us. For the first time ever, we would be facing the franchise in a league match as opposed to one of the cup competitions.

Chapter 55
BETRAYING OUR RULES

LOSING TO the franchise is the worst kind of defeat. Our first league game against them came in December 2016, at their place, and we were beaten 1-0. The result alone made the journey home wretched, but as I drove back I started receiving crank calls. That triggered an avalanche over the next few weeks, each abusive call – often in the middle of the night – getting more and more sinister.

I eventually tracked down the cowardly ringleader of a WhatsApp group and threatened to hand his name and address over to the police. Only then did the calls stop. But it wasn't until March 2017 that redemption truly came. We played the franchise at Kingsmeadow for the first time and won 2-0. Life was brilliant and, better still, we pretty much erased any mention of their adopted name inside our stadium.

Our match programme and tickets didn't include their name or badge, and our electronic scoreboard in the right-hand corner, opposite the main stand, only showed the letters MK.

Brilliant.

The game was given the highest priority billing by the Met Police, with around 150 officers standing by. Travelling fans were only allowed in if they'd arrived on an official franchise bus, and even then they had to walk the last 500 yards alongside a hefty police escort. Welcome to hell.

Brilliant.

Their directors were politely advised not to join any of us in our boardroom for 'security reasons'. Peter Winkelman spent the entire match standing in the away end.

Brilliant.

Then came the game: after a tense, goalless first half, Jake Reeves broke the deadlock on 61 minutes when he slammed the ball through a crowd of players. The elation was on another level and then it got even wilder nine minutes later when Lyle Taylor fired home.

Brilliant.

Everything was brilliant, Kingsmeadow was rocking and we were all feeling very pleased at the way we'd not only beaten the franchise, we'd also found a way of minimising their presence. It felt like a double whammy.

We met them again at home in September the following season. This time we lost, but we still managed to repeat everything we'd done before: their name didn't appear in all the places we'd find offensive. This time, though, the English Football League stepped in and charged us for not following their stupid rules. Apparently one of their 'new' regulations stated: 'all clubs are required to behave towards one another with the utmost good faith and not to unfairly criticise, disparage, belittle or discredit any other club.'

Oh, please, fuck off.

If anyone was guilty of breaking these rules, it was the franchise – not us. They were the ones who had disparaged and belittled us by stealing our club and our name; they were the ones who hadn't acted with 'utmost good faith'. How come they were still allowed to stick our name – Dons – in giant lettering on the outside of their stadium – when everyone knew it was inflammatory and provocative? How come nobody punished them, or ordered them to take it down?

We showed some balls and some defiance by refusing to acknowledge their existence: we behaved like our forefathers would have wanted us to. We handled it the Wimbledon way and I was proud that we'd done it. Predictably, the EFL scrambled for their rule books and charged us. They eventually dropped the charges seven months later so long as we agreed to behave.

After that, the only bit of ingenuity we showed came in 2019. We'd been drawn against the franchise in the Carabao Cup first round and the EFL made it clear they expected us to use their adopted name on our website, on tickets, in the programme, on the scoreboard – basically anywhere you might expect to see it. If we didn't, then we'd be heavily fined and God knows what else. So, we didn't bother printing a programme – which was our right – and the electronic scoreboard developed an unexpected technical problem. It wouldn't work that night.

Brilliant.

There have been attempts in the past to mend bridges but, in my mind, they have all been misguided. For instance, I was waiting for the players to emerge for a League One match at the franchise ground when, to my horror, I saw a small group of our officials walking out of the MK tunnel. They had clearly been inside the stadium but why were they coming down the bloody players' tunnel?

Those fuckers have had a cup of tea with them.

I was really distracted by it. Just before the break, I turned to my mate and said: 'Have a look over there, see what happens at half-time. I bet our lot get up and go down the tunnel, then come back out again for the second half.' Sure enough, as soon as the ref blew for half-time, they all got up – five or six of them – and trundled off down the tunnel.

It had always been our sacred code of conduct that absolutely nobody accepted any hospitality inside the franchise stadium. Fans, directors, anyone. And yet there they were, clearly crossing the line and doing exactly that. 'Look, look – there they go,' I screeched. 'What gives that lot the right to think they are so fucking different they can go inside there? They're having some form of hospitality. I don't care whether it's a bloody meat pie or they're just using a private bog, it's the thing we said we'd never do. It's completely out of order.' I really was furious, especially when I saw them coming back out for the second half. 'That's outrageous,' I ranted. 'If we held a public vote among our fans, there's no way they'd say, "Yep, go on, you enjoy yourselves."'

Not long after, Xavier Wiggins raised the issue at a Dons Trust meeting. Now it's fully agreed that nobody will ever accept any hospitality at the franchise stadium. If anything, their transgression reinforced that rule and it won't ever change – unless the franchise drop the Dons from their name. Which doesn't look like happening any day soon. And even if it did, I'd still say: 'Count me out.' The people who crossed the line that day represented themselves and not the will of our supporters. If recent matches are anything to go by, I'd say our fans feel stronger than ever before.

Chapter 56
THEY ALL WANTED NOLAN

A FORMER Premier League star, a real household name, looked destined to become our new manager in 2018 – which sounds great. Our senior execs were desperate to give him the job, but I wasn't so keen.

I wanted one of our club's own legends to take over instead.

Neal Ardley's reign had come to a sad ending on 9 November. The season had started diabolically – we'd lost 12 out of 14 league games and we looked relegation certainties.

It really was a bleak period for me personally. A few months earlier, I'd undergone an operation to remove a tumour from my lung. It wasn't cancerous, thankfully, but I was still in considerable pain – and the team's performances weren't helping.

Erik and I invited Neal round to my house, hoping to gee him up. He looked a broken man the second he walked in and we sat uneasily in my lounge, surrounded by my most treasured Wimbledon photographs and memorabilia.

The room really is a club shine. We tried to find different ways of saying, 'How can we help Neal, how do we solve this?' but everything sounded empty because what do you say to a man on the brink?

It was all platitudes: 'Neal, we'll do everything we can to support you' . . . 'Neal, you've worked miracles for our club, you're a great manager, you've done it before and you can do it again.'

And then the bottom line: 'Neal, you have to find a way to turn this round.'

There it was.

We couldn't give him any money – the one thing that might have helped most. We couldn't magic five new players outside the transfer window. And there was certainly nothing on my walls and shelves that could give him the solution he so desperately needed.

Then my mum died and my world fell apart. She needed a valve replaced in her heart, and the last words I ever said to her were on the night before her operation: 'See you tomorrow, Mum. Everything will be all right.' Only it wasn't. The op was a success, but she suffered a massive cardiac arrest soon after. She never regained consciousness: at least we were all there when the beeps suddenly stopped on her monitor.

Football had always been a massive crutch for me whenever something bad happened, but even that vanished when I needed it most. I was still in pain from my own op, my team was losing consistently, the manager I cared about dearly was in deep trouble and now my mother – an incredible woman, the matriarch of our family whom everyone loved – had passed.

It was a real low point, and I genuinely hoped things would improve when we travelled to Haringey in the FA Cup first round.

But no. Although we won 1-0, the performance was so wretched and Ards resigned immediately afterwards. Nobody was celebrating: this was a manager who had saved us on Survival Saturday, almost beaten Liverpool in the FA Cup – and then lifted us into League One. His departure was immensely sad.

Not long after, I got a phone call from another Dons legend – Wally Downes. We owe such a colossal debt to Wally. It's no exaggeration to say his blood runs yellow and blue: he adored the club when he was playing – and he adores it right now.

There'd be no Crazy Gang without Wally. He got that ball rolling, have no doubt. People think it was Vinnie Jones or John Fashanu or Dennis Wise – but it wasn't. They were all crucial, of course, and they became the public faces of the phenomenon and kept the legend alive.

But Wally got it started.

Wally was the first Dons apprentice to make it into the first team, and he went on to play in all four English divisions. Wally embodied everything Wimbledon stood for and helped instil an unbreachable togetherness among the players. Theirs was an 'us against the world' mentality, and that catapulted our club through the leagues and right to the top.

I first got to know Wally when he was a player and I was just a devoted fan at Plough Lane. He'd sometimes pass me and either ruffle my hair or give me a good-natured kick up the arse. Then, as we launched AFC Wimbledon, he'd message constantly for updates and news. As far as he was concerned, we were the true incarnation of the club he'd played for.

As soon as I answered his call, as soon as I'd said, 'Hi Wally, what's going on?' he immediately said: 'Should I apply, Iv?' I wanted to give him the job there and then. We needed somebody nuclear, and he was certainly that. He was calling from India, where he was working alongside former Crystal Palace and Manchester United legend Steve Coppell (who still advises our club and comes to our matches regularly).

'If you want to apply, then yes, but you must go through the process. How the fuck will you do it from India?' I asked.

'Don't you worry about that; I'll find a way.'

It seems so antiquated now, but Skype calls were the big thing back then and so we did a first interview with Wally using that while he was still out in Jamshedpur. I thought he was brilliant.

He talked about what we'd need: 'The players have got to be

much more resilient and certain positions definitely need strengthening,' he said. He'd been watching football's global video library, Wyscout, and seeing our games live. He clearly knew what had been happening.

'We need more togetherness; we've got to create a one-club attitude.' Wally talked a lot of sense and everyone agreed he deserved a second interview. However, that didn't go perfectly – after flying in from India, his video presentation was badly hampered by the IT system. It looked like his chances were sliding; instead, everyone was getting excited about the big Premier League name.

Kevin Nolan became an established Premier League midfielder at Bolton under Big Sam Allardyce. The club regularly finished in the top half of the table. He scored when they beat Man United at Old Trafford and he was a first-team regular when they qualified for the old UEFA Cup.

He continued to shine at Newcastle and then re-joined Big Sam at West Ham, where he was made captain and led them back to the Premier League.

His managerial career, though, was more checkered: strangely, his first club, Orient, sacked him when they were just two points off the play-offs. He then joined Notts County, saved them from relegation, but was axed a year later following a six-game run without a win.

I was wary. Yes, he was a big name, but how many times have big-name players totally failed when they switch to management? He had no history with our club and he didn't seem to be holding down jobs for very long, for whatever reason.

Was the gap between football management at our level and the more pampered world Prem players were used to just a bit too wide? We were lying second from bottom of League One and the air down there didn't smell very sweet.

I doubted Nolan had the managerial experience or the nous to save us – but I knew a man who did. For me, AFC Wimbledon badly needed an injection of Crazy Gang spirit and desire, and only one man could do that: Wally.

I made my views known. 'We are facing the trapdoor – we need to appoint someone who understands this club, who can inspire players at this level,' I argued. 'Someone who will be passionate, someone who will work at this 24/7 – someone who has yellow and blue blood in their veins.'

Nobody was listening. Maybe they were a bit start struck. Maybe Wally felt like a blast from the past. 'Oh, for fuck's sake, Ivor,' was the reply. 'Nolan is current, everyone knows who he is – he will give the club a boost just by walking into the dressing room.'

I understood their argument, but I doubted Nolan was cut from the same cloth as Wally. I was also puzzled why he'd been jettisoned by his previous two clubs. It didn't seem to make much sense.

I could see Wally's chances of getting appointed were doomed, though – until word reached me, via a personal contact I can't name, that Nolan was having his own second thoughts. My pal called unexpectedly and said: 'Ivor, trust me, he won't join – even if your lot offer him the job.'

'Why, though?' I asked, incredulously.

'I've no idea,' he insisted. 'But something has changed his mind.'

I kept this news to myself, not sure whether it was true or not. But sure enough, his agent contacted us a couple of days later and confirmed Nolan had decided to withdraw – just like I'd been told. I still don't know why – but I was massively relieved.

Perhaps the door would now open for Wally.

An emergency 'who-do-we-appoint-next?' meeting was held, and I immediately made my position clear: 'Well, there's only one candidate for me – and that's Wally.'

Then Erik did something completely out of character. Standing up, he banged his fist on the table and said: 'Fuck it, we'll give the job to Wally.'

Get in.

I'd never seen Erik do something like that ever before, and I couldn't wait to phone Wally.

'You've got the job,' I blabbered.

'You're fucking joking, aren't you? Fucking brilliant, Iv. Now I've got to get out of India.'

'How quickly can you do that?' I asked.

'Don't worry, I'll talk to Steve right now – he's a top bloke. He won't stand in my way.'

Our next game was against non-league Halifax in the FA Cup second round and, again, it was on TV.

We didn't make any announcement about Wally, but rumours started to spread. I'll never forget going to The Shay and seeing a banner hung over a terrace crash barrier that read: 'Where's Wally?'

It still makes me smile today. We drew Fleetwood away in the third round and none of us expected to win. Former Manchester City star Uwe Rösler was their manager, and it was a tough place to go.

But everything had started to come alive once Wally arrived. One of his first inspirational moves was to bring in another Dons legend, Glyn Hodges, as his assistant. It felt like we were witnessing a merging between the old Wimbledon and our new incarnation.

A renewed air of optimism developed and Glyn sorted a magnificent loan deal for one of Bournemouth's keepers – Aaron 'Rambo' Ramsdale. Yes, the one who later played for England.

We deservedly beat Fleetwood 3-2, reaching the fourth round for the first time since we'd reformed in 2002. We all prayed for a dream draw – and got one: Premier League giants West Ham United at home.

Chapter 57
HAMMERED

IT'S half-time at Kingsmeadow, we are 2-0 up against West Ham, and I'm about to have a bizarre conversation with their former owners David Sullivan and David Gold (RIP). One that completely underlined the chasm between the teams at the top and teams like us, scrapping ferociously to survive. Glyn had brought in a new winger, Dylan Connolly, from the Irish side Dundalk – and he'd just torn the Hammers apart in the first 45 minutes. I can still remember the two Davids collaring me at the interval and saying: 'Your winger – what's his name – he's rather good, isn't he?'

'Absolutely brilliant,' I cooed.

'Yes, yes. Actually, he's destroying us. He's very, very good. Where did you get him from?' asked Gold.

'We signed him from Dundalk. This is actually his first game for us,' I explained.

'Dundalk, Dundalk – where's Dundalk?' chirped Sullivan.

'Ireland.'

'We don't have any scouts there,' they said in unison, like it wasn't fair we'd found someone they hadn't in a country they'd overlooked.

'Perhaps you should do,' I countered.

'Yes, yes.' Then there was a pause as they absorbed what I'd said, until Gold continued:

'How much?'

'Five,' I admitted.

'£500,000?'

I nearly choked. 'No, no, definitely no: £5,000,' I clarified.

Then came another pregnant pause as they pondered some more.

'Blimey. You got an awful lot of player there for £5,000, didn't you,' added Sullivan.

'Yeah, looks that way at the moment,' I answered, before adding: 'We think he's really good. Perhaps you might want to buy him after this.'

'But what's the problem with him?' they asked. 'What's the snag?'

'Well, wages was a problem to be honest,' I replied.

'Yes, yes, it's always the wages,' said Gold. 'What happened then with the wages. How much is he costing?'

'Seven and a half,' I replied.

'You mean £7,500?'

'No, no, no . . . we had to go to £750 a week,' I smiled.

I'll never forget the look of sheer disbelief on their faces. A player they'd never heard of, who cost us £5,000 and £750 a week, had just bulldozed their multi-million-pound Premier League stars. The penny was beginning to drop for Messrs Sullivan and Gold, who had just splashed out a club record £42 million to bring in Brazilian international Felipe Anderson from Lazio.

I must stress, they weren't being big-time Charlies; in fact, they were both open and down to earth, to be honest. They'd just spent too long inside that Premier League bubble where everything gets inflated and distorted and everyone forgets what life is really like on the outside. They'd even innocently turned up in their West Ham United 1 and West Ham United 2 Rolls-Royces. I suspect it never dawned on them that both cars stood out like sore thumbs as they pulled up outside our humble Kingsmeadow entrance door. I believe both vehicles came in for some unwanted attention.

The fact we were 2-0 up against West Ham shouldn't really have surprised me. We've always saved something special for the FA Cup, and so it was on 26 January 2019. We were colossal underdogs, of course, and Wally's desperate bid to save us from relegation had taken a massive hit four days earlier when we were thumped 3-0 at home by Fleetwood. By contrast, West Ham had recently beaten Arsenal 1-0 thanks to a Declan Rice goal that put them ninth in the table. Their squad included stars like Andy Carroll, Michail Antonio and Javier Hernandez – and they were managed by the legendary Manuel Pellegrini.

We've no fucking chance.

Vinnie Jones didn't see it that way, though. He was part of the BT Sport commentary team, and I introduced him to my new partner, Lisa, for the first time and we all had a right giggle together before the game. I managed to hear some of his commentary before kick-off and remember the BT presenter asking: 'What do you reckon, Vinnie – surely this West Ham side will be too much for Wimbledon?'

His reply was classic Vinnie Jones: 'I don't fancy them at all – half of them are wearing gloves. Just you watch: Wimbledon are going to serve this up to them.' It made me giggle. If anyone could smell an upset, it would surely be Vinnie, who was also best pals with Wally.

None of us, though, could have foreseen just how brilliant Connolly would be. He battered the West Ham defence, launching a barrage of crosses into the box. Kwesi Appiah and Scott Wagstaff gave us a deserved 2-0 lead and it got even better after the break. I was still telling everyone about my chat with the two Davids, when – just 37 seconds into the half – Wagstaff struck again with a brilliant flick that left keeper Adrian stranded. Pellegrini had already brought on Anderson and Felipe Perez at half-time, and they both hit back to make the score 3-2. Our nerves were jangling but, two minutes from time, 19-year-old Toby Sibbick headed home to seal a famous 4-2 triumph.

It felt like the Wimbledon of old, like we were preserving a wonderful tradition that would have made Allen Batsford, the Crazy Gang and all the heroes from yesteryear extremely proud. The fact that it had all been masterminded by one of those very people, Wally, made it even sweeter and even more profound.

We were still bottom of the league, though. Could he now engineer a great escape? All the way through this period, Wally would talk in weeks. 'This is a three-point, six-point or nine-point week,' he'd say. 'Nine points up for grabs this week, but we'll settle for seven.' Or: 'This is a six-point week but if we get four we'll be doing all right.' It was a ceaseless mantra and it started to make sense. The rejuvenated players pulled off some significant results in some big games and the fans started to get increasingly excited. Suddenly, everyone was chanting: 'Wally's at the Wheel.'

We'd have a big win and it'd lift us agonisingly close to safety – only for another team to pull off an unexpected result and shunt us back down again. But the gap was definitely closing.

Nothing seemed to faze Wally. He definitely injected Crazy Gang resilience and self-belief into the players and kept repeatedly telling them: 'If you haven't conceded, you haven't lost.' Then he'd add: 'There is no finer result in football than a 1-0 win.' That meant we'd defended heroically and been too solid to break down.

The players bonded like never before. Rambo, in particular, embodied a new 'we have no fear' attitude. He was a magnificent keeper, powerfully built with lightning reflexes, but he was also a real presence – dominating the area and marshalling his defenders.

And Wally never wavered for a moment, even when we didn't get a result we'd hoped for. We went to Shrewsbury, who were also battling to survive, but only managed a goalless draw. Many of our fans thought that was the end: if we couldn't beat Shrewsbury then we were fucked. But Wally wasn't having that. 'It's another point to the total we need,' he'd say. 'Don't disrespect it.'

By early March, though, we were still nine points from safety. Then the Wally factor really kicked in and we amassed 20 points from the next 11 matches. By the last game of the season – away at already relegated Bradford – we only needed a draw to survive. Just to be in that position was a miracle.

We took over 2,000 fans to Valley Parade and they gave it their all, singing and chanting relentlessly. The match itself was completely sterile; in fact, I was more concerned about Dickie Guy, who was so wound up I spent most of the match watching him rather than the game. He looked like he would combust at any moment and, when the final whistle blew, I was more relieved to see he had survived than the actual team.

Then it sank in. Wally had indeed masterminded our great escape. Everyone was hugging and punching the air and applauding. Rambo led the celebrations, climbing up into the stands to orchestrate a mass sing-song. Our fans were running and jumping all over the pitch, but then the party was sullied when some idiot let off a flare. Of all the football grounds, that's the last place to do something so inexcusable and it was a genuinely embarrassing and uncomfortable moment. Some of the Bradford fans and directors were furious and justifiably so.

I made my way down to the team coach, desperate to give Wally a huge hug. 'What a fucking amazing job you've done,' I said.

'Yeah, yeah,' he replied, like it was no big deal. He was being very humble but I wasn't having it and continued: 'I reckon you're the only fucking person on this planet who could have got this club out of that situation in these circumstances.' And I truly believed that.

Wally was the right man at the right time and we owed him an enormous debt of gratitude. Which makes what happened next even more reprehensible.

Chapter 58
THE WALLY BETTING FIASCO

I ALWAYS knew Wally Downes had a self-destruct button but I never expected him to press it quite so stupidly. He fucked up big time and that was bad enough. Just as sickening was the way our club reacted. Instead of standing by the man who had engineered our relegation survival, who had masterminded our euphoric victory over West Ham, they abandoned him when he needed them most. They hung him out to dry.

There is no doubt the new 2019 season started abysmally: we didn't win a single league game in our first 11 matches, and lost eight of them. As unlikely as it sounds, we weren't actually playing that badly and I kept telling myself we'd be all right. It just needed one good win to turn things round. But the grumbles of discontent were undeniably spreading on the terraces.

I'd also noticed Wally didn't seem to be his usual ebullient, bullish self. It felt like there was something weighing on his mind but I hadn't a clue what – other than the results. We'd just lost narrowly yet again, this time at Peterborough, when Wally phoned.

'You all right,' I asked.

'No, not really. I've fucked up, Iv.'

I thought he was talking about the 3-2 defeat and said: 'Don't be ridiculous, we're only 11 games in and the team is actually playing well.'

'No, no – you don't understand. I'm being done for gambling.

Silence.

'What do you mean?', I stuttered.

'I've had around £35 worth of bets,' he answered.

In the past, people in football could have a bet on matches – so long as it wasn't anything they were involved in. However, that all changed in 2016 when it was forbidden for anyone in the game to bet on football at all. That included managers, coaches, players – and non-playing staff such as myself. Now I realised why he'd been looking more downcast than I'd ever seen before. It wasn't just the results. He was under investigation and shouldering the burden entirely on his own.

'What sort of bets were they?' I asked.

'It was just some women's football matches out in South America somewhere,' he replied. 'Me and the missus had a few drinks and placed the bets for a laugh. None of it was serious, it was just a bloody giggle.'

'Are you telling me they're investigating you just for that?' I asked, incredulously. 'Wally, are you absolutely sure you didn't have a bet on any of our matches – or any league games here?'

'Categorically not,' he answered with considerable indignation. 'I'm telling you, I never bet on any games here – either Wimbledon's or anyone else's.'

I believed him completely but I also knew he was in deep shit. It was typical of Wally to be in a mess of his own making. 'You knobhead, for fuck's sake,' I cursed – as much out of frustration as anger. This wasn't going to end well.

'What do you mean, Iv?' he said, almost innocently. He'd genuinely no idea where this might go.

'Do you want me to lie to you – or do you want the honest truth,' I replied.

'The truth.'

'Okay. Well, if you get any form of a ban because of this, you're fucking toast. There, I've said it, and I'm not joking. They'll bin you, Wally.'

There was a pause before he replied: 'That's a bit brutal, isn't it?'

'I'm sorry, Wally, but that's the way it is. You'll be done for if you're banned.'

'Well, I'm told I won't get a ban,' he insisted.

'In that case, you might just wriggle clear. But Wally, you need to start turning things round on the pitch as well because that's also counting against you.'

That came as less of a shock to him. 'Yeah, yeah, I know that,' he said. 'I don't mind getting dumped for football reasons. I can live with not being a good enough manager but I can't live with getting flung out because of so-called betting irregularities.'

Wally completely accepted that he'd screwed up and he kept apologising constantly because he knew I'd fought to get him the job, and he knew I was his biggest ally at the club.

'I'm so sorry, Iv, I've really fucked this up, I can't believe I was so stupid, I shouldn't have done it, I know. I'm so sorry.'

I kept telling him not to apologise. I didn't feel let down – I just knew he had the biggest self-destruct button in football. Could I ever be surprised by anything he did? I don't think so. Fucking up, without really meaning to, was part of what made Wally who he is. He's either calculated or completely wild – just like the Crazy Gang. And this was typical Crazy Gang behaviour.

I also knew him well enough to know he was telling me the truth. There were no tell-tale pauses or contradictions: he was letting it all tumble out freely and without censor. I instinctively sided with him. If Wally was deliberately trying to defy the FA, then I'm pretty sure he'd have wagered a hell of a lot more than £35. And I very much doubt he would have lumped it all on something as random as women's football matches in South America. But I also instinctively feared the FA would seize an easy opportunity to make an example of a household name and ban him. It's what bullies do.

I remember putting the phone down and feeling completely crestfallen. The knives were already out for him; there were people who had never wanted him in the first place – and I couldn't see any way that he'd be found not guilty. The only possible hope was that he wouldn't get banned. That was my way of reading it but it felt like a longshot.

I started to canvass other board members to see what they were thinking. To my dismay, there was a strong tide pushing to suspend Wally immediately – before the FA had made any decision. Our new chief operating officer Joe Palmer strongly believed the club had a duty to remove Wally from his position. 'The club's reputation is at stake here,' he argued. 'If we keep him in his current role, we will be sending out the wrong message. We have to be seen to be doing the right thing.'

I can't criticise Joe for wanting to handle the crisis in a corporate, fire-fighting sort of way. It was the way of the modern HR-driven world and everyone seemed to agree with Joe and not me. In the Crazy Gang days, the club would have closed ranks and stood together, refusing to be pushed around by the outside world. Those days were clearly over.

Then more wild accusations started to circulate. Reports conveniently emerged from the training ground that Wally had allegedly been placing bets while the players were physically training. I knew Wally owned greyhounds and sometimes they'd run at lunchtime meetings. It was entirely possible he was watching one of his dogs on a TV screen while his coaches were putting players through their paces. I don't know. It really seemed so insignificant to me. Nobody had mentioned it while we were beating West Ham or pulling off our great escape.

It sounded like bollocks but it suited the anti-Wally narrative that was gaining momentum. Rumours like that magically surface whenever people are looking for reasons to oust a manager. They wanted it to be true because it strengthened their argument.

A Dons Trust board meeting was called and I defended Wally passionately. 'We need to stand by our manager,' I argued. 'Suspending him is not the right way to go. If he's banned, then I accept there's nothing we can do but we should be supporting him until that actually happens – and we should be praying that it doesn't.'

My pleas fell on deaf ears, though. There was too much angst in the room and the board voted in favour of suspending him. Shortly after, I got a call from Joe, saying: 'Under no circumstances can you speak to Wally, or email or text him. You can't have any communication with him at all. We must handle this correctly. We must act responsibly as a club.'

'He's still our employee,' I protested.

'But he's under investigation, Ivor,' was his reply.

I was in no state of mind to follow orders and phoned Wally to talk it over. He was devastated and said: 'I know I shouldn't have done it but I expected a bit more support.'

'So did I,' I replied. 'I tried my hardest, Wally, but they just wouldn't listen.'

Then I wrote an email to every key person at the club, explaining why I thought their decision was outrageous. We should be supporting Wally, I argued. I agreed that we needed a procedure in place should he be banned – but until then, we should be working with him and representing him because he was still our employee. I was absolutely dejected and got even more pissed off when club legends started phoning me.

First up was Vinnie Jones. 'If Wally gets the tin tack over this, that's it – we'll never have anything to do with Wimbledon again,' he raged. Now I love Vinnie, I really do, but he was barking at the wrong person.

'Vin, honestly, that's harsh,' I replied.

'What do you fucking mean?'

'Wally's got a self-destruct button and he's gone and pressed it. You can't blame the club or anyone else. If he's banned, how can he seriously stay on?

'I'm not being a turncoat, Vinnie. When Wally rang me and told me what he'd done, that's exactly what I said to him. I'm doing everything I bloody can to help him but you can't blame the club. They didn't create this situation.

'I'll support Wally, I'll do everything possible but I'm not the silly cunt who put the bets on. He's the silly cunt who did that.'

To be fair, Vinnie took in everything I said. I knew he loved Wally deeply and desperately wanted this to blow over. 'Ivor, he fucking loves this club, he loves this job, you've got to do everything you can,' he said. And he kept on phoning me after that for updates.

Wally's old manager, Dave 'Harry' Bassett, was another on the phone, and there were plenty of other calls from all the leading characters. They were all unloading and I understood that. Wally was one of their own. 'If they don't treat him right, then that's it. I'm done, I'm gone.' That was very much the message I was getting from every one of them.

The Crazy Gang was for life.

I spoke to Wally all the time and we both felt optimistic when the League Managers' Association claimed he wouldn't get banned. But I increasingly realised that was no longer the issue: it was pretty obvious the club wanted him out, banned or not. Glyn Hodges had taken over in Wally's absence and results had started to improve. That helped the anti-Wally brigade enormously who argued we must stick with a winning formula.

About a month later, Wally was summoned to attend an FA hearing. As far as I am concerned, it heralded a new low and one of the most shameful moments in our club's history. Not one single representative from AFC Wimbledon went with him. The man who had saved us a few months earlier was literally thrown to the sharks, like he was a stranger to us all. He was completely abandoned and it still upsets me to this day. True to form, the FA did what it always does. Wally was fined £3,000 and banned for four weeks for placing eight small bets between 30 November 2013 and 12 July 2019.

As soon as I heard their wretched verdict, I called him and said: 'That's it mate, you know it is. There's no way back.'

Wally took it on the chin but his pride came out fighting. 'What matters now is the way the club announces it,' he said. 'If they're going to sack me, then it must be for football reasons and our bad run of results. I can live with that – but I can't live with the other.'

There's no doubt some influential people at the club wanted to throw him under the bus, and I never fully understood why. I started to wonder whether they were ashamed of our history and would prefer to see the club disassociate itself from the Crazy Gang and the Wimbledon spirit of old.

I really don't know but I do know things got increasingly heated. Wally asked one of football's real gentlemen, former Crystal Palace manager Alan Smith, to help mediate and a meeting was arranged at his house in leafy Surrey. I'd be there – along with Wally and Joe Palmer.

The atmosphere was tense, to put it mildly. We were in an office annexe: Wally was sitting on an individual chair, Smithy on another, while Joe and I were perched on a couch. Outside stretched a beautiful garden which I think we all stared at whenever we couldn't bear to look at one another.

It really was one of those meetings: Wally wouldn't look at Joe, Joe predominantly kept his eyes down, while Smithy was 'okay whatever happens, when we leave today we will all know which way we are going'.

Wally made his position clear right from the start. 'I'm deeply sorry for what's happened but you have to let me go for football reasons and nothing else.'

Joe didn't agree and insisted: 'I don't think that can be done,' while I interjected: 'Why not? I can't see one good reason why we can't do that?'

'Well it wouldn't be true for starters,' said Joe.

'But it is really,' I countered. 'Let's face it – the results were bad. Wally didn't win any games in the first 11 matches and now he's going to be banned for a month. We have to let him go to maintain continuity on the pitch.'

There was a lot of barbed exchanges after that and some unpleasant words were thrown around. Wally was losing his temper with Joe, while Smithy was flabbergasted that Wally had gone to the FA tribunal on his own. Mercifully, no punches were thrown. But Wally didn't shake hands with Joe at the end, which was uncomfortable to witness.

'No hard feelings,' said Joe, to which Wally snapped: 'Plenty of hard feelings.'

In the end, the club statement tip-toed precariously through a middle ground. 'Wally leaves on mutually agreed terms and with our sincerest gratitude for his time with the club,' it started.

It did reference the fact he'd been suspended when the FA charged him with 'alleged betting contraventions' but it didn't go into specific details and it didn't mention the punishment. Instead, it stated: 'While Wally's FA disciplinary process concluded last week, the board believe that a change of first-team manager is the best option to help the club maintain its recent upturn in performances.'

Looking back, Wally knows he fucked up and I know he fucked up. He was literally his own worst enemy. I'm absolutely certain the investigation affected him immensely and contributed towards our dismal run of results once the season started. He'd carried the burden entirely on his own and told nobody because he'd been told not to. As far as I'm concerned, the club handled the whole affair poorly. The way we treated an absolute hero was shameful and cast a very dark shadow over that period in our history.

I'm biased, I know. But I want to share the following true story because it absolutely sums up the Wally I know and love. From the moment we reformed in 2002, we were determined to make our presence felt within the community and support as many local causes as we could. Managers and players would be asked to turn up at events and Wally was no exception. With him, though, it was different. His attitude wasn't just 'I'll do it', it was truly 'I *want* to do it.' There's a big difference.

For instance, the Leyton Road Centre is very close to my heart. It does amazing work for adults with learning disabilities and one day they asked: 'Do you think Wally would come to the opening of our new centre?'

'Yeah, I think he will,' I replied. I gave him a call and his instant response was: 'Of course I will.'

We both arrived together and within seconds of walking in, he'd separated from me completely. He was off doing his own thing, spending proper time with people, communicating on their level and listening intently to what they were saying. Everyone was getting his attention.

I'd never seen a manager be so inclusive and genuine like that. The staff and the people there still talk about him to this day. 'Remember when Wally came in?' And every time they came to one of our matches, he'd come to see them – without fail.

Fucking hell, Wally.

Chapter 59
OUR FANS SAVE THE CLUB

EVERYTHING was in meltdown: we were critically short of funds, the company building our new stadium was threatening to halt work and two complete strangers were plotting to seize control of the club. Oh – and one more thing: the bloody Covid pandemic struck at the precise moment we were trying to build a new football ground. It really was calamitous. Our dream of a new home in Plough Lane looked increasingly doomed just when we looked so close to making it happen. There didn't seem to be any hope of salvation. We were faced with a barrage of catastrophes that dwarfed anything we'd encountered before. Everyone was holding emergency meetings but nobody was coming up with any solutions.

I didn't have any answers, either. But I knew who did. Our fans. From day one, they had been the one constant we could always depend on. When we needed them, they were there.

'You can't keep expecting the fans to dig us out of a hole,' I kept being told. I wasn't so sure. 'You never know until you ask them,' I'd reply. I believed they wanted Plough Lane as much as me. They had seen the cranes and bulldozers move in, they had seen the skeletal girders and pillars of our stands starting to rise and they had seen the beginnings of a new pitch starting to emerge.

They could imagine being there on a matchday, wearing their yellow and blue shirts, drinking with mates, making a noise, singing new songs, creating a fortress. They wanted to own that; they certainly didn't want two mystery outsiders suddenly owning the club they had helped raise from the ashes. When everything else looked doomed, I believed our fans would carry us home.

Once planning permission was granted, we plunged straight

into finding a company that could physically build our new stadium and eventually chose one in Swansea. They'd built the Liberty Stadium, where Ospreys rugby union club played. However, things started going wrong pretty quickly. Building costs had rocketed dramatically after Boris called in our planning approval; by the time we started construction, all our original budgets were way out. About two months after the Swansea contractors picked up the project, they backed off. They could see costs were out of control so they stepped away before work on demolishing the greyhound stadium physically started.

There then followed a very quick and short parade of who should step in. The Buckingham Group were the stand-out contenders: they were building Brentford's new stadium at the time, so they were almost on our doorstep already – and that really helped. Demolition work finally started in July 2018. By then, though, we had succumbed to an unforeseen temptation. Instead of ring-fencing every penny we got from selling Kingsmeadow, we spent some of the money on reinforcing the first team.

At the time, the side was struggling in League One and none of us wanted to be relegated – especially with a new stadium on the horizon. There should have been £21 million in the kitty from the section 106 and selling Kingsmeadow: instead, it was nearer £19.5 million. The shortfall was in the playing budget. In hindsight, it was a mistake, but I fully understood why we did it. We already had one of the lowest budgets in League One, the team badly needed bolstering, and we were all confident the new stadium would quickly bring in new revenue streams.

None of us knew Covid was lurking round the corner. Then came another huge blow: the ground where we wanted to build our new home needed cleansing. Asbestos had been used within the greyhound stadium and other pollutants were also found underground. The clean-up operation would cost us another £1 million we hadn't budgeted for. Add to that the £2 million Boris had cost us, and we were practically £4.5 million down before we even started.

Nevertheless, work got under way. Bulldozers and cranes and construction workers moved in and fans somehow repeatedly broke into the site on an almost daily basis to take photographs. Everyone was excited. Behind the scenes, though, we all knew there wasn't enough money to complete the build. Buckingham eventually twigged and threatened to stop construction altogether.

Around this time, Peter Miller, one of the club's longest-serving servants and a former director, met the founder of the ASOS online fashion chain, Nick Robertson, who lived in Wimbledon village. Miller invited him to a game and, although a Chelsea season ticket holder, he was captivated by the atmosphere at Kingsmeadow. Robertson liked the idea of supporting his local team and, as he became more aware of our plight, he injected £2.5 million into the club for a 10 per cent stake – just when we needed it most. He subsequently joined the board and now exercises considerable influence over the way the club is run. On its own, Robertson's investment still wasn't enough, though. In fact, it opened the door to two mystery investors, who each offered to match his £2.5 million. However, they fundamentally disagreed with fan ownership and would only invest if they could end up controlling the club.

It was a watershed moment. It felt like everything we stood for, everything we were and wanted to be, was on a precipice. Many feared it was the end of the road: the two mystery investors had us over a barrel. We either took their money and relinquished control, or we kissed goodbye to Plough Lane and even the club we had raised from the ashes. And that's when I said: 'We need to trust the fans. They will have a view on this.'

An emergency Dons Trust meeting was arranged just before New Year 2020. Sure enough, a miracle happened. Four passionate club supporters, Xavier Wiggins, Damian Woodward, Graeme

Price and Charlie Talbot, proposed the launch of a bond scheme, whereby fans could invest their savings and receive a much higher rate of interest than high street banks were offering at the time.

If anyone ever doubted what Wimbledon fans wanted, what motivated them, what they valued and what they cherished, then those doubts were erased there and then. The response was breathtaking. The bond became the most successful football club loan scheme in the UK, raising over £5.5 million. In fact, it was so successful that a second launch raised another £4 million.

The club also launched a crowdfunding scheme and that brought in a further £2.5 million. The fans had spoken: they wanted Plough Lane, they wanted to keep their club and they were willing to dig deep into their own pockets to make it happen. The two mystery investors could go fuck themselves.

Chapter 60

WE ARE HOME – 9,000 GHOSTS

IT WAS meant to be the pinnacle of everything we had been striving for: our return to Plough Lane. We'd saved our club, we'd got back into the Football League, we'd built a new stadium from our own pockets – and now we were going home. Ever since we'd played our last game there in 1991, we'd dreamt about this moment. Yellow and blue scarves and banners would be everywhere, 'A-F-C Wim-ble-don' would reverberate around our shiny new stands and we'd all be witnesses to a homecoming that we'd talk about for ever. And now the day had come. Our new stadium was complete and ready to host its first game on 3 November 2020.

There had been horrendous moments when we'd seriously discussed building just one main stand, with the other three sides roped off with nothing behind them. Just empty spaces like you see in park football. Our fans would have to cram into the one stand, somehow. But the Plough Lane Bond had put an end to that nightmare and given us the revenue to construct one showpiece stand – good enough for any Premier League club in my book – and three smaller, temporary stands that could be turned into something grander whenever we needed more capacity. One thousand construction workers had helped get us to this point.

Every day, I'd walk out on to the newly laid pitch, a carpet of grass deftly stitched into an innovative mix of artificial layers below. It was pristine and looked like a giant snooker table to me. Then I'd turn and look up in awe at the majestic main stand with its glass-fronted executive boxes and tiers of seating. I couldn't wait to join our fans there, hear their voices and see their banners with the profound messages that said everything: 'We Are The Resurrection And We Are The Light', 'There Is A Light That Never Goes Out' and 'In The Wider Interests of Football'.

Our long, torturous struggle was about to end: AFC Wimbledon would finally complete the circle with our final act of defiance. It would be historic; it would be symbolic. A bunch of scruffy-arsed fans like us had made the impossible happen. Plough Lane wasn't just a new stadium, it was a beacon for football supporters everywhere that underlined what fans can achieve. The moment our players walked down the new tunnel on to the new pitch, they'd not only hear the roar of 9,000 supporters inside our new stadium, they'd also feel the admiration of the entire football world.

Only none of that happened. Instead, as they walked out to face Doncaster Rovers, all they heard was silence. All they saw was 9,000 empty blue and yellow plastic seats – plus some cardboard cut-outs of our fans, fidgeting precariously as the evening wind threatened to blow them over. Our new home was deserted. The showpiece West Stand was mute. The tiered rows of seats were unoccupied; the bars and lounges and executive boxes closed and lifeless behind locked doors. All the people who desperately wanted to be there, the people who had earned this moment, the ones who had helped make it happen, were nowhere to be seen.

Instead of an explosion of noise and colour and excitement and joy, we stared out at 9,000 ghosts. The only people who witnessed Joe Pigott score our first goal back at Plough Lane – and an entertaining 2-2 draw – were me, a handful of staff and execs, and the 1,000 cardboard cut-outs. The pandemic had struck and our homecoming was one of its victims. Football fans across the country were banned from attending matches, without exception. Our stadium could open – but nobody would be allowed in. It was the saddest thing I'd ever seen and I actually felt physically sick. I realised there would be people who would have gone to that game – whom it meant so much to – who would never get another chance to experience what we'd built.

For instance, time had run out for my dad. He'd followed every step of our journey, he'd seen our new stadium being constructed, and yet he passed on 22 September 2020. There'd be many others who wouldn't see us cross the line. Every game from then on was horrible. We would not be home until our fans were allowed in. And that was riddled with uncertainty. We'd have to wait for vaccines to be rolled out and we'd need to stage test events so our new stadium could pass stringent safety regulations.

Even when the 2020–21 season ended, so much was still up the creek within the stadium itself. Everywhere you looked, jobs needed finishing off, snagging needed attention. Covid was still in the air and the number of builders allowed on site had to be limited.

A turning point came on 17 July when we were allowed to stage a test event against a Brentford under-21 side – in front of 2,000 fans. I remember walking along the main corridor in the main West Stand and seeing people arrive. Ian Cooke and his wife Pat were among the first and it felt great, really special. I walked along to the Gold Lounge (as it was called then) about 30 minutes before kick-off and was talking to Lynsey Coleman, marketing manager of the Centre Court shopping mall in Wimbledon. All of a sudden, I heard a little bit of clapping and cheering – then it got progressively louder and, for the first time, I got emotional. Tears were welling up in my eyes. For the first time, I'd heard the sound of life in the stadium. After everything we had been through, the sheer anxiety, the trials and tribulations of an 18-year project, the pandemic and all the unforeseen problems that triggered, I finally succumbed to the emotion of what it all meant.

People are here.

It was a bizarre moment. People were cheering our team and all they'd done was come out to do their warm-up. It absolutely broke me and the tears started to flow. We still needed to stage one more practice match against Scunthorpe. This time we had to get 4,500 fans in on 31 July – a tall order in the middle of summer – and we had to make sure some of them used the new lounges and bars. In the end, I got on to St George's Hospital and we gave away tickets to the staff there.

Then came 14 August 2021 . . .

Chapter 61
WE ARE HOME – JACK

IT WAS the drive that got to me. I hadn't physically driven to Plough Lane to see a match in front of a proper crowd for 30 years. Something made me want to retrace one of the routes I used to take: I wanted to see our fans strolling along the streets with their scarves and banners. I wanted to hear the buzz and feel the excitement in the air; I wanted to witness their journeys to the ground. It'd be part of coming home.

I got to the towering Prince of Wales pub, its whitewashed facade dominating Wimbledon town centre and there they were – groups of our fans, all in replica shirts, standing outside clutching pints. From there, I turned slowly down the Broadway and then went left, down Trinity Road. All along were clusters of yellow and blue and laughter and singing and flags.

By the time I reached Gap Road, I'd passed fans waiting at bus stops, or going into shops to stock up on snacks and sweets for their kids. That took me back to 2008 when I walked into Stephen Alambritis's office for the first time and said: 'Every time we play at home, Wimbledon's businesses will flourish.' These businesses were about to get the lifeblood pumping back into them because football was coming home.

By the time I reached the crossroads with Haydons Road, I was nine-year-old Ivor Heller all over again. The one who had been overawed by the waft of salt and vinegar as I'd passed Mr Bissell's chip shop; the one who had stood in amazement when I saw the Plough Lane floodlights for the first time. It felt like history was repeating itself. 'Walking down the Haydons Road, to see the Wombles' aces.'

Our opponents for the first game of the new League One season were Bolton Wanderers. I couldn't have wished for better: like us, they had a big, rich history. In 1995, we'd beaten them 3-2 in the opening game of the Premier League season. Was it an omen?

I had a lot of work on, hospitality was sold out, and I had a lot of people to look after, not least Mayor of London Sadiq Khan. I didn't give a damn about politics – Sadiq had resurrected our move back to Plough Lane after Boris Johnson had done his best to wreck it. Sadiq was more than welcome in my book.

Seeing the ground packed, and hearing the roar as the players came out was electrifying, of course. We'd done it. To be honest, though, I'd already had my emotional moments by then. I just wanted the game to match the occasion – and I wasn't to be disappointed.

Will Nightingale scored the opening goal, which was great because he was a local lad who had come through the ranks and truly loved the club. But Bolton threatened to wreck the party by storming into a 3-1 lead. We pulled one back with a penalty and then Dapo Mebude tore down the left wing, body-swerved lunging tackles, cut in, and curled an absolute beauty into the far corner. It was one of the all-time great solo goals and the stadium erupted. Everything about that goal embodied everything that had brought us home. Defiance, refusing to surrender, refusing to give in, fighting to the end – it was all packed into that sublime equaliser. Everyone went home ecstatic.

Behind the scenes, loads had gone wrong – especially with the catering – but it was all teething problems, stuff that could be sorted. What mattered most was what our fans thought of the stadium – and it was clear, they loved it. By the time I got home, I was elated but completely drained. Then my phone rang and a voice said: 'Ivor – you need to know this.'

'What?'

'One of our fans has died.'

'What on earth are you talking about?' I replied, a bit disbelievingly.

'A bloke called Jack has died.'

'What – how – when – at the game? What are you talking about? Who's Jack?'

The person who'd called didn't know all the details but my phone never stopped ringing after that. I eventually realised Jack was someone I'd known since he was a kid: Jack Lonergan. I'm still proud to consider his dad, Michael, a friend. He and Jack were as close as any father and son could ever hope to be. Jack had been our mascot at our very first game in the Combined Counties League against Sandhurst; he'd played for our youth team and was a very promising keeper. He was also a talented musician and had been in a band since he was 13 years old. In fact, he eventually became a music teacher because he wanted to give music to people who either had no access to it, or simply couldn't afford it. I think that says everything about Jack.

He was a massive Dons fan and became a volunteer for the

Dons Local Action Group, helping deliver vital food parcels during the pandemic. He'd gone to the Bolton game with his dad and I'm sure he went through all the emotions someone so connected to our club would have felt that day. The pair had returned home when Jack was inexplicably struck by the heart condition, sudden arrhythmic death syndrome. He was 28 years old.

Jack's tragic death became my overriding memory of our first proper game back at Plough Lane. How do you rationalise it? One of the last things he did in life was go to our new home with his father, see and experience everything we had built, and enjoy a thrilling game of football. But he should still be doing that now. He was far too young to be taken like that. No matter how obsessed we get, no matter how much we let it dominate our lives, there's one thing we must never forget. Football isn't more important than life and death and family. And Jack was family.

Chapter 62

MY ROLE FOR 21 YEARS

I CAN confidently say I raised millions of pounds for AFC Wimbledon during my 21 years as the club's commercial director. My big-hitting moment came right at the start, when Sports Interactive got in touch after hearing me talk on the radio. Our first front-of-shirt sponsorship with them in 2002 brought in more than most teams were getting in League One and League Two – and even the Championship. Only we were in the Combined Counties. Their sponsorship kept growing from there and was huge by the time we reached the Conference. They have made a crucial financial contribution to us over the years.

It was my job to bring in as much revenue as I possibly could from the outside world. In the beginning, that largely meant persuading local businesses to get involved and I launched The Dons Directory, which was hugely successful. It was a bit like the old Yellow Pages – but for Dons fans. Anyone could advertise their business in it for £100. All human life was in there: from the bloke who did garden fencing, to people who did embroidery on shirts, to solicitors to electricians, plumbers, carpenters and all sorts of trades people. They all shared one thing in common – they were all Wimbledon fans. Brendan Farrell, known as Benny, was a mortgage advisor. He went in the directory, picked up some clients, then next year paid for a perimeter board and an ad in the programme. So he went from spending £100 to £3,000 plus with the club. That's how it worked.

Even in the non-league years, we'd get £20,000 off companies to sponsor one of the end stands at Kingsmeadow, plus a further £30,000 for the main one. Businesses would phone us and say, 'We want to spend five grand,' and they'd frequently end up spending £10,000 instead.

I'd dabbled with life as a music promoter – organising a sell-out Mumford and Sons concert at Wimbledon Theatre in 2011, after discovering the lead singer Marcus Mumford was a huge fan of the team. It was an eye-opener, dealing with the band's requests and their laid-back attitude to something completely out of my comfort zone! They were absolute stars and did us proud, raising £40,000 in the process.

I even negotiated the rights to enable us to create our new mascot, Haydon the Womble, with the support of Wombles creator Elisabeth Beresford MBE. The original licensing agreement for Wandle the Womble, named after the nearby river Wandle, had expired shortly after the club was airlifted to Buckinghamshire. It was 2006 by the time we were able to renegotiate and there was nothing light-hearted about it – a complex legal agreement had to be drawn up with Rainbow Productions. A competition was held to choose the new name and Haydon was picked, after Haydons Road – the nearest railway station to both our old and new grounds in Plough Lane.

Dean Parsons has been Haydon ever since and pretty much morphed into a human Womble. Strict rules forbid anyone to see who is inside the costume, but Dean was powerless when a Luton Town thug pulled Haydon's head off as he walked along our pitch perimeter. A stunned Kingsmeadow then witnessed Dean grapple with his assailant before desperately pulling the head back into position.

I was given a revenue target to hit every season – and it would always go up. Erik was a taskmaster all right: he'd never, ever set it too low. As always, though, he'd listen. If the target was unrealistic, and I protested, he'd take on board my reasoning. Sadly, that wasn't the case in more recent years. For example, a lot of ill-conceived pressure was piled on me to get a new front-of-shirt sponsor and elbow Sports Interactive. I was horrified. How could our club even consider ditching such a loyal and vital partner?

'You won't get any better,' I argued. 'Their sponsorship is proportionately way better than anyone else at our level. Most companies would offer far less.'

Erik would have listened to that, every time. But the new regime thought they knew better. I'd always insisted on being upfront with people like Sports Interactive, so I went to their supremo, Miles Jacobson, and said: 'I'm truly sorry but I've been told to look for a new shirt sponsor because we need more money.'

Miles took it on the chin and replied: 'Well, if you can get it, great – but I very much doubt you will.' He knew the market better than the people at AFC Wimbledon did.

'There's no more money on offer from us but if you do find someone, then we will step aside and spend our money somewhere else within the club.'

By then, we'd contacted a renowned sports agency, believing they would help find a better deal. After a few months, the agency admitted they couldn't get anywhere near what we were already getting. 'I know,' was my response.

Covid was a particularly tough time commercially. Companies

were extremely reluctant to spend – why advertise to empty seats – but we were about to move into Plough Lane and needed our new stadium to bring in money, quickly.

During our final days at Kingsmeadow, I got a call from the huge waste management company, Powerday – founded by the Irish tycoon Mick Crossan. We talked and they were interested in an exclusive sponsorship deal, worth £60,000 to us. However, no other companies from the same industry could be involved with AFC Wimbledon. And that was a big problem. At the time, Cappagh were spending £3,500 with us, and Reston Waste a further £12,000. I got on really well with both Andrew Reston and Cappagh's Michael Ferncombe. I didn't want to jettison them – but £60,000 was too much to turn down.

I phoned Michael and explained the problem. 'This is leaving a sour taste for me,' I groaned. 'I feel blackmailed but there might be a solution – after all, you're a big company and I have a great idea.'

'Go on – what?' he replied.

'Why not become the first, historic sponsor of the main stand at our new ground in Plough Lane?'

'How much will that cost?' he asked.

He's interested.

'Well – it should be £60,000 but, if you twist my arm, I can make it 50 . . .'

'Consider your arm twisted then,' he replied.

And that was it, deal done. Then I went to see Andrew Reston and told him the same story. He was livid that an industry rival, Powerday, had tried to elbow his company out of AFC Wimbledon. So I offered him the chance to become our digital sponsor, which meant his branding would be on every single bit of communications we put out. He'd been planning to spend £15,000 with us. Instead, I got 80 grand. Even when Covid hit, I still got those deals over the line.

Overall, I managed to bring in £700,000 during the pandemic, which was phenomenal. I even created the cardboard cut-outs of our fans that filled the empty North Stand seats. Supporters simply had to send in a digital photo of themselves. Some even sent in pictures of their dogs! I then got one of our business club members to turn the images into cut-outs. It was a great earner for the club – fans paid something like £50 for the privilege, yet the cut-outs only cost us a tenner each to produce.

Nobody really acknowledged what I'd done during such a desperately tough period in our history – except Joe Palmer, who was chief executive at the time. I'll never forget his words: 'Ivor, you have shat an absolute miracle!'

Chapter 63
AGONY AND ECSTASY

IT WAS one of the lowest points in my life. I stared out onto our pristine, new pitch at our pristine, new home and tears unashamedly filled my eyes. I couldn't stop them.

My tenure as commercial director at AFC Wimbledon was over. I was distraught.

The more I stared at the pitch, the more the memories came flooding back. I was standing in one of our executive boxes and I couldn't help flashing back to the moment when there were four of us, in my little print-factory office, desperately trying to save our club. Filling in that London FA form and praying we'd be let into the football pyramid at any senior level. Getting excited and smiling when we said '1889' next to the question 'year formed'.

It seemed like yesterday, and everything that followed over the following 21 years had come and gone in a flash.

I let my gaze sweep around the entire stadium and all the empty blue and yellow seats. Everything we had been working towards was right there in front of me. We were home and it had been worth all the blood, sweat and tears.

But now it was over.

I had been commercial director for 21 years and pulled in our biggest commercial deals. But nothing can last forever. I understood that. The club wanted a change of direction, and there was no room for Ivor Heller in the brave new world.

I wept for the past, for the memories – but I also wept out of panic. I was terrified of losing my connection with AFC Wimbledon all together; the club was my umbilical cord to the moment nine-year-old Ivor saw the distant glow of floodlights for the first time as he walked down Haydons Road.

Ever since we relaunched in 2002, I had instigated the man-of-the-match ceremony and had proudly continued it at every home game ever since. I'd also wandered round our sponsors and hospitality guests on every match day to check everything was okay, and that they were having a good time.

But I wouldn't be doing any of that anymore.

I wouldn't be interviewing our matchday mascots to see whether they'd enjoyed their day. That's right – the kids who escorted our team on to the pitch. I used to chat to them on stage alongside the man-of-the-match winner. And I used to wonder which ones might make it into the first team one day.

Spike Brits was one of them: for six years he'd come on stage with keeper's gloves, given him by our goalkeeping coach Bayzo, and they were always way too big for him. I'd tease him over his height – he was shorter than me back then – but the last time he did it, when he was 13, he was so massive I didn't even recognise him.

He's at Manchester City now and winning England honours – after coming through our academy.

Everything I cherished most was coming to an end. I'd be losing all of it and that hurt like hell. I felt surplus to requirements, like someone had stamped a giant 'past his sell-by date' on me.

As hard as I tried I couldn't stop those tears.

In the end, I agreed a settlement package and that helped cushion the blows. I am now a life vice-president. I watch all our home games – and most of the away ones – from the directors' box. I am treated warmly and respectfully, and, in a small way, I still feel part of the inner sanctum. But only from a distance.

It's not quite the same as it was when I was at the centre of it all.

There are good people in the boardroom: people like Ian Cooke, David Charles, Paul Shippam, John Lynch and Dickie, of course. They rarely miss a match, home or away. And I have lost count of the amount of times Iain McNay's company, Cherry Red Records, has supported the club when it was needed the most.

Most recently, Dons Trust members voted overwhelmingly to change the ownership structure, so fans hold a 50-plus-one per cent stake in the club, instead of 75 per cent. I supported this because, if AFC Wimbledon is to continue growing and looking towards the Championship – instead of dreading a return to League Two – then it must attract outside investment.

I was always proud of the way we looked after our former heroes – whether they were ex-players or ex-staff or former super volunteers. I hope that tradition continues.

I freely admit I was in a bad place for many anguished months after my departure. I felt distant, disillusioned and depressed. Rightly or wrongly, I also felt judged. Had I become an afterthought?

Ivor Heller – wasn't he something to do with the club? Once?

That thought weighed heavily on me, wrecking my confidence and self-esteem. Then, out of nowhere, I got a phone call in September from Merton Council.

'Is that Mr Ivor Heller?' said a rather officious voice.

'Yes,' I replied, a bit apprehensively.

'Good morning, Mr Heller. This is to advise you that you are being considered for the honour of Freeman of our Borough. Once confirmed, you will be invited by the council to a formal presentation.'

What the fuck?!

'Are you sure?' I stammered. 'Why me – what's it for?'

'I believe it's for your outstanding contribution to the community and for resurrecting Wimbledon football club.'

I put the phone down in a daze. Seven months after exiting my club, seven months of feeling worthless and useless, I was now being offered the highest honour our local council could bestow.

I realised my charity work was one of the big reasons. I'd done a lot for the Leyton Road Centre (and still do); I'm a proud ambassador for the Dons Local Action Group and I've helped raise over £800,000 for St George's Hospital by organising fundraising dinners.

But the voice on the end of the phone had specifically said it was also for 'resurrecting Wimbledon football club'. The very same club that no longer had a role for Ivor Heller.

Now some new judges had come along – the council – and they were saying something entirely different. These judges were saying: 'This Ivor Heller is so appreciated we are going to bestow the highest honour we possibly can upon him.'

I think I can now graze my sheep anywhere I want in Merton and even walk them down the High Street. I'll be in good company, as well. I'm not the only freeman at AFC Wimbledon; the very same honour was also bestowed on Dickie Guy.

The council made me proud to be Ivor Heller again. It reminded me who I was and what I'd done. I'd felt crushed but now my spirit had been resurrected.

They know a thing or two, those people at Merton Council.

Chapter 64
THE BALL BOY

IT FELT like a gift from the heavens: Ronan Curtis scored in the 94th minute to beat the franchise 1-0. But it's what he did next that will for ever stick in my memory. Not only did he celebrate wildly as Plough Lane erupted with joy, he delivered the one thing I prayed would happen at AFC Wimbledon. Completely caught up in the drama, Curtis proved to me that our story, our fight, our struggle, our injustice – the whole shebang – was transcending generations. He probably didn't realise that as he went berserk. But it meant the world to me.

The moment came on 2 March 2024, in a League Two game at Plough Lane. After scoring his last-gasp winner, Curtis tore off his shirt ecstatically as he celebrated – then raced to a corner flag where he picked up one of our jubilant ball boys and hugged him like he was a long-lost son. The pair of them literally disappeared under a scrum of Dons players as the ground went mental – and that was when I knew our story would never die. More than anything, I wanted our young fans to understand what had happened to us, how we'd risen from the ashes and why beating the franchise really mattered.

It felt like the entire stadium zoned in on that ball boy. He embodied everything: our happiness, our love for our club – and our future. All around I could hear supporters saying, 'Did you see the ball boy?' and 'He's under that pile of players somewhere.' I think we were all a bit relieved when he finally emerged unscathed, still being held tightly by Curtis.

His name is Noah Johnston, he was 11 years old at the time, and it occurred to me that even he understood more than those misguided club execs who had foolishly accepted hospitality from the enemy. Plough Lane erupted because Plough Lane understood as well.

It will never stop. People who weren't born in 2002 are growing up learning the truth about the franchise. And the FA. And the three-man commission. And all the bastards who tried to keep us in a coffin.

Noah certainly knew our story. When we were campaigning and struggling and fighting to build the club, his mother – Nina – was one of our loyal volunteers. She still is, bless her. Nina has three sons, all three have been ball boys, and all three are fanatically committed to AFC Wimbledon. Curtis made a memory for that 11-year-old and it will never be forgotten by either of them and everyone else who was there because everyone got caught up in that moment of sheer joy. In 50 years, Noah will go to a game and somebody will turn round to him and say: 'Do you remember that day when Curtis scored the winner against the franchise and went and picked up the ball boy to celebrate.'

And Noah will turn round and say: 'Yeah, that was me. I was that ball boy.'

EXTRA TIME

Chapter 65

TWENTY-FOUR YEARS LATER

WE GOT there for 11 a.m. – me, Lisa and Dickie Guy – and the three of us sat on a bench on the right-hand side of Wembley Way as you look towards the stadium. For the next 30 minutes we watched in awe as great tidal waves of yellow and blue rolled past: our fans were making their way, noisily and joyously, to the 2025 League Two play-off final.

Their flags and banners and carnival hats almost obliterated the skyline. Every so often someone would recognise us, come over, have a chat and then carry on. Some wanted a photo, some even said, 'Thank you,' and, as they left, we'd shake hands and say, 'See you after the game.'

I'd never seen so many Wimbledon fans gathering for one match before. Officially, the club sold 28,500 tickets, but there were thousands in the hospitality and neutral areas and the vast majority were supporting us. It could have easily been 32,000.

We had nothing like that at the 1988 cup final, or the 2011 and 2016 play-offs. And what struck me most was just how generational it was. The old 'uns – who were there back in 2002 – looked like they were on a grand, military parade: I half expected to see rows of Wimbledon medals in a neat line across their chests as they proudly marched past, albeit a bit slower these days. Then came their kids – well into their twenties and thirties – and then, I realised, came their kids' kids, running around and screaming the loudest with their painted faces and oversized comedy hands.

Absolutely everyone was smiling and laughing and singing. It was like a gigantic outdoor party and I realised I was witnessing something I hadn't seen for 24 years. For the first time I was at a big game purely as a fan. I wasn't running around manically, sorting tickets, or burgers, or VIP guests or stewards or fucking problems.

Now, I was the one thing I had been at the very start, when I was nine years old going to my first football match for the first time. I was Ivor the Football Fan once more and I could actually soak in everything I'd somehow missed since 2002.

We were playing Walsall and I would go into the Royal Box, and sit next to Lisa and Dave Beasant. Dickie was a few rows in front and between us we would watch our club, the one the FA never wanted to see born, comfortably and very professionally win 1-0 to get back into League One. And, as I looked across a Wembley Stadium bedecked in yellow and blue, a thought flashed through my mind: 'Jesus Christ, what did we do?'

I thought back to those frenetic moments in 2002 when we had to find a ground and fill in the London FA's forms within the space of 12 manic days.

If we hadn't made those early calls when we did, if we hadn't found a ground and players and coaches and balls and cones and bloody bibs at breakneck speed, then I don't think the club would have ever started. I wouldn't have been sitting in the Royal Box at Wembley and Wimbledon would have been screwed because, let's face it, that's what the FA wanted.

My mind raced back to all the stuff that seemed so big at the time: launching the Dons Trust inside Wimbledon Theatre; showing fans the badges and shirts we'd designed and hearing them sing 'A-F-C Wim-ble-don' for the first time; holding trials on Wimbledon Common; failing to get into the Ryman League; sitting in a pub praying the Combined Counties would accept us and listening to old John moan about 'bloody players'; our first game at Bottom Meadow and marvelling at the Batsford Arms pub they'd recreated for us inside a marquee; watching powerless as all the tea ladies walked out of Kingsmeadow because they wanted to be paid in cash; arguing with Mr Khosla about the poxy ham slicer; burning the skin off my hands trying to cook breakfast for the Rugby World Cup final; standing on the pitch with Erik to tell Dave Anderson it was over; Terry Brown insisting he'd rather be lucky than good; meeting Stephen Alambritis; watching in awe as Erik led us back to Plough Lane and then witnessing our first game back there in front of a proper crowd.

Then came the triumphs and the glories and, above absolutely all of it, the greatest moment of them all: getting back to the Football League in 2011 at the City of Manchester Stadium. That was our redemption, our vindication, our two-fucking-fingers-to-the-FA moment and nothing ever beats that.

But there'd been so many great, insane, hilarious, painful, emotional, wonderful moments and I'd happily experience them all, all over again, in a heartbeat. I used to worry about squeezing 4,500 into Kingsmeadow and now we had seven times that inside Wembley.

What the fuck did we do?

The fact we won the 2025 play-off inside the FA's own home, Wembley Stadium, of course made beating Walsall – who'd looked like promotion certainties all season – even sweeter. Once Myles Hippolyte rifled home a half-volley from outside the box, we never looked troubled. Here we were, proving the FA wrong yet again.

Right from the start, when the FA wiped us off the map but we vowed to start again, I said we'd have great nights, great moments, great victories, great adventures.

'We will win cups,' I said, 'we will win leagues' and 'we will play the big clubs once more.'

Well, look what happened. In nine years we won non-league trophies and went from park football back into the Football League. And here we were again, this time getting promoted back to League One.

In between, we played Liverpool, West Ham, Chelsea, Newcastle, Arsenal and Tottenham – all as AFC Wimbledon.

We faced Millwall, Sunderland, Charlton, Portsmouth, Sheffield Wednesday – all big games against big, historic clubs. We were never disgraced by any of them. We were there by right and on merit.

In fact, our history against the big clubs has always been remarkable. Did we get the better of Liverpool? I'd say, 'Yes, we did.' We beat them in the cup final, we beat them at Anfield two years on the spin – and we gave them the fright of their lives at Kingsmeadow.

Did we get the better of Man United? Again 'yes': we did the double over them in 1986–87, and we beat them in the FA Cup at Selhurst Park, when they were the number one club of the nineties. How inconceivable is that?

We beat Chelsea 4-0, we smashed Tottenham several times, we went unbeaten in nine games at Arsenal. We even beat West Ham United at Kingsmeadow, when Manuel Pellegrini was their boss, and we beat the likes of Ipswich and Coventry.

We've had the last word every time someone has tried to put us in a box and keep us down. We even built ourselves a £33 million stadium in the one town the FA let us be dragged away from: Wimbledon, our home.

So who was wrong – me or the FA? I still hate them as much – if not more – than I ever did. They were the final betrayers. Instead of shovelling us off to Milton Keynes, they could have enabled us – the fans – to save the club in 2002. The FA could have worked with us. Instead, these educated, intelligent governors of our game, decided to let a club in Milton Keynes call themselves Wimbledon – and, to this day, Dons. How can they look themselves in the mirror? Are they not horrified by the absurdity of their decisions? Was that the best they could do? Were they in the wider interests of football?

They should have protected a football club in its local conurbation. You do not let a football club be taken out of its homeland when it's been there since 1889. But they were too scared to stand up for what was right.

I hated the FA from the moment they announced the three-man commission. They were building a wall around themselves because they didn't have the bollocks to do the right thing. They found a way whereby they could hold their hands up and say: 'Ah, well, this wasn't strictly our decision. It was the independent commission that did it and their decision was binding: 'Nothing to do with us.'

Except it was. When they added their extra nasty little bit about us 'not being in the wider interests of football', they never thought about the level of hurt that would provoke – or what such a dumb declaration might trigger.

They never realised the energy that was created as a by-product. And that's because they fundamentally don't understand football fans. They don't get what motivates us to turn up every week in all weathers and spend our last pennies on an away trip to some godforsaken ground, with no obvious way of getting home afterwards because the trains don't run after 10 p.m.

Today's FA are no better. The Premier League runs football from its lofty perch and the FA have been reduced to a fire-fighting organisation. They only flex their muscles against the small clubs, never the big ones. If the FA want to kick the shit out of us, or Carlisle United or anyone else struggling to survive, they'll do it.

The one creature I recognise above anybody else is the bully. I was bullied severely as a child, and it reared its head during my adult life as well. The FA are bullies. They throw their weight around when they know they can crush their victim. But they never stand up to the really big guys.

Were we in the best interests of football? Did we get it right? I'd say, 'Yes, we did.' We ticked every bleeding box. Those of us who kick-started our club were people with the right skills who just happened to be in the right place at the right time. We built a momentum and that was driven on by a relentless sense of injustice. We had to put right the wrong.

I think we are a miraculous story, one that is truly different from any other club. I don't think anyone has ever done what we've done, in the way we've done it. True football people get our story.

So what's left? For starters, the FA need to apologise. Below, is my open letter to them, spelling out what they should do to heal wounds that remain raw to this day. As for AFC Wimbledon, well, let's go all the way. Why not? We've set the bases, whether it happens in my lifetime or not. We have our team, we play at Plough Lane, so . . . fuck 'em all!

MY LETTER TO THE FA

Dear Sirs,

In 2002, your organisation oversaw the most calamitous decision in the history of our national game. An FA-appointed commission allowed our club, Wimbledon, to be relocated to a town 70 miles away from its natural homeland.

The decision caused immeasurable hurt to the Wimbledon community, where a football club had played since 1889.

I am writing now to assure you that hurt has not dissipated. While it may be impossible to turn back the clock, there is still time for you to at least repair some of the damage.

In the first instance, I would respectfully urge you to consider offering a formal apology. There has never been the slightest indication of contrition, regret or remorse – despite the untold misery your commission's decision caused.

Something else I find deeply offensive is the fact that they continue to use our historic abridged name 'Dons'.

There is simply no logical reason for this: it is deeply offensive, provocative and a constant reminder of the diabolical decision – as well as a continuous cause for tension. Forcing the club in Milton Keynes to drop the name Dons from their name would restore some calm and common sense.

To conclude, the pain your organisation caused on 28 May 2002 can only be resolved if you have a desire to address the root causes.

Everybody knows a terrible injustice was served upon our club, and a simple apology would be a huge step towards righting that wrong. And returning our abridged name to us, its rightful, natural and historic owners, would be a further step towards a more conciliatory relationship.

In fact, may I suggest, these modest actions would be in the wider interests of football.

Yours,

Ivor

25 YEARS AND MY 25 UNFORGETTABLE MOMENTS

1: Beating Luton on penalties at the City of Manchester Stadium in the 2011 Conference Premier play-off final. We were back in the Football League, and it only took us nine years

2: Our 2008 play-off win at Staines. We were 1-0 down with 10 minutes to go but two quick-fire goals triggered pandemonium and a huge party

3: Beating Plymouth in the 2016 play-off final at Wembley to reach League One. Amazing celebrations back at Kingsmeadow after the game

4: Our first match as AFC Wimbledon in 2002 at Sutton United. The first time I ever saw a peaceful pitch invasion to celebrate a 4-0 defeat

5: Beating mighty West Ham 4-2 at Kingsmeadow in the FA Cup, 2019. The most amazing atmosphere

6: Playing Liverpool at Kingsmeadow in the FA Cup in 2015. The whole nation was gripped as we levelled the scores at 1-1 only to lose to a Steven Gerrard wonder free-kick

7: Our first league victory against the Frannies – 2-0 at Kingsmeadow in 2017. I don't think the fans have ever been louder

8: Our first match back in front of fans at Plough Lane in 2021 against Bolton. An exhilarating 3-3 draw but tragically overshadowed by the death of Jack Lonergan (28) afterwards

9: Effectively sealing promotion to the Conference in 2009 with a 1-1 draw at Hampton and Richmond. We took over Wimbledon Village for a legendary knees-up

10: Beating Fleetwood 2-1 on last day of the season at Kingsmeadow,

2013, to avoid relegation back to the Conference. Most nervous I have ever been and massive pitch invasion afterwards including one Lord, a Baroness and an MP

11: Beating the Franchise 1-0 in 2024 at our new Plough Lane home with a 96th-minute Ronan Curtis winner. Watching him celebrate with a ball boy, who vanished under a scrum of delirious players. I got over 50 messages asking me whether the ball boy was ok

12: AFC Wimbledon's first-ever goal scored by 'Trigger' (the legendary phone hacker Glenn Mulcaire) against Bromley in 2002

13: Our incredible 2-2 draw at Accrington in the 2016 play-off semi-final. After winning the first leg 1-0, we trailed 2-0 on the night, scored, the lights went out – and then we scored again to win 3-2 on aggregate! Pandemonium!

14: Our first significant cup win in the FA Vase at Herne Bay. We took nearly 2,000 fans and centre back Matt Everard (aka The Caveman) got the late winner two minutes into added time

15: The Combined Counties League vote to let us in for the 2002/03 season. Without that, we would have never got started

16: Our worst nightmare when The Ryman League voted not to let us in. We never saw it coming

17: Wally Downes' amazing Great Escape in 2019, when our goalless draw at Bradford kept us in League One. Terrible game but an amazing celebration afterwards

18: Our first league match at Kingsmeadow against Chipstead, 2002. No seats left so I sat on the steps with our sponsor, Trevor Beattie, from the advertising giants TBWA

19: AFC Wimbledon's first-ever league game at rural Sandhurst Town, 2002. There were no stands, just hay bales for the fans to climb on. Phenomenal for so many reasons

20: Accrington Stanley away, 2015. Freezing, two down in 10 mins, 2-2 by 25 mins, 2-3 down on 36 mins, 3-3 after 44 mins – then we won 4-3 with a 64th-minute strike. Best road trip ever with David Charles, Jim Piddington and the eccentric Carlo Venditelli

21: Striker Jon Main's wonder goal as he runs the entire length of the pitch to complete a 3-1 win over AFC Hornchurch in the 2008 Ryman Premier play off